A WORLD OF
UFOs

A WORLD OF
UFOs

CHRIS A. RUTKOWSKI

DUNDURN PRESS
TORONTO

Editor: Tony Hawke
Copy-editor: Kaylee Baker
Design: Erin Mallory and Courtney Horner
Printer: Webcom

Library and Archives Canada Cataloguing in Publication

Rutkowski, Chris
      A world of UFOs / by Chris A. Rutkowski.

ISBN 978-1-55002-833-1

      1. Unidentified flying objects. 2. Unidentified flying objects--Sightings and encounters. I. Title.

TL789.R78 2008   001.942   C2008-903943-2

1   2   3   4   5   12   11   10   09   08

Conseil des Arts du Canada   Canada Council for the Arts

ONTARIO ARTS COUNCIL
CONSEIL DES ARTS DE L'ONTARIO

Canadä

We acknowledge the support of the **Canada Council for the Arts** and the **Ontario Arts Council** for our publishing program. We also acknowledge the financial support of the **Government of Canada** through the **Book Publishing Industry Development Program** and **The Association for the Export of Canadian Books**, and the **Government of Ontario** through the **Ontario Book Publishers Tax Credit program**, and the **Ontario Media Development Corporation**.

Care has been taken to trace the ownership of copyright material used in this book. The author and the publisher welcome any information enabling them to rectify any references or credits in subsequent editions.

J. Kirk Howard, President

Printed and bound in Canada.
Printed on recycled paper.

www.dundurn.com

Dundurn Press
3 Church Street, Suite 500
Toronto, Ontario, Canada
M5E 1M2

Gazelle Book Services Limited
White Cross Mills
High Town, Lancaster, England
LA1 4XS

Dundurn Press
2250 Military Road
Tonawanda, NY
U.S.A. 14150

CONTENTS

For Donna, my muse and amused

Acknowledgements

FIRST, I WOULD LIKE TO THANK MY FAMILY FOR THEIR patience and understanding when I disappeared into the study to write for long hours during the evenings and on weekends. Apparently, I now have a lot of chores and other household duties to perform.

I would also like to thank ufologists and researchers with whom I have discussed this material over the past years, and who have offered encouragement, suggestions, and ideas for incorporation into the book. These include Errol Bruce-Knapp, Grant Cameron, Barb Campbell, Jerome Clark, Peter Davenport, Geoff Dittman, Stanton Friedman, A. E. Gevaerd, Martin Jasek, Gord Kijek, Don Ledger, Jim Moroney, and Vladimir Simosko.

I would like to acknowledge members of my writers' group, including Susan Rocan, Kevin Russell, and Evelyn Woodward, and other writers with whom I have been acquainted and who have inspired me: Rae Bridgman, Samantha Day, K. C. Oliver, Duncan Thornton, and Nathan Town.

I thank my publishers at Dundurn, particularly Beth Bruder, Tammy Cabral, Michael Carroll, Tony Hawke, Barry Jowett, and Kirk Howard.

I thank Jennifer Wang and Susan Birdwise for assistance with illustrations for the book, and B.J. Booth for the cover.

Finally, special thanks to those individuals who have meant much to me throughout my writing: Alan and Cindy Anderson, John Robert Columbo, Geoff Currier, Chester Cuthbert, John Danakas, Rob Dyck, Gerry Goertzen, and Chester and Joan Lobchuk.

INTRODUCTION

UFOS EXIST. THIS IS A STATEMENT OF FACT THAT even a true skeptic cannot deny. Around the world, thousands, and perhaps even millions, of people have seen objects in the sky that they cannot identify. These objects are, by definition, UFOs.

This is not to say that these objects cannot ever be identified. Indeed, with some effort, many if not most are likely to be explained by UFO investigators as misperceptions of conventional or natural objects such as stars, aircraft, meteors, balloons, and the like. But to the witnesses who report them, they are mysterious and seem to have no immediate explanation.

For example, in March 2007, I received a call from an RCMP officer in a small northern Canadian community. Several people in and around the town had reported seeing a bright, star-like light changing colours as it danced in the southwestern sky, not far above the small mountains that surrounded the area. It was visible for several hours, from about eleven to three, almost every night. From the descriptions provided by the officer, I knew the object was likely Saturn, which was very bright and noticeable in that exact part of the night sky. I advised the officer to try to make further observations during the next two or three nights, just to confirm my theory. Sure enough, by the end of the week he had called back to say he had watched the object with one of the original witnesses, and it was definitely Saturn.

Star-like lights are one thing, but what about sightings that involve detailed observations of objects with more discernible shapes, like the archetypal flying saucer? Unfortunately, there are often similarly practical explanations for such sightings, as witnesses watching aircraft fuselages glinting in the sunlight are unable to see the wings from a great distance.

"But what about the *real* UFOs?" you ask. "Surely there are some good sightings of objects that don't have explanations even after UFO investigators have a go at them."

Indeed, there are. This book presents a variety of cases, many of which have explanations, but others that do not. I include both kinds because it is painfully difficult to sort fact from fiction where UFO reports are concerned, and the general public, when confronted with a story in a book, in a magazine, on a television program, or on a website, has no easy way to discern good information from bad, and to recognize less than perfect sources.

Some of the most famous UFO stories have explanations, or at least are strongly disputed. Some stories are downright bizarre, as if the possibility of alien spaceships flitting about our skies wasn't strange enough.

It should also be pointed out that every UFO story and case in this book is true. That is, someone actually reported the sighting and the case has been documented to some extent. References are given when possible, with citations, article sources, and web page URLs provided for further reading.

One of the problems with a book designed to give a global perspective or an overview of UFO sightings and ufology is that there is simply too much material to cover. It would be impossible to list all the UFO reports from every country in the world, or even to give details on a handful of cases from every district. I decided to present a selection of UFO cases from around the world, some well known and others documented here for the first time. I have tried to offer a representative sample from all continents so that the truly global nature of the phenomenon can be appreciated. I have also provided references where possible, so that more information can be found for specific cases and issues.

Avid readers may be disappointed that cases they personally view as the "best" from a particular country or continent are absent from this review. If so, I apologize; any effort to include everything that might be relevant to all readers and researchers will fall short in some way. I do think, though, that the cases noted in this collection are some of the most fascinating, interesting, unusual, and confounding that have been reported.

I will not attempt to convince skeptics of their stubbornness, nor believers of their folly. I will not offer proof that aliens are invading our terrestrial home, and I will not insist that UFOs do not exist. I will offer food for thought and give the reader a primer for understanding how the UFO phenomenon has manifested itself around the globe.

Later in the book, a series of short essays lead the reader through a host of UFO-related topics from A to Z. These come from my own views about the subject during my more than thirty years of investigation and research on UFOs and ufology. As an investigator, I have done hundreds of field studies and interviewed literally thousands of witnesses. As a researcher, I have scrutinized reports and case data from other investigators and writers, and have written about issues and aspects of the entire field of ufology. As an educator, I have given public presentations on the subject of UFOs, as well as astronomy and the possibility of extraterrestrial life. As an astronomer, I have gazed at the night sky through telescopes at the ridges and rilles on the moon, observed distant galaxies, guided willing skywatchers through lunar and solar eclipses, and been treated to brilliant bolides and fireballs streaking across the bowl of night.

I have been fascinated with the UFO phenomenon from a young age, and have been investigating UFO sightings since the 1970s. I have listened patiently to people who needed to tell their stories of seeing odd lights in the sky, or to those relating encounters with strange aerial craft and their occupants. Even if a sighting has a simple explanation, the occasion is often an excellent opportunity to educate and introduce people to the wonders of their world and the universe in which we live.

This, then, is my perspective on UFOs and ufology.

The Five
MOST FAMOUS
UFO Cases

OUT OF ALL THE STORIES ABOUT PEOPLE WHO HAVE
seen UFOs, a few have been repeated and related most often. Some have
been investigated and reinvestigated long after the initial event, and new
evidence seems to pop up unexpectedly every year. Sometimes renewed
interest in a story uncovers additional witnesses, documentation, and, in
some cases, conflicting information that raises new doubts and questions.

Most readers will be familiar with the cases presented in this section.
They have been featured in movies and books, and Internet searches
for information about UFOs inevitably bring them to front and centre.
Some of these cases have taken on lives of their own. Some have been
analyzed and discussed so much that there are many differing versions
and interpretations of the details, and it is sometimes impossible to get
to the truth within the stories.

These cases deserve some additional attention, not because they
are proof of the reality of the UFO phenomenon, but because they
have unusual or unexplainable elements, challenge preconceptions
about UFOs, or have other characteristics that I feel are remarkable.
Furthermore, my reviews of these cases include details that may not be
well known, even to people who are aware of the general stories. I have
tried to discern the truth, whatever that may be.

THE ROSWELL CRASH

Strictly speaking, the famous (or infamous, if you prefer) case involving the crash of a flying saucer near the town of Roswell, New Mexico, in 1947 is not a very "good" UFO report. Some of the objects seen around that time by witnesses may have simply been bolides and fireballs, and the person who actually found physical evidence did not actually see a UFO. In fact, were it not for a series of events that followed the sighting of an unusual bright object, the case might have remained obscure. But this incident has become possibly the best-known case in the annals of ufology, spawning books, movies, and a TV series, and achieving legendary status among both hard-core believers and the general public.

On July 2, 1947, business owner Dan Wilmot and his wife were sitting outside on their porch, enjoying the summer evening. At about 9:50 p.m. they saw a bright, disc-shaped object with glowing lights flying northwest very rapidly. In an interview with the *Roswell Daily Record*, Wilmot described the object as shaped like "two inverted saucers mouth to mouth," and an estimated six to eight metres (twenty to twenty-five feet) in diameter.

Over the next few days, other sightings of unusual objects were reported in the general area. Most were of bright fireballs, including one sighting on July 4 that was described as a "brilliant light" plunging to Earth, similar to an aircraft on fire and falling from the sky.

This handful of sightings was hardly remarkable. In fact, they have characteristics of astronomical phenomena known as bolides — pieces of comets or planetary debris that impact the Earth's atmosphere at high speeds and immediately burn up, leaving a trail of light that is often blue, green, or orange. Each year, many of these objects are seen and reported as UFOs, but later assigned an "explained" or "possibly explained" status by investigators and researchers. Even the sighting reported by Dan Wilmot has some characteristics of a bolide, and similar cases have turned out to be fireballs, even with the odd description of two bowls rim to rim.

If the Roswell case had rested solely on these relatively unexciting reports, it would have faded into obscurity; however, on July 4 another incident added to the evidence that a UFO had indeed been spotted in the area. Rancher Mac Brazel, watching the skies during a severe lightning storm, heard an explosive noise that didn't sound like a typical thunderclap. The next day he was riding his horse through a pasture when he came upon a large mass of debris unlike anything he had seen before. Scattered throughout a large area were numerous metallic strips that looked like dark tinfoil. Brazel examined them in some detail, and said that as he crumpled a strip in his hand and released it, it would assume its original shape without appearing bent or wrinkled. He also found sticks of a lightweight material like balsa wood that were inscribed with odd writing that resembled hieroglyphics.

Brazel collected some of the pieces, took them home, and showed them to his family and some neighbours. They all marvelled at the unusual quality of the material. Brazel notified the local sheriff, George Wilcox, who in turn contacted the nearby Roswell Army Air Field, since the men thought the debris had come from a military operation of some kind.

Major Jesse Marcel, intelligence officer with the 509th Bomb Group, drove from the base to Wilcox's office, where he interviewed Brazel and examined some of the debris he had brought into town. Upon hearing the details of Brazel's find, Marcel believed the debris had resulted from the crash of an aircraft. He decided to travel to the site with Captain Sheridan Cavitt, a counter-intelligence officer from the Roswell base. Marcel and Cavitt drove to the base in separate vehicles. When they arrived at the location it was too dark to be able to do an extensive search, so they decided to sleep there.

In the morning, they explored the area in detail and found material scattered throughout a large crash site just over a kilometre (three-quarters of a mile) long and as much as ninety metres (three hundred feet) wide. Just as Brazel had, they found pieces of debris that resembled tinfoil, as well as several lengths of a light material like balsa wood; however, unlike balsa wood, they could not seem to be bent or broken.

Cavitt left the site in the middle of the afternoon, while Marcel stayed and loaded much of the material into the trunk of his car. He finally headed towards home late in the evening, arriving at his own house in the early hours of the morning. He woke his wife and his eleven-year-old son, Jesse Jr., to show them what he had found in the desert. He told his family that he had discovered the remnants of a flying saucer that had crashed. Later, young Jesse told investigators about the strange metallic I-beams that had lettering like hieroglyphics on them, and that his father had been very excited about what he had seen.

Marcel went to the airfield and informed his superiors of the discovery. The 509th's press officer, Walter Haut, was ordered by his commander, Colonel William Blanchard, to send out a press release announcing that a flying saucer had been captured.

On July 8, under the headline "RAAF Captures Flying Saucer On Ranch In Roswell Region," the *Roswell Daily Record* announced the recovery of something by the Roswell Army Air Field. Soon, media were calling the base and Sheriff Wilcox's office for information about what had been found. However, the debris had been shipped to Brigadier-General Roger Ramey of the Eighth Air Force at Fort Worth, Texas. From there, Ramey called the local media and told them the debris was not from a flying saucer, but a weather balloon. The sticks and metallic pieces were actually part of a radar reflector.

On July 9, the *Daily Record* essentially retracted the previous day's story under the headline, "General Ramey Empties Roswell Saucer." The paper also ran a story about Brazel, indicating he was mistaken and that he was sorry to have caused such a commotion. That seemed to end the affair, and the incident was brushed aside.

After the fact, researchers found evidence that military personnel had visited radio and newspaper offices in the Roswell area, requesting the original copies of the first erroneous press release about the flying saucer. Furthermore, some military personnel later claimed that they either helped load, or witnessed others loading very unusual wreckage onto flatbed trucks or transport aircraft destined for Los Alamos, Fort Worth, and other classified locations.

Many years passed before anything more was learned about the Roswell case.

In February 1978, Stanton Friedman, nuclear physicist and outspoken advocate for the reality of flying saucers from outer space, was in Baton

Rouge, Louisiana, for a TV interview. While he was waiting to go on, he was told that a former air force officer named Jesse Marcel who lived close by had seen and touched some debris from a crashed flying saucer. Friedman was intrigued and looked up Marcel, who was then in Houma, Louisiana. Friedman interviewed him at length and learned that there was much more to the story than most people knew.

Friedman reopened the case and found additional witnesses who seemed to be able to corroborate the amazing story that an unknown craft of some kind had indeed crashed in the New Mexico desert. His investigations became the basis for *The Roswell Incident* (1980), a book by Charles Berlitz and William Moore.

In October 1978, while at Bemidji State University lecturing about UFOs, Friedman met a couple who told him that a friend of theirs named Barney Barnett, who had since passed away, had described seeing a crashed flying saucer in New Mexico sometime in the 1940s. Barnett was an engineer working for the government, and was deemed very reliable. His story seemed to match Marcel's, with one added feature — Barnett had seen several small bodies near the crash debris. While in Minnesota, Friedman discussed this story with William Moore, a high school teacher with a strong interest in UFOs. Friedman suggested that Moore research the Barnett story to see if it had any merit. Only a few months later, Moore found newspaper clippings that told the Roswell story.

Speculation about the incident flourished during the next decade. Friedman found additional witnesses, and in 1988 the Center for UFO Studies (CUFOS) sponsored a team to locate the crash site. In 1991, members of the CUFOS team, author Kevin Randle, and CUFOS investigator Don Schmitt, published their book *UFO Crash at Roswell*, claiming that the government had retrieved the debris and cleaned up the site, and was covering up its possession of several alien bodies.

One of the new witnesses that Friedman located was mortician Glenn Dennis. He said he was working in a funeral home in 1947, when he got a call from the base about whether small, child-size coffins were available. He also said that he was ordered to leave the base hospital one day in July after speaking with a nurse who told him she had assisted with autopsies on weird, tiny childlike bodies.

After the TV show *Unsolved Mysteries* aired an episode about the Roswell incident in 1989, a Missouri man named Gerald Anderson called in to say that he had also seen the crashed flying saucer while rockhounding with his family in New Mexico in 1947. What's more, he later told investigators he had seen three alien bodies underneath the hull of the saucer, and a fourth tending to its injured crewmates. Military personnel had shown up and ordered the rockhounds to go away and never tell anyone what they had seen.

Anderson's story seemed to be corroborated by another independent witness, Frank Kaufman, who said he was part of a military search party that had found a crashed saucer some distance away from the site where Brazel had discovered the debris. He too said he had seen a large craft half buried in sand, as well as a number of small humanoid bodies.

In 1992, a book co-authored by Friedman and Don Berliner came out with another theory — that two crashed saucers were actually recovered in 1947, along with their alien crews. *Crash at Corona* explained that Anderson's story was inconsistent with the Brazel discovery, as one saucer had exploded in mid-air, leaving only debris, while the other crashed almost intact.

What really happened at Roswell? The case, and its numerous investigations, has taken on a life of its own, with researchers debating one another on TV shows and in books and magazines. Even those whose evidence seems to support other writers or investigators seem to be at odds with others' statements. Each writer seems to add some new fact or suggests a new interpretation that supports the possibility that a saucer crashed, yet their versions may be at odds with one another. It is, sadly, a confusing quagmire of facts, anecdotes, and, very likely, fiction.

It's no wonder, then, that skeptics and debunkers have had a field day with the Roswell case. The late Philip Klass, who made a name for himself as a UFO arch-skeptic, took great delight in pointing out inconsistencies and problems with various theories.

In 1994, when the U.S. Air Force released a report on an internal investigation into the Roswell claims, the controversy reached a new plateau. The report claimed that in 1947 scientist Charles Moore conducted a secret program called Project Mogul in the Roswell area.

Moore supervised the launching of balloons carrying equipment to monitor Soviet nuclear tests. Each balloon had reflective materials that allowed radar tracking for easy retrieval. According to air force records, one of the Mogul balloon arrays was launched on June 4, and was lost by radar tracking near the Brazel debris site a few weeks later. The fact that some of the balloon package material was balsa wood held together with glue and packing tape, some of which was emblazoned with abstract designs and lettering that could have been mistaken for hieroglyphics, seemed to clinch the idea that the supposed UFOs were actually the Mogul balloons.

But in June 1997, the air force came up with yet another explanation for the Roswell debris. Another internal study discovered that shortly after 1947, a military project that involved dropping mannequins from high-altitude balloons to help understand injuries suffered by pilots and crew that had fallen from aircraft was underway. According to the air force, these one-metre- (three- and four-foot-) tall hairless mannequins were seen by Roswell witnesses and interpreted as aliens. Needless to say, this explanation hasn't sat well with investigators and researchers. Some point out that the mannequins were not deployed until long after the Roswell debris discovery. This is countered by the detail that eyewitness accounts of alien bodies did not emerge until decades after the fact, allowing the possibility that witnesses are confused about the year of their observations. The alien bodies story became even more confounding when a new theory published in 2005 suggested that the small bodies with large heads were actually those of human victims of progenia or other malformations who had been subjects in air force experiments.

Coming up with a viable and coherent explanation for all of the Roswell evidence and claims is difficult because the air force has changed its stance several times — first, the air force denied there was any event at all, then it suggested that the debris belonged to Mogul balloons, and then it added the mannequin explanation. This sounds suspiciously like an attempt to make the data fit the theory, and not the other way around. UFO researchers are probably justified in looking askance at these explanations. In fact, since the Roswell legend includes the idea that newspaper stories were switched to comply with military demands, the accusation of a cover-up may be valid. Even if the truth behind the Roswell crash stories is something militarily terrestrial, there is enough evidence to suggest a cover-up of some kind is involved. But is it an alien spaceship, or a top-secret military accident that is the subject of the cover-up?

Researchers note that the air base near Roswell was the only one in the United States with nuclear capability in 1947. Furthermore, the area was home to former Nazi rocket scientists spirited out of Europe following the end of the Second World War as part of Operation Paperclip, an attempt to obtain rocketry and nuclear secrets. Certainly some experiments designed by such treasures of intelligentsia would have resulted in at least a few accidents, all of which would have been highly classified.

One argument in defence of an apparent cover-up is that with all the secret projects underway in the area in the late 1940s, and because compartmentalization of knowledge is a typical military approach, it is possible that some high-ranking (and most low-ranking) military personnel would not have had knowledge of some experiments taking place right under their noses.

The most difficult issue to overcome while investigating the Roswell case is that of time. Ufology has just celebrated the case's sixtieth anniversary. Most first-hand witnesses are dead. All relevant official documents may have crumbled out of existence long ago, or been accidentally (or purposefully) destroyed.

In 2007, the publication of the contents of an affidavit signed by Walter Haut, the officer who sent out the original press release that stated that a UFO had been found, created a considerable stir within ufology. It was supposedly written in 2002 and sealed until after his death. Throughout his lifetime, Haut maintained that he had never seen any wreckage, and even explicitly stated this on *Larry King Live* on CNN in 2003; however, in the affidavit, Haut stated that he had not only seen, but handled wreckage from the crash site. Haut stated that it was "unlike any material [he had] ever seen in [his] life." He was later taken to a hangar where he was shown an object "12 to 15 feet in length, not quite as wide, about 6 feet high, and more of an egg shape." Most astonishingly, Haut reported that "from a distance, [he] was able to see a couple of bodies under a canvas tarpaulin." In his post-mortem confession, Haut stated that he was convinced that what he had "personally observed was some type of craft and its crew from outer space."

Skeptics have charged that there is no evidence that Haut actually drafted the affidavit himself, as he was already becoming frail and feeble at the time it was written. Indeed, when he appeared on CNN in 2003, he appeared confused and did not even stay through the entire planned interview. Yet, one ufologist insisted that when Haut was interviewed in 2001, he was clear of thought and knew precisely what he was talking about.

As for the change of heart about seeing the wreckage, there was no way that Haut would have admitted to seeing it while he was alive as he would have been liable for prosecution. He protected himself by admitting his falsehood on record. Despite the excitement within ufological circles about his testimony, even a signed affidavit by a key witness to the Roswell incident does not offer undeniable proof that the crash really occurred.

Furthermore, the Roswell crash is only one of several alleged cases where an alien spacecraft is said to have impacted Earth. Other cases have been cited and discussed elsewhere in the world, including Kecksburg, Pennsylvania, in 1965; Johannesburg, South Africa, in 1953; and Moriches Bay, New York, in 1989.

If military personnel recovered any alien debris near Roswell, it has long been hidden or disposed of. Public debate among believers and non-believers (or other believers with opposing theories) has contributed to an obfuscation of the true nature of the original event. In short, we may never get to the bottom of what occurred in the New Mexico desert in 1947.

The Roswell case goes far beyond the issue of whether or not an alien spacecraft crashed into the desert. Roswell has taken on a life of its own, with an annual celebration and a series of UFO conventions in the area. There are tours of the crash site, souvenir stands, museums, and yearly re-enactments of the incident. The town has held parades, costume contests, and even commissioned a musical theatre show to commemorate the event.

It's almost as if the case need not have been true anymore.

BARNEY AND BETTY HILL

The most celebrated and disputed UFO abduction case ever reported is that of Barney and Betty Hill. The American couple's experience in 1961 is considered the archetypal alien abduction scenario. It has been the subject of books, a movie, and countless magazine articles. Even after numerous retellings of their story, their testimony remained essentially unchanged. The couple said they encountered a strange aerial object that approached them and frightened them to the point that they began having nightmares and anxiety.

Skeptics usually state that the Hills' story only manifested after they underwent hypnosis, which resulted in false memories or a transference of dreams from Betty to Barney, but this is not so. The Hills told family members about their experience almost immediately because it had been so strange, and it was only after discussions with many individuals that they were encouraged to seek medical help, and later to undergo hypnosis to treat their anxieties.

It all started on September 19, 1961, as the Hills were returning to New Hampshire after a vacation in Quebec. As they drove, they noticed a bright, star-like object, which they believed to be a meteor of some kind that seemed to be descending and pacing their car. It stopped its movement and appeared to hang in the southwest for a while, then seemed to rise again. Betty told Barney to stop the car so that she could get a better look. After he did so, she watched the object through binoculars, having difficulty following it as it bobbed and weaved and then flew across the face of the moon.

When she gave the binoculars to Barney, he saw the object move erratically again; it seemed to be coming towards them and decreasing in altitude. He suggested to Betty that it was just an aircraft heading for Canada, and got back into the car and resumed driving. He continued to drive south towards home, and they stopped discussing the unusual object, which still was moving in the sky and seemed to be getting closer.

As Barney drove around a bend, the couple was startled by the appearance of the object almost right in front of them, only about thirty metres (one hundred feet) above the highway. It was close enough now that they could distinguish that it appeared to be a broad, disc-shaped craft that was motionless in the sky. Barney stopped the car and got out, holding up the binoculars to get a close view of this weird sight. It suddenly moved again, taking up a position over a nearby field. Determined to figure out what the object was, Barney grabbed the binoculars and his handgun just to be safe, and strode across the field towards it.

He had a good look at the craft, which he estimated was twenty-four metres (eighty feet) in diameter. It had two rows of rectangular windows along its edge, and in the windows, Barney could see strange creatures making odd gestures. Afraid for his life, he turned around and ran back to the car, hysterically telling Betty they needed to escape or be captured by them.

Barney drove off quickly, but the craft followed. The couple then heard some unusual buzzing noises that seemed to bounce off the car's trunk, and felt a vibration. They continued to drive without speaking, and later heard another series of buzzing sounds. Eventually, even though Barney was driving in a dazed state, the Hills reached their home.

Most versions of the Hills' story note that when they reached home, they realized that they were much later in arriving than they had calculated, leaving them to conclude that hours of their journey were missing; however, they did not realize this until later, after discussing their experience with investigators.

They both felt odd and uncomfortable, but were not able to determine why they felt that way. When Barney unpacked the car, he noticed that the strap on his binoculars was broken, and Betty discovered a pinkish powder on her dress. They began to talk with one another about their drive, but they did not seem to be able to recall the details of the trip. They both had vague memories of a large bright object sitting on the road ahead of their car, and they were both unnerved by it.

After a restless sleep, they began putting their clothes and other things away, and Betty had a feeling that she had been exposed to radiation of some kind. When she told this to her sister, she was advised to run a compass over the car; if the needle deviated, it might be a sign the vehicle was radioactive. (Note: This makes no scientific sense; furthermore, the metal on most cars will deflect a compass needle, regardless of the age or model of the vehicle.)

The next day, Betty phoned the local air force base, and she and Barney described their UFO sighting. Their observations of the odd light and the craft with windows were recorded. Air force investigators had concluded that the Hills' report provided "insufficient data," and contained inconsistencies that prevented an explanation from being provided, though it was suggested the object they saw might have been Jupiter. However, the Hills had no knowledge of the air force's conclusion.

The Hills' case began to take on a life of its own. Betty was bothered by the UFO sighting, and spoke with her sister and some close friends about her concerns. She began to have dreams about being escorted through the trees by several strange, grey-skinned men in clothing that resembled air force uniforms. In the dreams, Barney was walking near her, although he appeared dazed and did not respond when she called to him. They were both led towards a large, disc-shaped craft, and then up a ramp and into the craft. Once inside, she and Barney were separated because their abductors wanted to do some tests on them.

The beings spoke English, although Betty noted they had odd accents of some kind. One being that Betty called a "doctor," snipped some of her hair, looked inside her mouth and ears, and clipped her fingernails. He scraped her skin with an object that looked like a butter knife, and then made her lie on a metal table while he used a device like an X-ray machine to examine her more thoroughly. He then produced a long needle that he jabbed in her abdomen, telling her it was a pregnancy test. This is particularly interesting, because it was not until decades later that amniocentesis tests became common among terrestrial physicians.

In the dream, Betty realized that no one would believe she had met these creatures, so she asked the one that seemed to be the leader if she could take something back home with her. Betty indicated a book that was on a table, and asked if she could have it. An argument among the creatures ensued, and the book was taken away.

At one point, Betty asked the leader where he was from. In response, he went over to a wall and pulled a map out of it. Betty said it looked very odd, as if it were three-dimensional despite being printed on a two-dimensional sheet. She noted it was a sky map, with stars of varying sizes and colours, and lines connecting some of them. The leader explained that the lines represented expeditions. He then asked Betty if she knew where Earth was on the map, and she naturally said no. He said that because she did not know, there would be no reason to show her where he was from.

Even though the book she had hoped to keep had been taken away, Betty told the leader that she would remember their meeting. He retorted by saying that was unlikely, and even if she did remember, no one would believe her.

These images were brought out as nightmares from Betty's troubled mind. It's no wonder that she was having difficulty putting them in context. During an interview with UFO investigators from the National Investigations Committee on Aerial Phenomena (NICAP), weeks later the Hills realized that their drive home took at least two hours longer than normal. They tried to reconstruct the events of that night, but they still could not account for the missing hours.

They began making trips back to the area to jog their memories, but to no avail.

Barney was experiencing extreme anxiety for reasons he could not understand, and he began imbibing more than he should have. The stress was getting to him, and he sought the help of a psychiatrist. He told the psychiatrist about the UFO experience, among other things, and saw him for several months without any significant easing of his anxiety.

Then, in September 1963, the Hills were talked into speaking about their UFO experience at a meeting of the Two State UFO Study Group of Massachusetts and Rhode Island. In front of two hundred people, they spoke of their memories of seeing the object with windows, and Betty's subsequent dreams. They received an overwhelmingly positive response from the audience; however, the event seemed to increase Barney's anxiety, as he became more concerned by Betty's dreams with every telling. After continued suggestions that he undergo hypnosis, which were supported by people who had been in the audience that evening and had begun corresponding with the Hills, Barney asked his psychiatrist to set up an appointment with a clinical hypnotist.

In December, the Hills had their first meeting with Dr. Benjamin

Simon, an expert on traumatic amnesia who had a clinical practice in Boston. He outlined the limitations of hypnosis, and tested the Hills' susceptibility over the next few months. Finally, in February 1964, Simon began regressive hypnosis with the couple, working with them individually in a soundproof room, and warning them not to discuss their sessions with each other. It was not until April 1964 that the sessions were completed, and Barney and Betty could share their experiences.

Simon helped the Hills piece together a consistent narrative of their joint UFO abduction experience while under hypnosis. Betty's dreams were essentially "real" (the dreams might have reflected a subjective reality or an actual event) and Barney's involvement was related in considerably more detail, including his own physical examination at the hands of the aliens. It was this part of the experience that seemed to have been the source of much of Barney's anxiety. He had been unable to protect his wife during his examination, and his clinical treatment on board the UFO had been very demeaning to him.

Simon's therapy was ultimately successful, and their sessions were concluded later in 1964. The Hills' lives and psychological states improved and they tried to return to normal, although they still fielded requests for speaking engagements. Then, in 1965, a strong-minded reporter broke the silence and filed a story that was syndicated worldwide. The Hills' tale appeared many times in national magazines and was made into a TV movie in 1975. Barney never saw the film adaptation of their experience, as he died of a cerebral hemorrhage in 1969.

Simon's hypnotherapy has been criticized over the years by debunkers claiming that he only fostered the Hills' personal fears and fantasies, and that Barney's memories were contaminated by Betty's vivid nightmares. However, Simon's outstanding record of working with amnesiacs, and the extreme care he took while working with each of the Hills shows that there was no fault in his methodology. Simon himself did not believe that aliens were involved in the Hills' experience, and he thought that Barney was somehow influenced by Betty's dreams. One trouble with this view is that Barney began feeling anxious weeks before Betty related her first nightmares to him. In a final report, Simon casually stated that the Hills' anxieties had been caused by a "harrowing experience."

Under hypnosis, when Betty was describing the star map shown to her by the alien leader, Simon told her to draw it, but she initially refused. She said she couldn't reproduce it accurately because it was so unusual. He then gave her a post-hypnotic suggestion that she should draw it only when she felt she could do so with confidence. Eventually she did, producing an odd collection of dots and balls of varying sizes, some with connecting lines. The map was published in a number of sources.

In 1968, amateur astronomer Marjorie Fish, a Mensa member, decided to test the theory that the map represented a real array of stars. Using data from star catalogues that listed estimated distances and directions to known stars, she constructed a three-dimensional model of our local section of the Milky Way. Looking through the model from different angles, Fish searched for, but was unable to find, a match for the stars on the map. It was not until she adapted her model according to revised catalogues that she finally found a pattern that matched Betty's map.

The "home stars" on the map were Zeta 1 and Zeta 2 Reticuli, stars in a southern constellation that are much like our sun. The other stars on the map that were joined by lines were also sunlike in their characteristics, suggesting that they might have planets that support life, like Earth.

In later years, Betty became more and more involved with ufology. Other abductees sought her advice and experiential wisdom, and she became outspoken on the issue of contact with extraterrestrials. She had many other unusual experiences and seemed to be the target of odd phenomena, such as streetlights burning out as she walked beneath them. This suggested to her and others that she had a supernatural link.

Skeptics have argued that Betty's dreams were just that — dreams, and that Barney started having similar dreams after hearing about them from his wife. Other explanations have been less convincing; arch-skeptic Philip Klass at one time was certain that the Hills had encountered a very intense ball of plasma and become mesmerized by it.

In the end, there are only two possible explanations for the Hills' experience — either they hallucinated the entire series of events, triggered by an unknown catalyst, or what they described and recalled pre- and post-hypnosis actually happened.

The Rendlesham Forest Incident

It was just after midnight on the morning of Boxing Day, December 26, 1980. Near Suffolk, England, personnel stationed at bases RAF Woodbridge and RAF Bentwaters were enjoying a quiet time during the Christmas season. There were no planes in the air, none scheduled to land or takeoff, and only a skeleton crew was maintaining the bases.

Airman First Class John Burroughs was posted at RAF Woodbridge's back gate, called the East Gate. With him was Staff Sergeant Bud Steffens, a long-time member of the air force. As they talked to interrupt the monotony of their task, Burroughs noticed some odd lights hovering low in the sky, near the edge of Rendlesham Forest not far from the base. The lights, flickering and flashing red, yellow, and green, danced through the trees. Because they were certain they had not seen the lights before and they seemed to be close to the base, Burroughs and Steffens decided to investigate. They left their post and drove off the base, soon discovering that the lights were even closer than they had first thought. As they neared the area where the lights seemed to originate, another light, this one very bright white, appeared and moved towards them. Nervously they turned around and went back to the base to ask for help.

Back at their post, they called Sergeant McCabe inside the base and excitedly took turns telling him what they had seen. McCabe thought that the lights may have been from a plane crash and contacted the main security control centre, which dispatched Staff Sergeant James Penniston, the flight chief on duty that night at RAF Woodbridge. When Penniston got to the East Gate and heard Burroughs and Steffens' story, he went to investigate further, taking with him Burroughs and Airman First Class Ed Cabansag. Steffens was too anxious to join them.

The men drove along the edge of the base, following a logging road that quickly became impassable because of ruts and potholes. They decided to continue on foot, leaving Cabansag at the truck so he could remain in radio communication with the base. As Penniston and Burroughs left, they received word that Woodbridge had heard from London's Heathrow Airport that an unidentified object had been seen on radar near their area.

Back at the truck, Cabansag saw an unusual object through the trees near where his colleagues had gone. Just to the side of the beacon of a lighthouse just off the coast, he saw an egg-shaped object with lights around its middle, flashing blue, white, and red. Despite later suggestions to the contrary, he insisted that the object he had seen was not the lighthouse.

Penniston and Burroughs continued into the forest towards the lights, encountering many seemingly agitated animals fleeing the area. The men were getting uneasy, too. They realized that if the lights were from a burning plane, they would have seen evidence of a fire by this time. The lights seemed to be in a distinct group. For some reason, the hair on the backs of their necks and hands was standing up straight, as if they were near an electric field of some kind. Then their radios seemed to cut out. They became disoriented and began to feel as if they were struggling to take every step, as though "everything seemed slower than [they] were actually doing."

By this time, they had got close to the object on which the lights were arrayed. It was about three metres (ten feet) tall and three metres (ten feet) wide at its base, cone-shaped, and had blue lights around its middle. It was standing solidly upright, although no landing gear was visible. Penniston ventured close enough to touch it, noting its surface was smooth and hard, like glass. Penniston leisurely examined the object, taking notes in his logbook and photographs with his camera. He described it as "triangular in shape … at the left centre is a bluish light, and on the other side, red … a small amount of white light peers out the bottom." Some symbols were etched or embossed upon the side of the object, and when Penniston touched the lettering, the object's lights intensified, frightening the men. They moved back just as the object rose silently off the ground, then began to move erratically back and forth through the trees until it was about thirty metres (one hundred feet) away. It ascended over the trees, "and then literally with the blink of an eye it was gone."

The men found that with the departure of the object, their perception of the world returned to normal. They then saw another light moving in

Illustration by Jennifer Wang

Artist's conception of the cone-shaped object seen by military personnel at Rendlesham, England, in December, 1980.

the forest an estimated eight hundred metres (half a mile) away, and went towards it briefly before realizing they had been out too long already and turned back. When they returned to the clearing where they had seen the object, they found three triangular "landing gear marks" about three metres (ten feet) apart. They left the area, and rejoined Cabansag, then travelled back to the base.

At the base, they were told to keep quiet about what they had seen, but were also directed to go back into the forest to search for some physical evidence that would confirm and support their experience. They set out again, not knowing what they would find, but hoping to discover something that would confirm their story.

Back in the woods, they found the three indentations, as well as leaves that appeared to be scorched on some nearby trees. Plaster casts were made of the indentations, which seemed to verify their experiences. But when the local police investigated the area themselves, their report said only that lights had been seen and that marks like "rabbit scratchings" had been found. Penniston and Burroughs seemed very shaken by their experience, and became reclusive, even seeking out transfers from the base.

Later the same day, Lieutenant-Colonel Charles Halt, deputy base commander, returned from his short Christmas holiday and heard the story of what had transpired during the night. He interviewed Cabansag and was amazed at what had supposedly happened to the three men, but being a UFO skeptic, he doubted their story.

As it turned out, Halt was away from the base the following night, December 27, 1980, when more unusual events began unfolding outside the gate. This time, four men stationed there saw lights that again appeared to move over the trees before dropping into the forest. They received permission to drive off the base and entered the forest, where they heard a deep humming sound and saw fog laying over a field. There were lights embedded in the fog, and they also felt some kind of electricity in the air.

Another patrol had heard about the lights and went to investigate as well. Eventually, one of them found Halt and told him that the lights had returned. Halt organized an expedition of men armed with Geiger counters, cameras, tape recorders, sampling materials, and portable lights. When Halt and his team arrived at the edge of the forest, he met the other personnel who had been sent to investigate. He encountered difficulties with the personnel carriers he had brought, but nevertheless he found what appeared to be a landing site, with indentations on the ground and broken branches in the trees above. The Geiger counters seemed to register above-normal levels, and the men noticed that animals in the area seemed very agitated.

Suddenly, the men saw a bizarre object, only about 150 metres (five hundred feet) away. It looked like a large, glowing red eye, with a black pupil in its centre. It was giving off flashes of light, and was dancing through the trees, even appearing to wink at them. Halt later insisted to investigators that this eye was not the lighthouse, which he could see some distance away. The strange light disappeared, and when it reappeared, it was emitting sparks or smaller lights that fell towards the ground. The object appeared to explode before their eyes and vanish, but the men noticed three star-like lights close to the horizon in the north and south, which they believed were connected with the sighting. These lights remained in the sky, dancing about their positions and changing colours for several hours, sometimes shining what the men thought were beams of light to the ground, as if searching for something.

The third night of sightings was December 28, 1980. The main witness this time was Larry Warren, an airman stationed at RAF Bentwaters, another base near Woodbridge. The eighteen-year-old recruit had joined the air force only a few months earlier. Warren claimed that around midnight on December 28, and during the early morning hours of December 29, 1980, he had his own series of encounters with a UFO and met its alien occupants. He also described how his superiors on the base, who told him that aliens had a "permanent presence" on Earth, debriefed him. Warren's story, although very detailed and bolstered by transcripts of interviews with witnesses of the previous nights' events, remains unsupported by tangible evidence.

The Bentwaters case was leaked to UFO investigators only a few days after it occurred. Years of slow, careful investigation by researchers followed, and uncovered more and more details. Researchers found reluctant military witnesses eventually willing to give their testimonies, and obtained an official USAF memo that documented what had occurred. The memo was dated January 13, 1981, more than two weeks after the incidents, and indicates they took place a day later than witnesses recall. Although it is generally accepted that the error in dating the events was due to the delay in filing the report, it is certainly remarkable that an official air force report would contain such an error.

The audio recording made by Lieutenant-Colonel Halt on the second night of the incidents was made available to researchers as well, although much of the dialogue is unintelligible due to background and transcription noise. Nevertheless, it is a valuable piece of evidence that bolsters the credibility of the case.

There is no question that something remarkable occurred outside RAF Bentwaters and Woodbridge at Christmastime in 1980. There is enough evidence and testimony to indicate that a series of lighted objects was observed by civilian and military witnesses, though exactly what the lights were is a matter of conjecture.

Skeptics have often pointed to two known quantities when considering the case — the fact that a Russian satellite was re-entering the atmosphere around the time of the UFO sightings, and the existence of the lighthouse on the other side of the forest. Many people in Europe saw the flaming satellite debris as it streaked across the sky on December 25 and 26, 1980. It was later shown that at least a few people who had seen the bright light flashing through the trees had mistaken the lighthouse for a UFO. However, neither possibility can account for all of the details of the witnesses' observations. The objects seen at close range certainly were not re-entering satellite debris, nor were they a distant light source. Furthermore, the duration of the sightings make a short-lived re-entry display an unlikely explanation. Some witnesses who were familiar with the area insisted they saw the lighthouse in addition to the UFO. The military witnesses were familiar with aircraft crash scenes, having investigated many in their tours of duty.

One rigorous analysis of all the testimony, transcripts, site visits, and physical evidence explains the series of Rendlesham events as a combination of misidentification of meteors, stars, and the lighthouse, and effect of possible electromagnetic experiments at Orford Ness, a nearby military research facility. According to this theory, these experiments could have caused confusion in the minds of the witnesses, creating illusions that were enhanced by the real light sources.

Of course, the testimony of Colonel Halt, who insists his observations were not of any astronomical objects or navigation lights, remains puzzling. Something happened in Rendlesham Forest that Christmas, but what?

THE TEHRAN INCIDENT

On September 19, 1976, at twelve-thirty in the morning, the Imperial Iranian Air Force (IIAF) was contacted by a civilian airport at Mehrabad, near Tehran, regarding calls they had received from citizens about UFO sightings over the capital. One person described the object as "a kind of bird," and another frightened resident asked the airport to "tell this helicopter with a light on to get away from [their] house." Not surprisingly, according to the IIAF, there were no helicopters in the area at the time.

Brigadier-General Yousefi, assistant deputy commander of operations at the base, contacted the Mehrabad tower operators and determined that the object that had been reported was not on any air defence radar screens. Yousefi went outside, and saw a large, bright star-like object that he considered unusual. He decided to order the scrambling of a F-4 fighter jet from Shahrokhi AFB, about 240 kilometres (130 nautical miles) southwest of Tehran, to investigate the light.

The plane lifted off at about one-thirty local time and headed north towards the object, which seemed to be about 112 kilometres (seventy miles) away. Even flying at Mach 1, the pilot was unable to close in on the object. As he reached a point about 40 kilometres (twenty-five miles) away from his target, he lost all communications with the base. Following procedure, he broke off his pursuit of the target and turned back towards the base. When he was on a path towards home, his communications came on-line again.

On October 1, a transcript of a tape recording of the pilot's conversation with the control tower was released to the media. The operator had told the pilot, IIAF Lieutenant Jafari, to return home if he was unable to close in on the target. When he turned to go back, he told the tower: "Something is coming at me from behind. It is [fifteen] miles away ... now [ten] miles ... now five miles ... It is level now. I think it is going to crash into me. It has just passed by, missing me narrowly." The tower then guided the agitated pilot back to the base.

At 1:40 a.m. that night, a second F-4 was sent out. This time, the jet's radar operator got a lock on the object, placing it at fifty kilometres (twenty-seven nautical miles) away and at a twelve o'clock high, closing in it at 240 kilometres (150 miles) per hour. When the pilot had closed to within forty kilometres (twenty-five miles), the object moved away at a pace that maintained its distance from the jet. Judging from the size of the radar return, the object was estimated to be comparable to a Boeing 707 tanker, but visually, it was difficult to ascertain the size of the object because the light coming from it was dazzling. It seemed to have flashing strobe lights in a rectangular pattern, alternating blue, green, orange, and red, sequencing so quickly that all the colours could be seen at the same time.

As the jet continued its pursuit, another bright object, described as half as large as the moon, seemed to emerge from the first object. It headed straight towards the plane at a high rate of speed. The pilot attempted to fire an infrared-guided missile at the rapidly approaching object, but when he did so, his weapons control panel shut down and his communications system went dead as well.

The pilot then went into a turn and dove to evade what he believed was an enemy offensive manoeuvre, but the object followed his action and chased him at an estimated distance of three or four miles. The second UFO seemed to move into the inside of his turn before moving away to be close to the first object.

Flying at an altitude of almost eight thousand metres (26,000 feet), the pilot continued to watch his pursuers. A third object appeared, again seeming to emerge from the first one. The third object quickly headed directly toward the Earth. It descended, then suddenly decelerated, illuminating the surrounding area, and either gently stopping a short distance above the ground or hovering slightly above it. The pilot reduced his altitude and made a note of the object's location, then flew back to the air base. Curiously, the pilot and his crew had lost their night vision, probably as a result of observing the bright objects, and had some difficulty vectoring in on the runway.

As they approached the airport, there was considerable interference on their communications, and when they turned in a certain direction the on-board communications went out completely. A commercial aircraft that was in the area also reported electronic interference, but did not see any UFOs.

On approach to the runway, the F-4 crew saw yet another UFO, this time cigar-shaped, with bright lights on each end and a flashing light in the middle. This object was also not on the airport's own radar screens. The night scramble ended with no further incidents.

The next morning, the F-4 crew travelled by helicopter to the area where they believed the third object had landed, but found only a dry lake bed. Just west of the spot they detected a signal on their radio that led them to a small house. Landing, they asked the residents if they had seen any unusual activity the night before, and were told about a loud noise and bright lights that had disturbed their sleep.

In January 1978, the tabloid *National Enquirer* announced that the Tehran UFO case was "the most scientifically valuable" of all the ones its "Blue Ribbon Panel" of experts had studied. They found the testimony of the pilots' observations, plus the jamming of the planes' electronics, were very compelling evidence that something truly mysterious had occurred.

Arch-skeptic and aviation journalist Philip Klass disagreed. He pointed out many problems with the case in his book *UFOs: The Public Deceived*. He noted that for a spectacular case that involved military confrontation with what was apparently extraterrestrial craft, the details of the case were, amazingly, unclassified. Klass noted that there were indications that the American government was not taking the case very seriously, including the fact that there was no evidence that a follow-up investigation was conducted, and that the report on the incident was made available to the public fairly quickly.

But researcher Martin Shough countered Klass's argument by observing that the absence of any evidence of a high-level investigation is not proof one did not occur. He reasoned that it was possible that the USAF was very interested in the case and conducted its investigation at a level of secrecy far beyond the classification levels of anyone Klass interviewed.

Klass quoted a Tehran newspaper as stating that the UFO was observed flying to the south of the city, which is clearly at odds with the statement of the first F-4 crew that had been north of Tehran. As noted by Shough, skeptics are often critical of proponents who use newspaper accounts as a basis for supporting the facts of a UFO case, yet Klass was guilty of doing so too. A UFO sighting in the south, as reported by the newspaper, would actually support the second crew's testimony. Without speaking directly to the Iranian crew, Klass suggested that they reported the communications malfunction in error, but did not consider the possibility that the newspaper account or the statements provided to the USAF were somehow inaccurate. One further misinterpretation comes directly from Klass's own version of the story. He notes that the pilot who reported that the UFO came at him "from behind," contradicted himself by speaking of chasing the UFO. While Klass uses this contradiction as another reason to dismiss the case, a careful reading of the pilot's account shows that by the time he noted the UFO was following him, he had already turned his plane around and was heading home. The directional confusion that Klass points out does not actually exist.

Shough's remarkably detailed refutation of Klass's debunking of the Iran case addresses key points and suggests that there was something truly anomalous in the sky over Tehran that night. This is not to say that there are no other possible explanations for some elements of the sighting. Klass noted that about the same time, there were sightings of very bright fireballs far to the west along the coast of Africa, and reasoned that it was possible the Iranian pilots had seen another salvo of these. He further found evidence that the flight crews may not have had the highest level of training, although Shough disputed this as simply Klass's opinion, rather than a fact based on documented evidence.

THE PHOENIX LIGHTS

The night of March 13, 1997, will be remembered for many years in Phoenix, Arizona. On that night hundreds of people watched formations of lights move over the city and the surrounding mountains, giving rise to the general belief that a huge, mile-wide aerial craft was manoeuvring over this populated area. In the case of the Phoenix lights, not only does eyewitness testimony support the event, but there are many photographs and video as well.

The first reports of odd lights over the Superstition Mountains east of Phoenix came at around 7:30 p.m. A cluster of six or eight amber-coloured lights was seen moving slowly in the sky, then a group of eight or nine additional lights was seen as well. Sightings continued throughout the evening thereafter.

At 7:50 p.m., five to seven blue-white lights in a V formation were seen leaving Nevada and entering Arizona airspace. They eventually passed over Prescott on their way south, and were videotaped just north of Phoenix at 8:28 p.m. By this point, they were moving slower and had changed to an amber colour, apparently flying along Interstate 10 heading for Tucson. Witnesses said the lights seemed to be getting in the way of aircraft flying in and out of Sky Harbor International Airport, although the airport radar was not detecting the formation. As the lights flew along I-10, they hovered over a carful of people driving on the highway, who reported that at that point the lights were reddish in colour. Then, as witnesses watched, the formation appeared to break into separate lights, and each one flew off in a different direction. Some of the lights hovered over Phoenix.

At about eight-fifteen, five white lights in a V formation flew slowly from the northwest towards Prescott, where witnesses said they could see that the lights were on a single large "chevron-shaped" object. It rotated in the air over a witness's house and the lights turned red, shifted to form an arc instead of a V, and zipped away at high speed. Some witnesses in downtown Phoenix watched the object approach quickly and slow to a crawl before the lights shifted back into the V formation. Some observers insisted the object was only thirty metres (one hundred feet) above them, flying at close to a walking pace of only about fifteen to twenty-five kilometres (ten or fifteen miles) per hour.

The first report to the UFO hotline of the National UFO Reporting Center (NUFORC) in Washington came in at 8:16 p.m. local time, from Paulden, Arizona. The caller was a former police officer who said he and his family had just seen a "cluster of distinctly red-orange lights" in a V formation, with an additional lone light that was "standing back from the others."

At 8:23 p.m., several witnesses in Phoenix reported a huge object with five or six lights in a triangular formation travelling at "blimp speed," hovering, then speeding up before slowing to a crawl as it passed by. At 8:45 p.m., far to the southeast in Tucson, an identical object was seen, although one of its lights was seen breaking off from the main body of the craft and flying around a bit before returning and resuming its place in the formation.

The largest of the objects was seen at about eight-thirty moving over north Phoenix. Several real estate brokers watched as a giant black triangular object, whose wingspan crossed two streets that were nearly three kilometres (two miles) apart, moved low overhead. The witnesses said they saw a multitude of little lights along its edges, along with rows of windows in which silhouettes of figures could be seen. Witnesses driving on I-10 as it flew overhead reported that it took up to two minutes for it to pass over them completely! It was reported to be blue-grey in colour, with definite structure and panels of some kind underneath.

In Mesa, just east of Phoenix, a family said that at about nine o'clock, they had watched a large object with a clearly defined structure moving overhead. They described it as triangular in shape, with lights at its corners and another light in its centre. They claimed they could even see a "grid" of metallic panels on its sides, proving that it was a physical craft.

At around ten o'clock, the same or a similar group of lights was observed over the Gila River and then over southern Phoenix, where thousands of people saw it. To many it looked like the lights were on one enormous craft. During the rest of the evening and into the morning hours of March 14, many witnesses attested that they had seen a

V-shaped group of lights flying in the sky, and photographs and videos were taken of the mysterious nighttime visitor.

At 10:20 p.m., a retired airline pilot and several others watched as a different object, this time circular in shape, flew over Scottsdale Road in Phoenix. It was estimated to be 1.5 kilometres (about one mile) in diameter, and had yellow lights around its edge. It flew away over South Mountain and out of sight. One witness to this craft, a retired United States marshal, said that as it flew overhead, he could see the city lights reflecting off its underside while it blocked out the stars above.

There are many reports on record from people who said they saw F-16 jets from the nearby Luke AFB take off in pursuit of, or to intercept, the various objects or lights. Stories have even surfaced from workers at the base who insist that jets were scrambled and that some gun-camera footage was taken; however, none of this can be substantiated or proven. In fact, in a letter replying to ufologist John Greenewald Jr.'s query about military aircraft responding to the Phoenix lights, a spokesman explicitly stated that "Luke AFB aircraft were not involved in any way with the phenomena reported on the night of 13 Mar 97."

This statement is completely at odds with a report received by NUFORC on March 14, 1997, at 3:20 a.m. A caller to the UFO hotline stated that he was on staff at Luke AFB and had seen two F-15C jet fighters sent to intercept a large triangular object flying at eighteen thousand feet over Phoenix. The object did not have strobe lights as a military or commercial aircraft would, and its lights dimmed all at the same time before they went out completely. The caller noted that the F-15C jets were part of the "Air Force One Protection Group," and were on standby when needed. He also claimed that the jets had gun-camera film of the object, but that their radar showed only "white noise."

What were these mysterious lights and V-shaped craft? As with many complex cases, there may not be a single explanation, but a series of possibilities. First, there have been some very detailed analyses conducted on individual components of the Phoenix lights flap. Regarding the large object that was seen flying south over I-10 between about eight and nine o'clock, debunker Tim Printy located witnesses who saw that it was not a single large craft, but was composed of several individual aircraft. A pilot who saw the formation of lights and watched them with binoculars, described what he witnessed: "I saw five aircraft with [their] running lights (red and green) and the landing lights (white) on. They were also flying fairly slow and in the delta formation. As they went over me I could see stars going between the aircraft so it could not have been one large ship."

Other pilots also said they saw planes flying that night, which is something that proponents of the alien visitation theory don't usually mention. But wouldn't the airport radar pick up the planes as they flew overhead? An air traffic controller at the Phoenix Airport confirmed that no radar returns were detected, but explained that in a formation of planes, only the lead plane would have its transponder on. If for some reason its transponder was malfunctioning or was turned off, no information about any of the planes would be painted on the radarscope.

Of course, this information doesn't answer the question of who was flying in formation that night, and why. Despite all the publicity surrounding the case, no group of pilots has ever come forward to admit that they were the ones seen flying over Phoenix that night.

Another possibility is that the strings of lights were flares dropped from military aircraft during a training exercise. This theory is very popular among skeptics and seems entirely reasonable. Ufologist Lynne Kitei, who interviewed hundreds of witnesses and made many public comments about the lights, spoke with information officers at both Luke and Davis-Montham air force bases about the possibility of flares. She was told that aircraft out on nightly flying missions over Goldwater Range near Phoenix do drop flares, but that they "never fly over populated areas." She was also informed that no planes were in the air that night; however, on July 25, 1997, the *Arizona Republic* carried a story that stated that while it was true that planes from the local air force bases were not flying over Phoenix on March 13, 1997, a visiting Maryland National Guard squadron was in the area, flying overhead and dropping flares as part of an exercise. Records showed that several planes flew through the area between 8:15 and 10:30 p.m., but later investigations indicated that the planes had landed by 8:30 p.m., so while some of the sightings may have been planes, not all could be explained this way.

Peter Davenport, NUFORC director and the recipient of dozens of reports from witnesses of the Phoenix UFOs, felt that the lights could not have been from aircraft because they were "witnessed by many people to hover silently … because [the object] apparently covered the distance between Paulden and Prescott, AZ — not less than 30 miles — in approximately 1–2 minutes … [and] the lights seen on it were not consistent with any type of strobe lights, or navigation lights on any type of known aircraft, either private or commercial."

Davenport also acknowledges that military personnel have said the Phoenix lights were caused by flares dropped at nine-thirty by USAF A-10 aircraft that were over the Gila Bend bombing range southwest of Phoenix. He notes that this exercise, "if it did take place, occurred at approximately 2130 or 2200 hrs, some 45 minutes after the UFO sighting had already occurred over northern Arizona, Phoenix and Tucson."

In other words, the flares can explain some of the sightings, but certainly not all of them. Printy makes a strong case that some of the other observations were aircraft, although the planes' identities remain a mystery. They certainly weren't part of a regular flight because the sightings weren't repeated over the next several months or years. If aircraft were responsible for the bright lights over Phoenix, the flight of March 13, 1997, was quite unique.

On June 19, 1997, Arizona Governor Fife Symington III, pulled a bizarre stunt during a news conference in Phoenix. He appeared with his aide, Jay Heller, who was dressed as an alien in a metallic jumpsuit, sporting handcuffs, and wearing a large rubber alien mask, and announced that he was ordering the Arizona Department of Public Safety to conduct an investigation into the Phoenix lights. He later admitted he did it all in fun because many Arizonians were in a frenzy over the UFO flap, stating that he "wanted people to lighten up and calm down," but that he "never felt that the overall situation was a matter of ridicule."

In an interview in March 2007, ten years later, Symington confessed that he, too, had seen the Phoenix lights, but had not wanted to go public with his sighting at the time. He had seen an "enormous and inexplicable," object with lights and "a geometric outline, a constant shape." He added that the triangular object he had spotted "couldn't have been flares because it was too symmetrical."

During a news conference in 2000, Senator John McCain, Republican candidate for President of the United States and a friend of Symington, commented on the Phoenix lights: "That has never been fully explained. But I have to tell you that I do not have any evidence whatsoever of aliens or UFOs."

THE FIVE
MOST BIZARRE
UFO CASES

MOST UFO SIGHTINGS ARE OF SIMPLE LIGHTS IN THE
night sky. Such cases could be explained as any number of things: stars, planets, airplanes, and so forth. The sightings that can't be explained easily, like those of a light moving in the night sky that suddenly makes a ninety-degree turn and heads off in a different direction, are odd and puzzling. But what about cases where a witness sees a large metallic craft, meets alien creatures, and reports unusual side effects? Now those cases are more than puzzling — they are very bizarre indeed.

The Kelly-Hopkinsville Close Encounter

Dr. J. Allen Hynek, the leading UFO researcher during the early days of ufology, said the Kelly-Hopkinsville case seemed "preposterous" and offensive to "common sense." Despite this, the case as a whole is difficult to refute, and many investigators consider it a solid example of a close encounter of the third kind.

At around seven o'clock on the evening of Sunday, August 21, 1955, nearly a dozen members of an extended family began experiencing encounters with strange monkey-like creatures surrounding their farmhouse. The Suttons and Taylors were enjoying an evening together in their home near the towns of Kelly and Hopkinsville, Kentucky.

When Billy Ray Taylor went outside to the well to get some water, he saw a flying saucer move through the sky and drop down into a gully running along the farmyard. He ran back inside the farmhouse to tell everyone, but

Illustration by Jennifer Wang

A Hopkinsville "Goblin," seen August 21, 1955.

they just thought he had seen a meteor and weren't that interested.

That is, until about an hour later when their dog started barking loudly just outside the door. Billy Ray and Lucky Sutton opened the door just in time to see the frightened dog scramble under the house. It seemed to be running from a short, strange silver-suited creature approaching from the field. It was monkey-like, about three-and-a-half feet tall, with a large head, bulbous glowing eyes, pointy ears, and clawed hands at the end of long arms that were raised over its head.

The men reached inside for their guns and shot at the creature. It appeared to have been hit because it did a backwards flip and righted itself again. When the buckshot and bullets hit the creature, it sounded as though the men had "shot into a bucket." They went inside when they saw the creature clamber up the side of the house. Soon, it or a similar creature appeared at a window, and the men shot it point-blank through the screen. It flipped again and dropped out of sight.

Billy Ray went outside, and everyone watching his exit immediately saw a clawed hand reach down to his head from the overhang. A family member ran past Billy Ray, and, from the yard, shot the creature on the roof, which again flipped over and ended up on the other side of the house. Another creature was seen up on a tree branch, and when it was shot it floated gently down to the ground and scampered off. Throughout the next hour, creatures seemed to scurry in the shadows around the house, dashing around trees and outbuildings. The family heard scraping noises on the roof of the house, as if clawed feet were moving around up there.

Finally, after about three hours of being trapped in their own house by these strange creatures, the family made a dash for it, getting into their two vehicles and speeding to the sheriff's office in Hopkinsville, eleven kilometres (seven miles) away. They explained breathlessly what had happened, and the police officers accompanied them back to the farm, but there was no sign of the intruders. The police left around two o'clock, and the family nervously went to bed. Alas, the creatures seemed to return when the coast was clear, and family members saw them again, poking their heads in windows and darting around the outside of the house.

Reporters interviewed the seven adult witnesses several times over the next few days. Skeptics assumed that the witnesses had been drunk or hallucinating, leading the family to simply stop granting interviews after a short while. Another theory was that the family had seen monkeys that had escaped from a zoo, but the witnesses insisted that they had been close enough to see that the creatures were not ordinary animals.

While under questioning, the witnesses provided a clearer picture of the creatures. Their bodies were thin, like "a formless straight figure," with arms almost twice as long as their legs, but their hands were "huge, bulky-looking things." Their heads were round and completely bald; their eyes were large saucers set about six inches apart, and they seemed to wrap around the sides of their faces. The creatures' mouths were "not much more than a straight line across the face." Each of the seven witnesses gave identical stories of the events that transpired that night, and virtually identical descriptions of the odd creatures.

Once word got out about their experience, the family was subject to a great deal of ridicule and negative publicity. Understandably, they soon refused to discuss the matter with anyone. One investigator noted that, "the Suttons seem never to have been tempted to recant and get back into the good graces of society," and added that "neither adults nor children so much as hinted at the possibility of a lie or mistake — in public or to relatives; there was no trace of retraction."

So, the family either made up a story so fantastic that no one would believe them, or something unusual happened at their farm that night. It's easy to dismiss the case as a fantasy, but the witnesses were adamant that what they claimed to have happened really did happen, and not one of them changed his or her story.

JOE SIMONTON'S PANCAKES

One of the most tired clichés regarding UFOs in popular literature is that of an alien that steps out of its flying saucer and announces to amazed witnesses, "Take me to your leader!" However, I don't recall any case in the UFO literature in which this actually has been reported.

An odd variant of this scenario is a case that has become part of ufology folklore. On April 18, 1961, just before lunch, farmer Joe Simonton heard a strange noise outside his home. He ran outside just in time to see a silver, egg-shaped object land in his yard. It was about four metres (twelve feet) high and nine metres (thirty feet) across, and Simonton saw that it was hovering over the ground rather than actually resting upon it. He bravely walked over to the object as a hatch opened, and inside he could see three "men," who looked "like Italians," with dark complexions and dark hair. They each wore a uniform consisting of a kind of turtleneck sweater and close-fitting headgear. Simonton could hear a whining sound, as if from a generator, and he observed that the interior of the craft looked like black "wrought iron."

One of the "men" saw Simonton, and, holding up a silvery jug with a handle, he motioned to him in such a way that Simonton understood that he wanted it filled with water. The unflustered farmer stepped forward hospitably, taking the jug and going inside his house to fill it from a tap.

When he returned with the desired supply of water, Simonton saw that one of the "men" was sitting at a flat counter, apparently cooking something as if on a stovetop. The farmer gestured to the chef and conveyed his curiosity about what was on the grill. In reply, one of the men passed Simonton three "pancakes" — small, flat cookie-like things with numerous holes in them.

As Simonton examined the mysterious product, one of the men attached a cord or harness to the inside of the hatch, and pulled it closed from the inside, leaving no visible seam. Within a matter of seconds, the craft rose about six metres (twenty feet), rotated slightly, emitted a blast of gas from exhaust tubes on its exterior, and then flew away at high speed.

Illustration by Susan Birdwise

Aliens who gave Joe Simonton some "space pancakes."

Remarkably, there may have been another witness to the event. Investigators noted that around the time of Simonton's encounter, an insurance agent named Savino Borgo was driving along Highway 70, about a mile from Simonton's farm. He reported seeing "a saucer rising diagonally into the air and then flying parallel with the highway."

When the local sheriff investigated, there was no physical evidence to prove that such a craft had ever been there, except for the pancakes. One of these was eventually given to the U. S. Air Force to be studied, another went to a civilian UFO group, and Simonton attempted to eat the other. He noted that it tasted like cardboard. The USAF directed the Food and Drug Laboratory of the Department of Health, Education, and Welfare to test the object. The laboratory later reported that "the cake was composed of hydrogenated fat, starch, buckwheat hulls, soya bean hulls and wheat bran … [and] the material was an ordinary pancake of terrestrial origin." The cakes were made from a decidedly healthy recipe. If they were indeed made by the visitors to the Simonton farm, those aliens were health nuts!

The case was widely publicized because it was so fantastic. The National Investigations Committee on Aerial Phenomena (NICAP) made public statements about their investigation of the case, but some ufologists noted that "when the press interest died, NICAP dropped the whole thing."

Simonton received more support from the Aerial Phenomena Research Organization (APRO), whose investigators were impressed with his veracity. When one debunker suggested Simonton had simply been hypnotized (although entranced would have been a more accurate term), APRO representative Cecile Hess in Wisconsin scoffed at the suggestion, saying, "If I ever saw a sincere and honest man, it was Simonton."

Nevertheless, Simonton became fed up with the accusations about him. Sometime after the incident, he told a UPI reporter that if the same thing happened again, he didn't think he would tell anybody about it.

THE TULLY SAUCER NESTS

Probably the best-known historical UFO case in Australia is that of the Tully saucer "nests." A possible precursor to the famed crop circles of England in the 1980s and 1990s, the incident occurred in a remote area known as Tully in north Queensland on January 19, 1966. There are marked differences between the Tully case and what was reported in England decades later, including some possible meteorological explanations and the likelihood that hoaxers were not involved.

At around nine o'clock on a clear, warm summer morning near Horseshoe Lagoon, banana farmer George Pedley was driving his tractor along an access road on a neighbour's property when he heard an odd hissing sound. Thinking that one of his tires had sprung a leak, he stopped and climbed down to check. Walking around the tractor, he was surprised to see a grey, football-shaped object that looked like two saucers glued rim to rim, rising from the ground about twenty-three to thirty metres (seventy-five to one hundred) feet up the road. It seemed to be about eight metres (twenty-five feet) in diameter and slightly less than three metres (ten feet) thick, and it appeared to be spinning. The UFO was already about nine metres (thirty feet) in the air and was rising above the trees very quickly. In a matter of only fifteen seconds, it had ascended to about eighteen metres (sixty feet) in the air. It then flew off towards the southwest.

When it had gone, Pedley travelled up the road to the marshy area where the object seemed to have been. He found a circular spot that had been swept clean of reeds, and some of the water in the marsh, in an area of approximately the same dimensions of the object, was rotating slowly.

When he returned a few hours later for another look, he found marsh grass swirled in a clockwise direction, with no scorching or evidence of burning. The grass appeared green when it had first fallen, but turned brown quickly.

Pedley went to tell the marsh's owner, Albert Pennisi, what he had seen. Pennisi noted that his dog had been in a frenzy and barking in the direction of the marsh that morning; furthermore, he told Pedley that he had been having odd dreams about a UFO landing on his property. He went with Pedley to visit the area where the incident had taken place, taking

Illustration by Jennifer Wang

The spinning saucer-shaped object that was seen to create the Tully "nests" in Queensland, Australia.

photographs and even wading into the swamp and diving underneath the floating mat of reeds to discover their roots had all been cut away.

That evening, Pedley reported his experience to Tully police, and an officer visited the site the next morning. The nearby Royal Australian Air Force Base was contacted, and two days later the military office there asked the Tully police to file a formal UFO report and take samples of grass from the affected area. The report was filed a full week after the incident took place. Although Royal Australian Air Force records confirmed that there were no aircraft in the area at the time of the sighting, the police investigator was of the opinion that the swirled patch in the grass had been caused by a small helicopter. The investigator also felt that Pedley had mistaken sunlight gleaming on its rotating blades for a disc-shaped craft.

Other explanations were offered for the sighting, including the possibility that a waterspout had sucked up water from the swamp and uprooted the marsh grass, leaving it in a circular pattern. It was also suggested that there was nothing really unusual about the "nest" formed by the marsh grass, as a strong downdraft during a severe thunderstorm could have caused the "lodging" of the grass — a common occurrence whereby standing grass or wheat is blown flat by the force of wind. However, these explanations did not account for the object Pedley claimed to have observed.

During the next month, several other "nests" were found near the site of the original discovery. Cane farmer Tom Warren and schoolteacher Hank Penning found two more "nests," only twenty-three metres (seventy-five feet) from the first. They were considerably smaller than the original at only three metres (ten feet) in diameter. One mass of reeds was swirled clockwise, while the other was counter-clockwise. Three more "nests" were found within a week by another cane farmer. Two were about 3.5 metres (twelve feet) in diameter while the other was the smallest of all of the sites at only 2.5 metres (eight feet) across. It was speculated that these "nests" had been caused by further visitations or whirlwinds, or that they were the product of copycat hoaxes.

Queensland and Brisbane universities and the Royal Australian Air Force all conducted some studies on the affected reeds, but could not come to any conclusion as to what had caused the circles in the marsh.

ANTONIO VILLAS-BOAS

There are close encounters — and then there is what happened to Antonio Villas-Boas in 1957. He had what could be described as the *closest* encounter. You see, he didn't just see a UFO — he went inside one. And he wasn't just abducted — he was violated.

At about eleven o'clock on October 5, 1957, twenty-three-year-old farmer Antonio Villas-Boas was in his house getting ready for bed. He lived with his family near the town of Sao Francisco de Salles, in the state of Minas Gerais, Brazil. Looking out a window, he was surprised to see that their corral was illuminated from above by a strong light, although he could not see what was producing it. The light seemed to play upon the ground, and it eventually moved across the yard and onto the house, appearing through cracks between boards before going out.

Just over a week later on the evening of October 14, Antonio was plowing a field with his oldest brother at about nine-thirty when they saw a dazzlingly bright light appear at the opposite end of the field. It was about three hundred feet in the air and seemed to be shining from an object that was hidden by the glare. Although his brother was too frightened to move towards the object, Antonio bravely walked closer to see what it was. As he did so, the object flew to the other end of the field. He went towards it again, but it moved back. This continued for several minutes before the object suddenly disappeared.

The next night, Antonio was plowing at the same location, and at about one o'clock in the morning he noticed an odd, red-coloured star in the sky. It was moving towards him and getting perceptibly bigger as it approached. The object eventually took up a position about forty-five metres (150 feet) over his head. It appeared to be an egg-shaped object that cast a very bright pinkish light around his tractor.

Antonio thought about running away, but the object had proven the night before that it could move faster than he could run. Besides, it was too late; the object dove from its position and landed only about ten metres (thirty-five feet) in front of his tractor. He could now see that the craft was oval-shaped with three spurs arranged as a tripod on which it rested, and a lighted, rotating ring on top. Completely "freaked out,"

Antonio started the tractor and attempted to drive off, but its engine died. He then opened the door that was farthest from the craft and bolted outside, but a small creature in a strange uniform grabbed him from behind. He shoved the being away, tossing it several feet, but as soon as he made another dash for safety, he was accosted by three more creatures. They lifted him in the air and despite his struggles, managed to carry him to the craft and through a door in its side.

Once inside, Antonio saw that he was in a small room with shiny metal walls and ceiling, and what seemed to be fluorescent lighting along the wall. Five of the small but powerful creatures were restraining him, and he was guided through a doorway into another larger room. This room had a support beam running from floor to ceiling, and held a table and several small, one-legged stools. Antonio was kept there by two of the creatures while they and the others spoke to one another in dog-like grunts and growls.

The beings were similarly attired in seamless, one-piece "siren suits" that resembled skin-divers' outfits, grey in colour, that covered them from neck to feet. They wore helmets that attached with metallic plates to their suits, and that had eye coverings that looked like goggles. The helmets were larger on top than would be necessary to accommodate a human head, and three tubes that extended behind the creatures and into their suits stuck out from the top of each helmet. Their leggings blended into their footwear, which had thick soles and odd turned-up toes, much like a jester's shoes.

The creatures stopped talking, apparently having come to a decision, and began forcibly undressing their captive. Antonio fought them, but nevertheless ended up in his birthday suit. To make matters worse, one of the beings approached him with some kind of soft cloth, and began giving him a sponge bath with a thick, clear, odourless liquid. He was then led towards a door over which there were red squiggly letters that Antonio did not recognize as any language he had ever seen. He was taken into the next room by two of the creatures.

In this room, the creatures produced two thick pipes that they applied to Antonio's body to suck out some of his blood, leaving painful scars. They then exited the room, leaving Antonio shivering in the cold metal prison alone. Exploring the room, he walked over to a long, low table that he found to be a bed or cot, without legs or headboard. It was covered with a soft and comfortable material that was very inviting, so he lay down. But he noticed an unpleasant smell in the room, and when he got off the bed to investigate, he found that puffs of smoke or coloured gas were being emitted from thin tubes located along the top of the walls. His discomfort increased and he became nauseous, eventually vomiting in a corner of the room.

Antonio lost track of time and may have lost consciousness, for he was startled by the door opening suddenly. Looking up, he saw the unmistakable figure of a naked woman approaching him with a curious expression on her face. She wasn't quite human; Antonio described her as beautiful, but not like an Earth woman. She had long, silver-blond hair that looked as if it had been bleached, parted in the centre. Her eyes were almond-shaped, and extended farther around the side of her face than a human's. She had high cheekbones and an oval face with a small nose and a decidedly pointed chin. Her lips were thin and pale and her ears seemed "normal."

The female alien who seduced Antonio Villas-Boas in Brazil.

Illustration by Susan Birdwise

Antonio described her visual anatomy as that of a well-developed human female. She was shorter than him by about ten inches. Her skin was pale white, although she seemed to have many freckles on her arms and back. He also noticed that the hair in her armpits was red, instead of the silver-blond colour of the hair on her head.

This alien female moved towards Antonio and immediately made it clear what she wanted. She hugged him tightly and rubbed her body against his, then rubbed her head on his face, much like a cat. Antonio said he became uncontrollably aroused, which he attributed to the gas or liquids that he had been exposed to. He was somewhat put off by the growls and guttural sounds she was making, and they apparently did not complete their actions.

Before long, the experience was over. As the female alien exited the room, she turned back to him and pointed to her belly, then upwards, which Antonio interpreted as meaning that she would return to take him with her to her home. When she left, one of the creatures came into the room with his clothes, clearly indicating that he needed to get dressed. After he did so, he was led into another room where several of the creatures were sitting around a table. They appeared to be discussing the situation, and as they did, Antonio realized he had nothing to prove what had happened to him. He noticed that on a table near them was something that resembled a clock, and he nonchalantly sidled over and made a grab for it. One of the creatures caught on to what he was doing, ran over, and roughly shoved Antonio away. Nonplussed, he tried another tactic and inconspicuously attempted to scrape the walls with his fingernails, but found that the texture was too smooth to gather even a minute sample.

As Antonio was led through other rooms, he tried to note details of their appearance. He was taken back to the exit and down a ladder to the ground outside. Before long, the craft had sealed up once again. It took off from its tripod landing gear and rose into the air, spinning and making a loud noise. It ascended to about thirty metres (a hundred feet) then moved away with great speed, and was gone like a bullet within a few seconds.

Antonio walked over to his tractor and tried to start it, but found that the engine wouldn't turn over. He discovered that the battery leads had been disconnected. Antonio assumed the aliens had done this so that he wouldn't have been able to make a getaway if he had somehow escaped from the craft.

When he eventually got home, Antonio found that he had been gone more than four hours, as it was now about five-thirty. Exhausted, he slept through the day, and awoke at suppertime feeling refreshed. But he slept poorly or not at all during the next week, experiencing vivid nightmares about being captured again. During the next month, this trend reversed and he was excessively tired, even nodding off more than usual. When examined by doctors, he had some sores and purplish marks on his body, but was otherwise physically normal.

Dr. Olavo Fontes of Rio De Janeiro brought the case of Antonio Villas-Boas to the attention of the Aerial Phenomena Research Organization (APRO) in the United States in 1958. Fontes had examined Villas-Boas and was puzzled by his story and physiological symptoms. He was convinced that Antonio had not simply made up the story, because he had been reluctant to come forward with the details. Furthermore, if it had simply been a sexual fantasy, surely he could have done better. The female alien didn't even have lips for kissing!

Antonio kept to himself for many years, refusing all interviews, but in 1978 he agreed to be interviewed on Brazilian television to set the record straight about the many different versions of his story that had emerged over the intervening years. He was a learned man, having become a practising lawyer in Brasilia, and was married with several children. He had not discussed his experience in any detail, even with his family. Until his death, he maintained that his experience had been real, and that he had not made up any of it. He did not use his story to gain profit or fame, though he certainly could have if he had wished.

THE MANHATTAN ABDUCTIONS

In contrast to Antonio Villas-Boas, who refused interviews and went to great lengths to stay out of the limelight, the case of Linda Napolitano is one of notoriety and public attention. And rightly so, as many of the claims surrounding the case are fantastic and allegedly involve prominent individuals. The fact that it is said to have occurred in downtown Manhattan, in New York City, is also remarkable.

In May 1989, Napolitano began corresponding with abduction researcher Budd Hopkins about some odd experiences she had that seemed to be related to aliens. Six months later, on November 30, she called Hopkins in great distress because of a very traumatic dreamlike memory she had of a bizarre encounter with "them" during the previous night. She said she remembered waking up at about 3:15 a.m. and finding small alien creatures around her bed. She had tried to wake her sleeping husband, screaming at him, but he wouldn't stir. The aliens seemed to be speaking in strange language and telling her to be quiet. Before she knew it, she was somehow floating outside her downtown Manhattan apartment in her nightgown, many storeys above the ground, beneath a bright bluish-white light.

The light was revealed to be a large object that resembled a clamshell. The object opened, and Napolitano was taken inside. Within the craft, her body was examined by small creatures with large heads that poked and probed her with some kind of medical instruments, including a rod with a ball on its end that they put inside her nose. Eventually, the examination was over and she found herself back in her bed beside her snoring husband. The bedside clock showed that it was nearly five o'clock in the morning.

As remarkable as her story is, Napolitano's abduction experience by itself would hardly have merited much discourse, as literally hundreds of such cases are documented each year by abduction researchers around the world. Hopkins's files alone contain the accounts of many, many abductees, whose cases are at various stages of investigation, including regressive hypnosis, on-site investigations, and other therapies.

Illustration by Susan Birdwise

Linda Napolitano was seen to float over downtown Manhattan with several alien creatures.

But in February 1991, Hopkins received a letter from someone identifying himself as a police officer who wrote of an amazing experience he and his partner had in November 1989. Very early one morning they had been in a patrol car underneath the FDR Bridge in Manhattan when they suddenly noticed a bluish light near a tall apartment building in front of them. They were even more surprised to see the figure of a woman floating in the air beneath the light. She was accompanied by three odd-looking creatures that were also suspended in mid-air. They entered the light, which had now been resolved to that of an oval object, and it then flew off behind the Brooklyn Bridge where the astonished officers watched it descend and enter the water, disappearing from sight.

This observation greatly unnerved the men. In fact, after their experience, they had been troubled with guilt because they had been unable to do anything to prevent the woman from being abducted. The implications of what had transpired also caused the men to experience extreme anxiety — they had seen that aliens were indeed real, despite official denials of such things, and they had witnessed a close encounter over a populated area. One of the men even had a nervous breakdown of sorts, taking time off his beat and spending many nights parked outside the apartment building wondering what had happened to the woman.

Hopkins immediately realized the significance of this report; if true, it would be the first outsider eyewitness account of a UFO abduction that could corroborate an abductee's memory of her experience. He told Napolitano about the letter from the police officer. He recommended that if the policemen contacted her, she should not to tell them any details, so that their testimony would not be contaminated by anything she said to them. Hopkins reasoned that they would eventually show up at her door and want to talk with her, and ideally, he wanted to talk with them first.

Sure enough, a few weeks later, a very agitated Napolitano contacted Hopkins with the news that the two men had shown up at her door. They had said they were not actually policemen, but detectives named Richard and Dan. She said that Dan acted strangely during their visit, but that Richard seemed genuinely concerned about her well-being. They were puzzled about how she had managed to float in mid-air outside her apartment building, and wanted to know "how she did it."

A few days later, Napolitano was at a bus stop when Richard showed up, wanting to talk with her. A few days later he confronted her again, this time as she and her family were entering church to attend Mass. She informed Hopkins of each meeting, and he advised her of what to say and not to say. Hopkins asked Napolitano to tell the men how to contact him. A few weeks later, Hopkins received an audio tape from Richard, describing in detail what he had seen that morning. He also received a letter from Dan, who described how upsetting the experience had been for him.

Shortly thereafter Hopkins received another letter, this time signed not only by Richard and Dan, but also by a third person, whom Hopkins identified only as "Him." The story in this letter was different from the earlier versions. Richard and Dan were not police or security guards, but bodyguards hired to protect and escort "an important political figure." This third man had also seen the object and Linda's aerial abduction, even though Richard and Dan had made him lay down out of harm's way in the back seat of the vehicle.

Other ufologists speculated that the third person was Javier Perez de Cuellar, former Secretary General of the United Nations. Hopkins refused to reveal the man's identity, and Cuellar himself denied the claim. Another name bandied about was that of Canadian Prime Minister Brian Mulroney, who had apparently been in New York for a meeting at the United Nations that Cuellar had also participated in. His being in the car with Richard and Dan has also not been verified.

The case became even stranger as Linda and members of her family had both chance and prearranged meetings with Richard and Dan throughout the next several months, and as more letters and audio tapes came to light. At no time did Hopkins ever meet Richard or Dan, leading some researchers to suggest that the entire thing was an elaborate hoax perpetrated by Napolitano herself.

The case was complicated by other events such as Napolitano's abduction in broad daylight from a street corner by none other than Richard and Dan themselves. She claimed that they physically dragged her into a car then drove off, abducting her to interrogate her about her experience. She said that at one point Dan accused her of being "one of them" — an alien-human hybrid with "alien blood" coursing through her veins. Her captors even examined her feet to see if she had toes, as they insisted that aliens do not.

On another occasion, Dan, who was driving a red sports car, abducted Linda off the streets of New York, again in plain sight of many passersby. Perhaps such things are relatively commonplace in New York City, but skeptics challenged Linda about why she did not report the incident to police. Her reply was that because the kidnapping was done under the auspices of national security, it was technically legal. Dan drove her to a remote oceanfront location on Long Island where he forced her to put on a nightgown similar to the one she was wearing the night of the alien abduction. He also attempted to have sexual relations with her, twisting her arm and overpowering her, then forcing her head underwater when she resisted.

Linda was saved by Richard, who appeared suddenly and in the nick of time. He brought Dan, who was babbling incoherently, under control and protected Linda from further danger. Richard drove her home, and she immediately contacted Hopkins to arrange an emergency meeting. He verified that she appeared dishevelled and had sand in her hair when they met.

Hopkins eventually received a letter from the mysterious political figure who had witnessed Napolitano's abduction. He advised that the aliens were directly involved in Earth's political process and that they were striving to achieve world peace in co-operation with terrestrial agents. He also warned that any attempt to contact him directly would seriously threaten the proceedings.

As if things weren't complicated enough, Hopkins received reports from additional witnesses who had seen the UFO outside Napolitano's apartment.

Towards the end of 1991, Napolitano showed Hopkins an X-ray of her head that had been taken by a person whom she said was a doctor and a friend. She had been bothered by some discomfort in her nose and the X-ray clearly showed a strange opaque object about one centimetre in length with a curly protrusion at one end. This has been interpreted as an alien implant, possibly used by the aliens to track and locate their subjects.

Debate has raged within the ufology community regarding this case. Napolitano's credibility has been attacked, as has Hopkins's objectivity. It has been suggested that Hopkins was the victim of an elaborate hoax perpetrated by a number of people in cahoots with one another. It has even been suggested that the case bears an uncanny resemblance to the plot of a science-fiction novel, *Nighteyes* by Garfield Reeves-Stevens, which was published in April 1989, only months before Napolitano first contacted Hopkins.

The Five
MOST INTERESTING
UFO Cases

OUT OF ALL THE UFO CASES THAT HAVE BEEN REPORTED, only a select few are what I would call "interesting." A witness's sighting of lights in the night sky can be puzzling, but not as puzzling as multiple-witness observations of structured craft flying, landing, and perhaps leaving behind some physical evidence. This is not to say that nocturnal light sightings are not important. In fact, in terms of UFO case data, sightings of lights in the sky are very valuable in helping to understand the UFO phenomenon.

What constitutes a good UFO case? In the annual Canadian UFO Survey, we note the difficulty in assigning an evaluation or conclusion to UFO reports. If we use a ten-point scale to evaluate cases, and if the least credible is assigned a one and the most impressive is a ten then obviously we're more interested in cases with higher values. We note:

> The evaluation value is a subjective value imposed by the investigator or compiler (or both) with a scale such that the low values represent cases with little information content and observers of limited observing abilities and the higher values represent those cases with excellent witnesses (pilots, police, etc.) and also are well-investigated.

But the criteria mentioned above may not be enough to allow us to sort the wheat from the chaff. Perhaps a case rating a nine has been thoroughly investigated, but is simply a well-observed light or set of lights in the sky. The Phoenix lights qualify as a higher-valued case, since there is a great deal of documentation and witness testimony of what took place that night. True, some witnesses saw very large objects attached to the lights, but the entire affair didn't grab the attention of the public in the same way that, say, the Betty and Barney Hill abduction case did.

In picking my top five most interesting cases, I was looking for an indescribable "something" that made a particular incident stand out, or a case that had a subtle difference that piqued my curiosity just a little bit more than others. The following cases did just that.

FATHER GILL

In 1958, Father William Booth Gill, an Anglican priest, was working as a missionary in Papua New Guinea. He had heard of reports of odd lights in the sky over the large island near Indonesia, but wasn't sure what to make of them. He and other missionaries in the region had discussed such reports in their correspondence, but Gill was skeptical. In fact, when one of his friends reported a sighting in October 1958, he believed the lights that had been spotted actually belonged to the Soviet satellite, Sputnik, which had been launched recently.

On April 9, 1959, Gill was at his mission near the town of Boianai when he saw a light on the side of a mountain some distance away. The light vanished, but reappeared ten minutes later on the other side of the mountain, a distance impossible for a person carrying a lamp or torch across that difficult terrain to cover so quickly.

Gill became even more curious when his indigenous assistant, Stephen Gill Moi, reported to him a few months later, on June 21, that a saucer-shaped object had been seen in the air over the mission. Gill puzzled over the incidents but remained skeptical about the notion of flying saucers.

That is until June 26 at 6:45 p.m., when he was standing outside the mission and saw a bright light in the northwest. Gill noted that this bright object was above the planet Venus in the dusky sky, which he had been watching the past few nights. He called to some of the other missionaries so they could see it as well. As they watched, villagers joined them until more than three dozen people were all looking at the "sparkling" object. It came closer to them until it was hovering nearly overhead. It was resolved to a disc-shaped object with four "legs" on its underside. Witnesses said that on its sides were several "panels" or "portholes." Gill estimated the size of the craft to be about ten metres (thirty-five feet) across, and only about 90 to 120 metres (three to four hundred feet) away in the sky, although without reference points, he admitted this was only an estimate.

On the upper surface of the saucer, four humanoid figures could be seen through the glare of the light emanating from the object. They seemed to be doing some chore, moving around and occasionally moving out of sight. A "shaft of blue light" seemed to be shining up from the object into the sky, illuminating the figures on the deck. After about forty-five minutes, the object was obscured by clouds and lost to sight. It reappeared in another hour, accompanied by several smaller lights, and vanished into the clouds again after a few more hours. Gill had the wherewithal to have many of the crowd sign a written account of the group's observations, showing his awareness of the scientific and investigative process.

The next evening at six o'clock, the strange craft returned, with its crew again clearly visible on its upper deck. Two smaller objects flanked the larger "mother ship." Two figures could be seen, bending over and moving their arms as if they were "adjusting" something. After a while, Gill noticed that one of them appeared to have turned and was looking down at him, leaning over the side of the saucer with its hands on a "guard rail."

Father Gill decided to wave at the "man," and was surprised when he received a response. A native man watching with Gill joined the fun and waved at the figure on board; this time, a second figure on board waved back as well. As Gill and his companion waved together, all four figures on the craft waved back. "There seemed to be no doubt that our movements were answered," he noted.

Gill realized that purposeful communication with the craft's occupants was possible. Because it was getting dark, he asked that a flashlight be brought to him. When it arrived, he shone it in the direction of the craft, turning it on and off repeatedly. In response, the entire craft swayed back and forth in a pendulum motion, which Gill interpreted as a good sign. As they continued to alternately wave and shine the flashlight, either the figures or the craft would respond with movement. By about 6:25 p.m. the two-way communication ceased as the figures on the object moved out of sight. A blue "searchlight beam" shone out of the craft a few times, although Gill and the other observers did not know if it was in response to their actions.

At six-thirty Gill went inside the mission to have dinner. This fact alone suggested to skeptics that this entire story was a hoax, for what reason could there be for anyone to stop watching a flying saucer from another planet hovering over your head? Gill addressed this very question and others during an interview nearly twenty years later. He explained that since he had watched what appeared to be the same object for four hours the night before, and since he believed it was actually just an American "hovercraft" staffed by military personnel, he didn't think it was all that unusual. He did pop his head outside the door at about seven o'clock, and noted that the object was still in the sky, but had moved away slightly. When he checked again at 7:45 p.m., the sky was completely overcast and the strange craft could no longer be seen.

The UFOs were back the following night at 6:45 p.m., when as many as eight objects formed a line across the sky over the mission. This time they were not close enough for any figures to be seen on board. Gill and the villagers watched the lights intermittently until about eleven-thirty, when he went inside to bed. Just before he did, there was a loud metallic "bang" on the roof of the mission, as if something heavy had been dropped down onto it. The next day when the roof was examined, nothing was found, not even a dent.

The observations of Father Gill, his colleagues, and the townspeople have been debated among ufologists and debunkers for nearly fifty years. In 1960, the Department of Air, Commonwealth of Australia, issued a statement that noted that although it could not come to a "definite conclusion," it believed that what was seen could be explained as "reflections on a cloud." The Royal Australian Air Force later concluded that three of the lights seen were Jupiter, Saturn, and Mars, and implied that that this fact explained the entire series of observations.

Harvard astronomer Donald Menzel, known for debunking UFO reports, stated that Gill's saucer was likely the planet Venus, since Gill "never mentions [Venus] as a point of reference." In fact, as noted earlier, Gill did describe both Venus and the strange craft in his account, completely negating Menzel's explanation. Later, Menzel stated that Gill's observations of the creatures on board the craft were likely due to his not wearing glasses, since Gill suffered from astigmatism. But Gill told an investigator that he always wore his glasses, and that other witnesses who had good eyesight had seen the creatures as well. Yet another debunker suggested that Gill simply made up the UFO stories to entertain his colleagues. Again, this ignores the testimony of dozens of other witnesses, and disregards the dozens of other UFO sightings reported in the area about that time.

THE BELGIAN TRIANGLES

One of the most remarkable series of UFO sightings in recent memory occurred in Belgium from 1989 to 1991. This case involved multiple witnesses, military and government investigations, countrywide skywatches, and both photographs and video of something strange moving in the night sky. The number of reports involved is staggering — about 3,500 sightings, a quarter of which were investigated by ufologists. In surveys of ufologists asking them to rank the best cases of all times, the Belgian wave is often cited.

The case began with a rather spectacular multi-witness UFO sighting on November 25, 1989, near Limbourg, that was, unfortunately, explained relatively easily. Many people reported seeing large disc-shaped patches of light moving about the clouds, that sometimes circled overhead then darted away. Investigators quickly found that the owner of a popular nightclub had been using a strong spotlight projector to shine a rotating beam of light on the underside of the cloud cover. It was such a striking display that Belgian Air Force jets had been scrambled to intercept the intruder one night, eventually leading officials to pull the plug on the searchlight.

The Belgian wave began in earnest on November 29, 1989, at about five-thirty. Two police officers were driving from Eupen to Kettenis when they saw a bright light moving slowly over a field near the road. They decided to head it off by driving to the spot where it would pass over the highway. Sure enough it did. They watched as the object noiselessly moved over the road, stopped, made a U-turn and headed back from whence it came. The witnesses said it was a dark object in the shape of a triangle, with three bright lights, one at each corner, and a red flashing light, "like a fire truck," in the centre.

The officers drove back to Eupen, and learned that there had not been any civilian or military aircraft scheduled in the area. At six-thirty, they drove back out to the countryside to a place that would afford a better view of the surrounding area. They reported seeing the object again, this time stationary and low over a lake. But it seemed to be more internally active, with beams of light and what appeared to be "fireballs" shooting out of it.

Suddenly, they were surprised to see another group of lights rise into the air from behind some trees. The lights appeared to be connected to an object that also looked like a dark triangle, this time with a greenish pallor. It appeared to have a row of "windows" on its side. It turned in flight, and moved in a spiral path before heading away and out of sight by about eight-thirty.

Other police officers who had been listening on their radios as the sighting unfolded also reported seeing odd lights in the sky. An officer who actually saw the triangular object, with its white lights and central red light, also noted a "turbine" spinning at its trailing edge. Others heard the distinct sound of a generator or motor whirring. This led some investigators to suggest that the triangular object may simply have been a blimp or an ultralight aircraft manoeuvring in the night without a flight plan. As for the stationary object near the horizon that was shooting beams of light, investigators noted that the planet Venus was in the exact direction that the object was seen, and that no witness reported seeing both the planet and the UFO.

The next major sighting was on December 1, 1989, when a Belgian Air Force meteorologist and his daughter saw a triangular object moving slowly in the sky over the town of Ans. Then, on December 11, many people in Liège and other cities saw several lights moving about in the night sky. One man said he even saw an egg-shaped object apparently stuck in a tree, and making a loud humming noise. It also had three bright white lights and a structure of some kind. After a short while, it freed itself and flew away. Investigators combed the area and examined the tree the next day, but had no explanation for what was seen, other than a possible nighttime blimp.

A remarkable press conference was held on December 12 in Brussels. The conference was a co-operative venture of the Belgian Air Force, the Eupen police, and a civilian UFO group called the Société Belge d'Etude des Phénomènes Spatiaux (SOBEPS). Media were told that an official investigation into the sightings was underway, and that the origin of the UFOs would be found through in-depth investigations. A unique partnership was formed between government, military, and civilian organizations, and hundreds of cases were soon under investigation.

Things happened quite quickly. On December 21, 1989, the Belgian Minister of Defense released a statement about the investigations. He noted that the UFOs were not related to military activities, and were not radar patrols, American F-117A fighters, remote control drones, or ultralight aircraft. Some ufologists believed that the information provided in the statement was simply a cover, and that the UFOs were secret military aircraft. However, it was announced that if there were another reliable sighting of a triangular craft, the Belgian Air Force would scramble American F-16 fighters to investigate.

Sightings continued off and on throughout the next several months. Perhaps the most remarkable event of the entire UFO wave occurred on the night of March 30, 1990, hundreds of people reported seeing UFOs in the skies over Belgium. Most were stationary lights, but some seemed to be moving about. At 10:50 p.m., a police officer in the village of Ramilles reported seeing a UFO, and police in Wavre confirmed his observation. They notified a Belgian Air Force radar station at Glons that three lights in a triangular formation were again flying nearby, and the NATO base at Semmerzake confirmed an unknown target.

The Belgian Air Force made good on their promise, and two F-16s were sent out. One pilot was directed to videotape his radar screen, while the other was told to tape what was taking place directly in front of him. No visual images were recorded, but the radar showed that thirteen separate unidentified targets were locked on. Some of these targets moved slowly, at about 270 kilometres (170 miles) per hour, before accelerating to 1,770 kilometres (1,100 miles) per hour. At times, the targets appeared to drop from an altitude of 2,700 to 1,500 metres (nine thousand to five thousand feet) in only a few seconds. One even crossed directly in front of the jets without being seen at all. The Belgian Air Force reported: "Each time the pilots were able to secure a lock on one of the targets for a few seconds, a drastic change in the behavior of the detected targets occurred."

The radar tapes were analyzed, and it was said that the activity that had been recorded could be explained as the result of processing defects within the on-board computers. At least one of the lock-ons was one F-16 accidentally targeting the other! The other targets were nothing but ground clutter, and the lights in the sky were bright stars and planets.

These explanations did not satisfy members of the Belgian public or the international community, who were suspicious of official pronouncements about UFOs. They found this dismissal especially difficult to believe because on March 31, the day after the radar case, a man in Brussels shot a video of the infamous triangular craft. It had all the earmarks of the classic Belgian triangle: three white lights, a red flashing light, and steady movement. But even SOBEPS had to concede that the video was simply of a plane taking off from an airport.

Only one photograph taken throughout the Belgian UFO wave has held up to scrutiny. It has been regarded as proof that something strange was occurring in the skies over Belgium. A member of a photography club near Petit-Rechain, near Liège, took a photo that clearly shows a dark, triangular object with three bright lights on its corners and a fourth red light in its centre. SOBEPS and other ufologists believe that this is an authentic photograph of the object that harassed Belgian townspeople for more than two years. The three corner lights show some structure, as if they were composed of a group of smaller lights. Even this evidence is problematic, as the exact date of the sighting and photograph is unknown, and there are no reference points on the image to indicate how large it is or how far away it is from the observer. Further, the validity of the photo is additionally complicated by the story that it was supposedly put in a drawer and forgotten for four months, until a reporter questioned the photographer (who remains anonymous) about it.

Ultimately, as with all UFO waves, the large number of cases that composed the Belgian wave can be boiled down to a relatively small number of unexplained events, while the other incidents can be explained as misidentifications of ordinary phenomena.

One of the more unusual cases took place on the night of October 21, 1990, near the town of Bastogne. Two people were driving home when they were shocked to see a pair of bright lights coming down from the sky, apparently heading for them. The lights disappeared behind some trees, but as the car came around a hedge the occupants were confronted by a strange lighted object only about fifteen metres (fifty feet) away on their right side. They continued to drive, panicky, but the object kept with them until they finally stopped in fright. They could see it was actually a dark craft, about thirteen metres (forty-five feet) in diameter, with a ring of seven or eight lights on its underside. It continued to move, and rose swiftly into the air before vanishing from view.

By the middle of 1991, the Belgian UFO wave was over. Sightings had dwindled to a trickle, and residents were left wondering what had really occurred during those frenetic few years.

TRINDADE ISLAND

Trindade Island (not to be confused with Trinidad in the Caribbean) is a small dot on the map, off the east coast of Brazil. During the International Geophysical Year of 1958, scientists gathered data throughout the world on changes in the Earth's climate.

Brazilian scientists working with that country's navy selected this small island as a location to gather samples and launch weather balloons with instrument packages. A base was set up and several ships were anchored offshore to facilitate research activities. Personnel aboard the navy ships tracked and retrieved the balloons to collect data. Curiously, some of the researchers reported seeing odd lights and other objects at high altitude near the balloons, but could not identify them.

On the morning of January 6, 1958, Commander Carlos Bacellar, chief officer at the scientific base, watched the launching of a weather balloon with an attached instrument package. It was fitted with a radio transmitter that sent out signals as it ascended, allowing easy tracking. As Bacellar monitored the receiver inside the base hut, the signals faded and then stopped unexpectedly. This occasionally happened in high winds and stormy conditions, but the day was clear with few clouds.

Bacellar went outside to see what might have happened to the balloon and found it well within sight, gaining altitude and nearing a cloud. As he watched, the balloon and its package were suddenly drawn upward into the cloud. After ten minutes, it reappeared over the cloud but without its package. Using binoculars, Bacellar watched as a silver crescent-shaped object moved out from behind the cloud and then away. A technician with Bacellar also saw the object through his theodolite. As puzzling as this was, what happened next was even more remarkable.

Not far away, off the coast of Trindade Island, the Brazilian Navy ship *Almirante Saldanha* was anchored as scientists packed up their experiments before returning home. Among the forty-eight passengers and crew was Almiro Barauna, a civilian with expertise in underwater photography. At 12:15 p.m., he was on deck with some of his camera gear when a retired Brazilian Air Force officer called to him, drawing his attention to a bright object in the sky over the island.

As he looked in the direction the officer was pointing, another officer ran towards them, also gesturing skyward. Barauna saw the object flash in the sunlight as it moved over the ocean toward the island, and watched as it passed in front of a cloud. He quickly took two photographs of the object before it flew behind a mountain on the island. It reappeared on the other side, apparently closer to the witnesses because it seemed larger. It was metallic grey, and its shape resembled the planet Saturn — that is, it was an oval with a ring. Barauna took one more photo, but was being jostled by the excited group of witnesses on board and couldn't get any more clear shots off. The object flew off across the ocean away from the ship and could no longer be seen.

Once it was gone, Barauna took the film out of the camera and joined the animated discussions about the object that were taking place on deck. An hour later he took the film into the ship's darkroom with a Brazilian Air Force officer, and developed the photos. There was no photographic paper available, so he couldn't print the negatives, but these were examined and seen to contain images of the object.

When Barauna got back to his home in Rio de Janeiro, he printed the negatives and took them to the navy office. A few days later, he was called to the office and interviewed about the circumstances surrounding the photographs. Over the next several days, officials discussed the case at length, and eventually decided to release the photographs to the media. They caused a sensation. Newspaper reporters worked hard to get the testimony of additional witnesses, and politicians argued about the incident in Brazil's parliament.

A carefully worded news release by the Brazilian Navy stated: "This Ministry cannot make any statement about the object sighted over the island of Trindade, for the photographs do not constitute enough evidence for such a purpose." It was noted, however, that the object was not a weather balloon or a stray missile. Another statement noted that there were "indications of the existence of unidentified aerial objects."

Originally, debunkers explained that the photos were actually of an aircraft viewed head-on, giving the impression of an egg-shaped body bisected by a line that was interpreted as the ring. Later, it was said that Barauna, in collusion with one or more people on the ship, had simply faked the photos. This ignores the fact that several witnesses testified that they had seen the object flying overhead, although the navy failed to get official statements from any of them except Barauna! Finally, one critic discovered that Barauna had exposed a previously photographed UFO in Brazil as a fake in a magazine. The implication was that he had learned from his subject and created a hoax that would stand up to scrutiny.

Debunker Donald Menzel described how he thought Barauna had created the photos: "In the privacy of his home the photographer had snapped a series of pictures of a model UFO against a black background. He then reloaded the camera with the same film and took pictures of the scenery in the ordinary fashion. When the film was developed, there was the saucer hanging in the sky." Supporters have countered that no such model ever turned up in Barauna's possession, although this in itself doesn't offer enough proof to dismiss the allegations.

Menzel did state that only Barauna and one other person, who he believed to be an accomplice, actually said they saw the object. This conflicts with statements made by investigators, who listed several witnesses of the event.

Recently, the issue of photographic trickery was again raised among ufologists discussing important cases. The magazine in which Barauna offered his expertise at faking flying saucer photos was translated into English from Portuguese to allow greater accessibility. Barauna's Trindade photos were placed beside some of his fake saucer photos for comparison, and there is no question that they do look similar.

Brazilian ufologist A.J. Gevaerd defended Barauna in a detailed rebuttal to skeptics in 2008, pointing out that the published article on fake UFO photos was well known; Barauna had never denied it. Gevaerd noted that Barauna was not the only witness to the sighting. In fact the same magazine that published the fake saucer photos, also printed an article about the Trindade case that noted that many witnesses saw the object pass over the ship.

Gevaerd argued in favour of Barauna's veracity, stating: "I can tell you that no one has ever caught him in any kind of dishonesty or even in a small lie. On the contrary, he is still remembered by everyone as a serious, reputable and decent person." In 2008, Gevaerd made public an English translation of an interview with Amilar Viera Filho, a witness to the Trindade UFO who was on board the Brazilian Navy vessel. Filho was not interested in UFOs, and was only on board the ship to deliver supplies from the mainland. He said that Brazilian Air Force Reserve Captain Jose Viegas saw the object first and called out to Barauna, who began photographing it. By the time Filho saw it, the object had already moved over the island. He described seeing "a gray object which turned bright then went away slowly then increased speed until it disappeared on the horizon." Filho insisted that the "object was really in the sky," and added: "I can assure that because I saw it and I'm saying that I'm sure!" He also noted that the Brazilian Navy had asked the witnesses not to disclose anything.

This case is most interesting because it continues to spark discussion and controversy. More details about the sighting continue to emerge and are becoming accessible to ufologists.

TRAVIS WALTON

On November 5, 1975, a logging crew was heading home after a long day of thinning new growth in the Apache-Sitgreaves National Forest in northern Arizona. Among the seven-member crew was twenty-two-year-old Travis Walton, who shared duties with the others, cutting scrub with a chainsaw and gathering branches into piles. The foreman of the group was Mike Rogers, an experienced forester. Rogers and his crew were working hard to complete a contract with the U.S. Forest Service, but had been running behind and had already been given an extension. As a consequence they didn't finish until about six o'clock when it began to get dark.

The entire crew climbed into their pickup truck and headed along a dirt track through the rocks and trees, with Rogers driving and Walton by the passenger door. As they turned a corner, they saw a glow that resolved into a blue, disc-shaped object hovering in the air over a clearing not far away from the track. The object was lit from inside, as if it was an opaque fluorescent light, and was covered in black lines dividing it into facets, like a diamond. Judging from its position in the clearing, it appeared to be about six metres (twenty feet) wide and just over two metres (eight feet) high.

Walton suddenly opened the passenger door and jumped out. He had thought the object would zip away, and wanted to get a really good look at it before it did. He ran towards it, and stopped nearly underneath it, gazing sharply upward at the strange craft. The object started to emit a pulsating rumble and tilted down slightly towards him. He backed off and hid behind a log, but he was frightened. Walton rose and had begun to turn back towards his friends when he felt a shock as if he had been electrocuted, and blacked out.

His co-workers in the truck saw a brilliant flash of blue light hit Walton, raise him off the ground slightly, and throw him about three metres (ten feet) away onto the ground like a rag doll. Spooked, Rogers put the truck in gear and sped away, with the panicky crew shouting behind and beside him. He didn't want to suffer the same fate as Walton. Eventually, he stopped the truck almost half a kilometre (about a quarter of a mile) down the road, and after some agitated discussion with his companions, he turned back to search for Walton.

Walton and UFO, however, had disappeared without a trace.

Rogers and the others called the sheriff's office from a shopping mall when they made it back to town at about seven-thirty. The police who arrived were suspicious of the foresters' bizarre story, but observed that the men were highly emotional and some were even crying. The officers went back to the site with Rogers and some of his crew, searching the area with flashlights. They were concerned because Walton was not dressed for the cool weather. Later that evening, Rogers and a police officer went to the home of Walton's mother, about sixteen kilometres (ten miles) away, to break the news to her. The officer was surprised when Walton's mother didn't fall apart at the news her son was missing; in fact, she was relatively unemotional. This observation led skeptics to later charge that Walton and his mother had conspired together to fake his disappearance.

During the next several days, search parties combed the area but did not find any trace of Travis Walton. Suspicion fell on Rogers and the rest of his crew, and eventually they were implicated in Walton's apparent homicide. Each man was even given a polygraph test to see if he had killed Walton or knew where he was. Incidentally, they all also passed the polygraph question asking whether they had actually seen a UFO that night.

Late in the evening on the fifth night after Walton vanished, one of his brothers-in-law received a phone call from someone claiming to be Travis, saying he was at a phone booth by a gas station in a town about fifty kilometres (thirty miles) away. Initially leery because pranksters had been calling the entire Walton clan all week, he was eventually convinced that it was the missing Walton, and agreed to pick him up.

Travis Walton was found gaunt and exhausted in the phone booth, barely able to stand. As they drove, he talked about creatures with large eyes and how he had been very frightened. He asked to be taken to see a doctor, but did not want anyone else to know he was back.

Duane, Travis Walton's brother, was approached by many ufologists once the strange story had been made public through the police investigation. One of the ufologists was Bill Spaulding, representing a group call Ground Saucer Watch (GSW), who impressed Duane with his credentials and his claim that the group had many affiliated professionals, including doctors. When Travis asked to see a doctor, Duane took Spaulding up on his offer. Unfortunately, the doctor to whom the Waltons were referred did not even have a licence to practice, and was only a hypnotherapist without professional accreditation.

Fortunately, another UFO group soon set the Waltons up with licenced physicians, who came to their home to examine Travis. Two anomalies were found: a red mark on the inside of his elbow, and the absence of acetone in his urine sample, which normally builds up when someone goes without food for several days.

Skeptics have noted that the urine sample was not actually produced by Walton at the time of the medical examination. In fact, the sample had allegedly been produced at Spaulding's suggestion not long after Walton had come home after his ordeal, and preserved. Skeptics also suggested that the mark on Walton's arm could have been an indication that he had injected himself with a hallucinogen, leading to his bizarre story.

And what a story! Walton said that after blacking out, he woke up on his back, fully clothed, in a small, sterile room similar to a hospital room. He was tired and thirsty, his body was sore, and his vision was initially blurry, though it cleared slowly. He seemed to be lying on a bed of some kind, with a curved piece of a hard material arched around his chest, possibly acting as a restraint. He was shocked to see three strange creatures standing near him.

These beings were less than five feet tall, with large hairless heads, and no eyebrows, eyelashes, or beards. They had large, staring eyes and slit-like mouths. They were delicate creatures, soft and fragile, with whitish skin and slight builds.

Walton realized they were not physically threatening, and because he was angry with his captors, he lashed out, hitting one and watching as it fell against the others and knocked them over like dominoes. He grabbed a short rod off a ledge along a wall and waved it menacingly in their direction. They stopped advancing towards him and turned about, leaving the room.

He followed them out warily, and found himself in a curved hallway. He progressed along it and came to another open doorway. Inside was an almost empty room, except for a single captain's chair with panels of buttons and switches. When he approached the chair, the lights dimmed, and the ceiling and walls appeared to dissolve into a dome of stars that resembled a planetarium. When he backed away, the room returned to normal.

Suddenly, another door opened and in walked a tall being with a bubble-like helmet on his head. This creature was obviously different from the smaller aliens; he was wearing a tight-fitting garment that showed he was very muscular. This formidable being took Walton by the arm and led him out of the room, down the hallway, and into yet another room. This area was very large, and they soon walked down a sloped ramp into what could only be described as a hangar. Walton saw that he was exiting a craft shaped like the one that had zapped him back in the forest. Other craft sat silently not far away.

Walton was led by the tall being across the hangar to a doorway that opened into a long, wide hallway. They continued walking along the corridor until they reached a set of doors that opened into a room where three other beings that looked like his tall companion were sitting, all without helmets. They came up to him, forced him down onto a table, and placed a device that resembled an oxygen mask over his face. He passed out almost immediately.

He woke up lying on the highway near the gas station. He looked up just in time to see a craft that looked like the one he had first seen in the forest hovering over the road. Suddenly, it shot up and out of sight without making any sound whatsoever. He immediately ran over to the pay phones, trying three before finally getting one to connect, and called his brother-in-law.

Whether or not Walton made up the entire story has been debated by skeptics and proponents since the case became known. As is typical of abduction stories, there are elements that seem absurd and suspicious. Could the story just be a grand lie orchestrated by Rogers because he knew he couldn't finish the contract on time? In theory, he could have coerced his workers to help with the scheme, but one wonders why, once the police investigation began to turn towards murder, the hoaxers would not have simply admitted their ruse? What would have happened if Walton had not turned up?

During their investigation the police examined the phone booths for Walton's fingerprints, but found none. Lie detector tests on Walton, Rogers, and the other foresters were either passed or inconclusive. One psychiatrist stated that in his opinion, Walton only imagined the abduction experience, although he could not explain "five witnesses having the same basic story and passing lie detector tests about it." Could the entire forestry crew have collaborated in a conspiracy to defraud the government by fabricating an alien abduction?

THE GIANT YUKON SAUCER

The best-documented and most thoroughly investigated recent Canadian UFO case was a multiple-witness event in the Yukon on December 11, 1996. The lead investigator on this exhaustive case was ufologist Martin Jasek, who has devoted much effort and expense studying the UFO phenomenon in the North.

Through the course of his diligent investigation, Jasek came to believe that this particular case was of critical importance to ufologists because there did not seem to be a conventional explanation for what had been seen over the Yukon that night. He was so certain that the object that was sighted must have been detected by military or government installations, that he sent copies of his forty-five-page report to the federal and provincial governments, the RCMP in Whitehorse, and the Department of Defence base in Yellowknife.

None of the sightings of the object in this case were reported to the military or government institutions at the time. Using a compassionate approach and assuring his witnesses' anonymity, Jasek managed to obtain detailed testimony from people who feared ridicule and lack of support if they were to make their sightings widely known. Furthermore, Jasek interviewed each of the twenty-two witnesses separately and at length. They provided him with drawings of the object that were consistent with observations that had been made from different distances and perspectives. Jasek pieced together a complex and consistent series of observations of a remarkable object seen over the course of 320 kilometres (two hundred) miles over Fox Lake in central Yukon.

At around seven o'clock on December 11, 1996, four people were travelling north nearing the town of Carmacks when they saw a group of lights in the northwest above some nearby hills. They pulled off the highway to get a better look, and saw that the lights appeared to be attached to a larger object moving across the sky. There were several large orange lights in an oval pattern, and dozens of smaller white lights on the main body. One witness saw only three large orange lights in a row with the other smaller lights to the right side. The object was very large, covering an estimated sixty to ninety degrees of sky. It moved ponderously across their view, and vanished suddenly after approximately ten minutes.

At the same time in the town of Carmacks, a family sat watching their television, which was positioned in front of a large window with a view to the northeast. They saw a row of lights that reminded them of a Boeing 747 jet airliner slowly moving over trees to the northeast. Three young children believed that it was Santa Claus coming early. The silent object, estimated to be at least thirty metres (one hundred feet) across, had four large red and yellow lights in a row, with smaller orange and green lights trailing. Additionally, there seemed to be "white sparkles" dropping to the ground from the bottom of the object. As it made its way east, the lights went out one by one, as if the object was moving behind trees. It was lost to sight after about five minutes.

Driving north along the Klondike Highway from Whitehorse to Carmacks, another witness saw a bright white light over the far end of Fox Lake. He watched it during his sixteen-kilometre (ten-mile) trip along the lake, noting some cars parked at a campground halfway along. When he reached the northern end of the lake, he could see that the light seemed to be on a larger object, and was partly illuminating a curved surface. He lost sight of the object briefly, but then saw three rows of rectangular lights slowly moving over the crest of a hill on the east side of the highway away from the lake. He stopped at Braeburn Lodge and excitedly related his sighting to the owner over a cup of coffee, even drawing a picture of what he had seen for the bewildered proprietor.

At about seven-thirty, two cousins heading for Carmacks left Whitehorse in separate vehicles, and began travelling along the Fox Lake road. The first was nearing the Fox Lake campground when he looked west and saw a large, football-shaped object with a rim of lights hovering over the lake. Astounded by what he was seeing, he pulled over to the side of the highway. His cousin stopped at the side of the road a few hundred feet south of the other car because he too had seen the UFO. They both watched from slightly different perspectives as the large object moved towards the highway. The first of the two cousins looked directly up at the underside of the craft, which was featureless except for a large bright white light in the centre. The craft continued to his right, and passed over the mountains out of sight. While watching the object, he tried to use his two-way radio, but its band was filled with static.

The cousin who had been travelling behind watched the object move over the road ahead of him. Having a more oblique view, he saw that the large object was lighting up the surrounding countryside. His view was spectacular, to say the least. The object looked like a domed, oval-shaped craft with two rows of rectangular lights along its midsection. Small, diffused white lights outlined its upper and lower surfaces, while there were two stacks of red rectangular lights on either side of the smaller "windows." As he watched, the UFO brightened and moved across the highway out of sight.

He walked towards his cousin up the road, where they confirmed each other's sighting. They agreed to get back in their vehicles and drive to a nearby campground to discuss it. While they were there, another car pulled up and two people got out to ask if they had seen the UFO as well. To them, the object looked like a row of rectangular windows with flashing lights at either end, and an additional rotating "searchlight beam" on the right side. They believed the object was quite large, and they judged it to be about six to eight kilometres (four or five miles) away, near the campground. One of them thought he had also seen several very dim white lights in the shape of an arc or dome above the "windows." After a while, they all got back in their cars and drove north to the Braeburn Lodge where they, too, told the owner about their sighting.

Meanwhile, a trapper was working his trapline about fourteen kilometres (nine miles) east of Pelly Crossing at around the same time as the Fox Lake sightings. He was looking west when he saw a row of lights moving over the hills in the distance. As they approached, he realized they were on an object so large that he had to turn his head from side to side to look at all of it. The object stopped about three hundred metres (a thousand feet) away, blocking out the stars across a wide expanse of sky. He estimated the craft was a kilometre (three-quarters of a mile) across and was positioned about 240 metres (eight hundred feet) above the trees.

The trapper noted the row of lights was comprised of as many as one hundred individual rectangular "windows," which were each approximately two by six metres (six by twenty feet) in size. Above these and centred on the middle of the craft were seven white or yellow rectangular lights. A beam of white light was projected from the bottom of the object, playing upon the ground in front of him. The object made no discernible sound, and was in view for about four minutes before moving behind some trees to the east, where it abruptly vanished.

Two more witnesses were driving north along the Klondike Highway when they noticed what appeared to be a "cluster of stars" moving together through the sky. They recognized the stars of the Big Dipper above this group of moving stars, and figured that they covered at least as much sky as the constellation. The cluster consisted of a middle row of lights surrounded by several others above, below, and to the sides. The lights moved slowly to the east over the hills and trees. The lights appeared to turn off as the object vanished in the distance. The time was between eight-thirty and nine o'clock, and the object had been in view for approximately three or four minutes.

At about eight-thirty, four students were taking a break from classes at Yukon Community College in Pelly Crossing when one of them noticed some odd lights in the sky. She called the lights to the others' attention, and they all watched a horizontal row of lights move from the northwest to the northeast. The yellowish lights appeared to be on an object about the same size as a large aircraft that was travelling slowly and making no noise. One student thought the object had square windows, noting that there were larger ones at the leading side that appeared to taper to the rear. Another described the object as a large oval with rows of lights on either side. They all watched the object for about three minutes until it was lost to sight behind a hill in the north.

Another witness was walking across a bridge in the area when he saw the large UFO flying towards him. He was so frightened that he fell prostrate on the ground as the object passed only a short distance above the bridge. A family member later verified that he was in an agitated state when he eventually got home.

In total, Jasek interviewed twenty-two people who witnessed this remarkable event, and received second-hand information about many other witnesses across the Yukon and Northwest Territories. He sorted through the testimonies, and calculated distances, directions, and times to piece together what happened that night. He checked with airports and military bases, but was told that there was no activity in the area at the time of the sightings.

Jasek considered a dozen possible explanations for the event, ranging from hoaxes and hallucinations, to satellite re-entries and military aircraft. He rejected all of these, as none adequately explained the data. In his widely circulated report, he concluded: "The sightings of a giant UFO in the Yukon Territory on December 11th, 1996 by at least 31 people were most likely a product of non-human intelligence and a technology far beyond current scientific knowledge reported by mainstream science."

Jasek sent his report to a host of officials, including his local member of Parliament. He asked them to consider the subject of UFOs more seriously, and to note the Yukon case in particular. He called upon the Canadian government to initiate an inquiry into the matter and suggested several things that could be done to put an end to what is perceived as an "atmosphere of witness ridicule and government silence on the UFO topic." These were:

1. Ask the Government of Canada to assess what was likely the cause of the sighting of a giant (at least 0.88 km long) UFO on December 11th, 1996, at Fox Lake,

Carmacks, Pelly Crossing, and Mayo, Yukon. Most importantly, they should make their conclusions public.

2. Ask the Government of Canada what conclusions they have reached about the large quantity of other UFO data that they have collected and specifically the reports that are highly suggestive of non-human intelligence.

3. Ask the Government of Canada what actions citizens should take if they are confronted with intelligently controlled vehicles of apparent non-human intelligence.

4. Ask the Government of Canada to educate the public and civil servants about the potential seriousness of UFO sightings to encourage witnesses to report their sightings as well as feel free to discuss them openly.

5. Explicitly list "Ridicule of Witnesses" as a form of discrimination.

6. Encourage scientific study of the phenomena by sharing data that the Government of Canada has collected and conclusions (past and recent) it may have reached.

7. Ask the Government of Canada to encourage and support Universities and Colleges to study the UFO issue/topic much the same way they support other scientific programs.

8. Ask the Government of Canada to establish a government-sanctioned UFO study committee including both military and civilian investigators such as has been done by the Government of Chile.

The last point refers to a report that the Chilean Air Force had set up a special committee to investigate UFO sightings. It had been noted that "reputable sources such as pilots and air traffic controllers had sometimes reported seeing objects for which there was no immediate explanation."

Whether or not Jasek's recommendations were embraced by any department within the Government of Canada, his noble effort to bring the subject of UFOs to the attention of politicians and Parliament is commendable. Jasek's outstanding and thorough investigation of a well-witnessed, well-documented UFO flap stands head and shoulders above many other UFO investigations.

SO CONTINENTAL

IN A SINGLE BOOK, IT IS DIFFICULT TO GIVE EVEN THE most basic overview of notable UFO sightings around the world. The best I can do is to give readers a flavour of the types of sightings that are reported in various countries. Entire books have been written about UFO cases in specific countries, and where possible I have given some references for further reading.

The UFO phenomenon is truly global, with sightings reported from literally all corners of the world. Most countries have at least one UFO group of some kind, with varying degrees of interest. Most of these groups investigate and discuss UFO sightings reported within national boundaries. They usually have a presence on the Internet, and are in communication with colleagues in other countries through e-mail and web pages, although the latter become out of date and go off-line as groups come and go.

While we have already looked at some significant UFO cases around the world, in this section, I will note some additional reports that have been made on each continent to paint a clearer picture of global UFO sightings. Sources for these cases are provided so that readers can judge their reliability and put them in context. It is not known how much investigation has been done on each individual case, only that they have been discussed among ufologists, and in some instances presented in other works on the subject.

Asia

On July 14, 1947, the Associated Press reported that an "enormous platter" that "emanated luminous rays in all directions" was seen in the skies over China. The information was released by the Chinese Palace of State, and showed that the Kenneth Arnold sighting in June 1947, in the United States was not a phenomenon unique to the West. While on an aerial search near Mt. Rainier in Washington state, Arnold, a pilot, had reported seeing a group of crescent-shaped metallic objects reflecting the sun, dipping slightly now and then as they flew like "saucers" skimming across water. (This was the origin of the term "flying saucers.")

One would think that a country as populous as China would produce more UFO sightings than any other in the world. In North America, polls suggest that one in ten people believe they have seen a UFO. If the phenomenon was truly global, then China should have a very significant number of cases on record; however, China's break with the West, which occurred shortly after the 1947 "platter" report was released, made information about UFOs in that country difficult to obtain. In fact, the subject of UFOs was at one time considered counter-revolutionary. In recent times, though, news about sightings of UFOs in China has been much more forthcoming, and we are learning that the phenomenon has been present there throughout the decades, just as it has in the West.

In October 1963, passengers and crew on a Chinese airliner flying from Kuangtung to Wuhan saw three luminous objects that chased the plane for fifteen minutes. The pilots were in radio contact with civil aviation authorities during the entire encounter, and when they landed the crew was interrogated and the passengers were told not to speak about what they had seen.

A few months later, residents of Shanghai watched as a large cigar-shaped object flew slowly through the sky. Chinese fighter jets were scrambled but were unable to get near the object. It was later reported by the Chinese news agency that the object was an American missile. The military was also involved in chasing a spherical object that rose from behind a rocky ridge near Dingxian City in Hubei Province in September 1971.

Perhaps the most remarkable UFO sighting in China took place on July 24, 1981, at about ten-thirty at night. Literally thousands of people in twelve provinces across China reported seeing a large bright object shaped like a spiral flying through the night sky. Some witnesses in Guizhau likened it to a "dragon" while others called it a "flying saucer," suggesting that some information from Western media had been making it to the Chinese population over the years. Several students at Kunming Medical College in Yunnan Province watched it through binoculars as it progressed rapidly through the sky. The object had at its core a disc or lens that had a row of "windows" on its upper part. The centre was bluish-green, and it was surrounded by a spiral of light, making the entire thing appear to be about four times as wide as the full moon. A farmer described the object as a moon-sized disc from which sprouted a tail that made a spiral as it rotated. The New China News Agency published stories about the sighting throughout the next few months.

In August 1980, many people reported unusual lights in the skies over Tientsin and Bo Hai, and only a few months later on October 16, 1980, a UFO was tracked on radar near Tientsin. Air traffic control was tracking routine air traffic when a return they assumed was an expected incoming flight appeared on the screen. The blip mysteriously disappeared and the controllers contacted the pilot to see what had happened. To their surprise, they realized the airliner was not the return they had detected, as it was not yet in range. When the plane did come into view, the mysterious blip appeared once again, crossing their screens in the opposite direction of the airliner. As another flight came by, the unknown object vanished, then reappeared again. In addition, radio interference was heard by the air traffic control tower, causing some concern.

Shortly before this, on October 5, 1980, a schoolteacher in Tangshan was awakened by a bright light outside her window shortly before four o'clock in the morning. She woke her husband and the two of them watched an illuminated cigar-shaped object with a ring around its middle fly slowly across the sky towards the southeast. Investigators found four other witnesses who had seen the same object while fishing on a beach.

In Ghizhou Province on February 9, 1995, yet another radar UFO case was reported. An air traffic control operator picked up an unknown object about two miles from an incoming commercial airliner, and informed the pilot of the object's presence. The pilot told the tower he could not see anything there, even though the plane and unknown object were travelling on parallel courses. Suddenly, the pilot reported that the anti-collision alarm on board the plane had gone off. The pilot had to climb through a cloud layer to avoid the perceived danger.

Hundreds if not thousands of people are now members of various UFO groups in China, attesting to the intercultural fascination with the phenomenon. In 2005, a World UFO Conference was held in Dalian, a port city in Northeast China's Liaoning Province. It attracted a large crowd, including more than the approximately four hundred people who were reported to be members of the Dalian UFO Society, most of whom had college degrees. At that time, the Beijing UFO Research Association had 110 members, "mainly from official organizations and research institutes." Ufologist Stanton Friedman, who attended the Dalian conference as an American representative, was impressed with the conference proceedings and discussions.

In 2007, a recording of an exchange between an air traffic controller and a pilot was played at a UFO seminar in Shanghai. The tape was made on March 18, 1991, when a pilot radioed an airport tower to report that he had seen a fast-moving object near his plane. The object was about ten or fifteen feet long, red in colour, and "spraying fire-like gas and transforming into two objects, a ball and a cube." The object made several mid-air turns, first heading northeast, then southeast, then west, and finally north as it split into the two shapes. The objects then climbed higher and moved out of sight of the pilot, who was mystified by what he had seen.

Many citizens of India are also interested in the subject of UFOs. Among the most recent reports in this country was a case that took place on March 7, 2007, at about nine-thirty in the morning, when air traffic control radar in Delhi detected two UFOs. The slow-moving objects, flying about seven miles apart, both passed over Safdarjung before heading east and vanishing off the radar. Both air traffic control and the air force tried to establish radio contact, but failed. Safdarjung is only two miles from the prime minister's residence, and UFOs flying over a secure area might indicate a security threat.

The Indian Air Force claimed it was informed about the UFOs only when the objects were within five miles of Safdarjung. The air force also said that the objects had vanished from the radar with five minutes, so there was no time to scramble jet fighters to the area. The Civil Aviation Ministry said there had not been any other reports of UFOs over Delhi. The air force conducted an inquiry into the incident, but did not come up with an explanation for what had taken place.

Just two months later, at about nine o'clock on May 28, 2007, a group of brothers in Bangalore saw a bright, slow-moving group of lights in a triangular formation heading to the northwest. One of the brothers reported it was "definitely not an aeroplane." They watched it for about half an hour and managed to take several photos of the object.

On October 29, 2007, the manager of a company in Kolkata got up at about 3:15 a.m. to get a drink of water. When he came back to bed, his wife told him to draw the curtains because a breeze was coming in their ninth-floor apartment window. As he was at the sill, he looked east and saw a bright star-like object about thirty degrees up in the sky. He was puzzled by the object, and took out his video camera and began filming it.

After zooming to maximum magnification, the object appeared through the viewfinder as "a white ball with flaming sides which changed colour and shape." Then it seemed to be "dotted with red bulbs but with a white patch in the middle." After a while, the witness described it as looking like a "jaguar-shaped plane with a blue flame at the top and yellow and green in between." He continued watching and recording the object until it became lost in the lightening dawn sky at about 6:20 a.m.

He was convinced that the object was not an aircraft, which were a regular sight from the apartment window. The sighting was reported to Indian authorities who verified that there was nothing on radar in that direction at the time. The sighting sounds very much like a star or planet scintillating through the hazy atmosphere, and is similar to cases recorded elsewhere in the world. It appears that misidentifications are a global phenomenon.

Probably the strangest UFO story to come out of India is one that has several variations and is recounted from year to year, so it is difficult to verify. In August 2002, a mysterious object was said to be terrifying villagers in Uttar Pradesh by flying into their homes and causing injury and even death! One survivor said the object looked " like a big soccer ball with sparkling lights." She reported that it burned her skin, and that she continued to experience pain after the incident. Near the village of Darra, seven people were reported killed, one with "his stomach ripped open," and many others had been scratched and burned. Doctors in Lucknow explained the effects as mass hysteria, while police in the Mirzapur District believed the deaths were caused by a type of bug, described as three-and-a-half inches long with wings. It was said to cause rashes and superficial wounds when it bit. So many people were afraid of being attacked in their beds that when police dismissed their hysteria, as many as ten thousand rallied and protested, requiring police to issue warning shots over their heads.

In Japan, people have been reporting unusual objects in the sky for so many years that some ufologists have even suggested that "ancient astronauts" made appearances in the Land of the Rising Sun before recorded history.

The most significant post-war sighting in Japan turned out to be singularly dramatic — a luminous object dangling in the air from an enormous, darkened craft, was witnessed by many observers over Tokyo Bay in the summer of 1952. The objects were also picked up by radar, prompting jet fighters to scramble to intercept. The huge aerial contraption proceeded to elude the military aircraft with manoeuvres never thought possible. In the early days of the Cold War, with the Korean conflict still brewing on the other side of the Sea of Japan, the thought of a surprise attack by unknown Soviet technology was fresh in every strategist's mind.

In June 1974, an F-4 Phantom with the Japanese military locked on to a mysterious quarry, and experienced the closest of close encounters — a head-on collision with a UFO. The pilot and his weapons officer thought the object approaching at high speed on their radar screen was a Soviet aircraft, as these planes would often would play cat-and-mouse with the Japanese. As it moved within visual range, the crew was surprised to see it was not a plane, but a twelve-metre- (forty-foot-) wide disc with square openings on its side. When the Japanese crew locked its weapons on the UFO, it increased speed and collided head-on with the jet's nose cone, forcing the crew to eject. Unfortunately, the weapons officer died as a result of the accident. According to one published source, the Japanese government never acknowledged the encounter with the UFO, attributing the in-flight accident to "a collision with an unknown object at 30,000 feet."

In February 1975 near Kofu, two boys claimed they watched a UFO land, and were brave enough to walk up to it, noting it had "oriental characters" on its side. As they watched, a "ladder" came out of the craft and a silver robot-like creature descended and headed towards them. Not surprisingly, the boys panicked and ran away to the safety of home, where one of their parents observed an object rising into the sky. Later that year, a UFO followed a Japan Airlines DC-8 for twenty minutes until the plane landed safely at a local airport.

Early in the morning on October 17, 1976, as many as fifty people in Akita reported seeing a gold-coloured, disc-shaped object that hung in the sky for ten minutes. Air traffic controllers at the airport advised approaching flights to avoid the area because of the unknown craft. Witnesses included Japanese media that had been filming a documentary at the airport, so the sighting attracted considerable attention.

In 1991, at an International UFO Symposium held in Hakui City, Japanese Prime Minister Toshiki Kaifu expressed his opinion that it was "time to take the UFO situation seriously." Prior to the symposium, on June 24, 1990, Kaifu had written a letter to Mayor Shiotani of Hakui City endorsing the upcoming event. In the letter, Kaifu said that Japan was "an underdeveloped country with regards to the UFO problem," and wrote that the country needed to "take into account what should be done about the UFO question ... to solve the UFO problem with far reaching vision." Kaifu also expressed his hope that the symposium would "contribute to peace on Earth from the point of view of outer space, and take the first step toward the international cooperation in the field of UFOs."

Compared with other Asian countries, less information about UFO sightings is available for Japan despite its high population. Yet, interest in UFOs is said to be high. OUR-J was a Japanese UFO group formed in 2000, and by 2003 it had several hundred members — but as of 2008, its

Illustration by Jennifer Wang

In Akita, Japan, on October 17, 1976, many people saw a disc-shaped object hanging in the sky.

website was closed and no information was available. When OUR-J was active, the group held periodic skywatches for UFOs and also published newsletters. During one such skywatch on October 11, 1999, as many as sixty transparent, luminous rings appeared in the sky over Meiji Jingu shrine in Harajuku, Japan. They were witnessed and photographed by OUR-J founder Junichi Kato and many other members of his group, who "just gasped" at the extraordinary sight. An analysis of the OUR-J data indicated that the UFOs seen in Japan are most commonly described as being shaped like "pachinko ball[s]." Oval and lemon-shaped UFOs were also reported.

UFOs have also been reported in most other Asian countries. One case occurred in Vietnam on June 19, 1966, during the time American soldiers were heavily engaged in the conflict there. The case received very little attention at the time, even though there were hundreds, if not thousands, of military witnesses, since Nha Trang was a heavily defended coastal base in South Vietnam, with more than forty thousand troops and about two thousand American personnel. A civilian UFO group, the National Investigations Group on Aerial Phenomena (NICAP), investigated the incident and interviewed one of the military eyewitnesses.

The Nha Trang base was in a valley, on a south-facing beach along the ocean. On the night of the incident, bulldozers were clearing roads west of the base, small aircraft were being readied for flight on an airstrip to the east, and a Shell Oil tanker was anchored in the bay to the southwest. At eight o'clock, many of the troops had gathered in an open area of the base to watch an outdoor movie, the projector powered by a diesel generator.

At around 9:45 p.m., a very bright light like a flare suddenly appeared north of the base. Since flares were often deployed, this wasn't particularly surprising, but this light was moving erratically. According to a witness: "It dropped right towards us and stopped dead about 300 to 500 feet up. It made this little valley and the mountains around look like it was the middle of the day."

As the mass of soldiers watched, the object began moving again and rose swiftly out of sight within a few seconds. One soldier reported that while the light was over the base, the "generator stopped and everything was black and at the Air Force Base about ½ mile from here all generators stopped." Even the engines on the aircraft at the airfield nearby stopped running. The witness noted that no cars, trucks, or planes ran for "about four minutes." The ship anchored offshore experienced the same power blackout. Later checks of all the generators and engines at the base could not find anything wrong with them.

The soldier further noted that following the incident, "a whole plane load of big shots from Washington" arrived to investigate. Apparently, news of the event was broadcast widely on military radio stations, although nothing was ever reported in the stateside media. The case would certainly have created cause for concern, since it temporarily crippled a major military base during a period of operations in an intense conflict.

The subject of UFOs in Russia and the former Soviet Union has been of great interest to Western ufologists. The fact that the American government and military establishment have undertaken several studies of UFO reports makes it likely that parallel studies have been conducted behind the Iron Curtain. Since UFOs are a global phenomenon, the number of cases throughout the Eastern bloc should be considerable.

Indeed, since the opening of the Russian states and Eastern Europe to Western examination and interaction, a great deal of information about UFO cases in the former Soviet Union has come to light. Many of these cases are of the same calibre and detail as major cases in the United States and other countries, and have been investigated by officials and military personnel. Several books have been written about UFO sightings in the former Soviet Union and present-day states, each providing a wealth of information about what has been seen and experienced.

Stories of unusual aerial objects and encounters with otherworldly visitors from the land east and south of the Urals date back many centuries. In relatively modern times, on July 30, 1880, a large bright object flew over St. Petersburg, moving in a triangular formation with two smaller objects. They moved together without making any sound across the city, in view for three minutes.

Probably the most talked-about historical case of a strange flying object in Russia took place on June 30, 1908, over Siberia. Early that morning, hundreds of people in and around the Tunguska region reported seeing an oval fireball pass overhead, changing direction and speed, with a luminous trail behind it. A massive explosion was felt throughout the continent, and seismic stations in Irkutsk and Tashkent registered tremors. The sky glowed so brightly that people could read newspapers at midnight in Moscow, Paris, and even London.

It was not until 1927 that an expedition funded by the Soviet Academy of Sciences managed to visit the swampy wilderness area, and what they reported was more astounding than anyone had imagined. A wind-driven firestorm had swept the area, uprooting and charring trees in a region measuring several thousand square kilometres in diameter. Many theories have been proposed to explain the event, ranging from asteroid impact, a comet, a black hole, a nuclear blast, and even an alien spaceship. Most scientists now believe the damage was most likely caused by a comet.

A more traditional UFO sighting, if one can be so described, took place in August 1958, close to Tsarina's Mountain near Leningrad.

Members of a topographical survey were doing some work there when one of them called the others' attention to a strange object moving noiselessly through the sky. It was cigar-shaped, like an airplane's fuselage, and had a shiny metallic surface, but no doors, windows, or stabilizers. It veered unexpectedly and flew out of sight rapidly. There were no rocket ranges in the area, and the scientists could not explain the event.

Although not over Russian soil, a case that took place a few years earlier in 1956, involved famous Soviet pilot Valentin Akkuratov. Akkuratov was with a crew on a mission in the far north near Greenland when his plane descended through clouds into clear sky, and he saw an object flying parallel not far away. It was lens-shaped with "pulsating edges," off-white in colour, and had no wings, windows, or visible exhaust. Since the Soviet crew believed it to be an American craft, they ascended again into the clouds. After flying for forty minutes, they came out of the clouds and were surprised to see the same object, still pacing them. They decided to approach the craft and altered their course to intercept it, but it turned as well and continued to maintain a constant position relative to their aircraft. After fifteen minutes of this game, the object increased its forward velocity, flying away and then higher into the atmosphere.

A more remarkable UFO case took place in the Soviet Union on August 13, 1967, near Yalta on the Black Sea. At around eleven o'clock at night, a fighter pilot was on a training flight, flying at nine thousand metres (thirty thousand feet), when he looked up from his instrument panel to see an oval light to his left side, very close to his aircraft. He radioed his commander about the object and was told that there were no other planes in the area. He banked and as he did so, the object's light dimmed considerably. Suddenly a bright beam of light appeared in the sky ahead of him. The pilot tried to avoid it, but he could not change course in time and the beam impacted his plane's left wing. He was shocked to see the beam of light shatter into a collection of sparks like a fireworks display. When it did so, the plane shook and rattled, and its instrument panel malfunctioned. Soon, the light and its solid beam vanished. When the pilot returned to his air base, he noted that the surface of the plane's wing shone mysteriously, even several days after the incident.

On September 10, 1976, a British airliner en route from Moscow to London at an altitude of ten thousand metres (33,000 feet) had just entered Lithuania when the pilot saw a "blinding" stationary light off his starboard side. It was estimated to be sixteen to twenty-four kilometres (ten to fifteen miles) away and slightly below them at about 8,200 to 8,500 metres (27,000 or 28,000 feet). The yellowish light was of constant intensity. It was too bright to look at for any length of time, and was reportedly illuminating a cloud bank below it. The pilot radioed Soviet air control, but was told not to "ask questions" about the object. After ten to fifteen minutes, the British plane had progressed far enough that the object was no longer in sight.

The pilot of a Russian MiG encountered a UFO in October 1981. He was flying on a routine mission when a ball of light, estimated to be about five metres (sixteen feet) in diameter, suddenly appeared nearby. As the pilot continued to fly while watching the object, his radio stopped working and his engine cut out. The object moved to a position behind the plane, and an explosion was heard and felt in the tail section. The object vanished and to the relief of the pilot, the plane's engine started functioning again and he was able to land safely. Investigators believed the event was caused by highly charged plasma.

A year earlier, on June 14, 1980, a retired colonel in the Soviet Army claimed that he had begun hearing a strange booming noise in the evening, and had seen a spherical object hanging in the sky only ninety metres (three hundred feet) away from him. When he ran towards it to investigate, he found himself struggling to make progress, as if he were wading through thick molasses. Finally, when he was within about forty-five metres (150 feet) of the object, he found he could walk normally. He approached the object, which he could now see was hemispherical on its underside, and bulbous above. The booming sound was now accompanied by a whizzing noise that sounded like an aircraft engine. The object emitted three blasts of light towards the ground and ascended higher into the sky. It hovered in place for a few seconds, moved a short distance away, then vanished completely.

The officer looked around and saw another strange, lighted object over some trees, and when he went inside his apartment building and looked out from an upper-floor window, he could see other objects as well. About thirty other people, among them more military personnel and scientists, had also observed these or similar UFOs that same night. Investigations revealed that two Soviet satellites had been launched that night, and it was suggested that these were what witnesses had seen, although the colonel's experiences suggest something more than this.

The Moscow "jellyfish" is one of the best-known UFO cases to come of out of the Soviet Union. On June 14, 1980, an enormous object shaped like an upside-down U was seen over Kalinin, near Moscow. It had several strands of glowing gas, like tentacles, that streamed downward, and it was seen by hundreds of people, including many scientists. Some residents were so concerned by the appearance of the phenomenon that they ran into the streets, convinced that it was an American nuclear attack. The sighting caused considerable controversy that persisted for years, and it was only after the Soviet policy on secrecy was loosened somewhat that an explanation for the sighting was given. We now know that the "jellyfish" sighting coincided with the launch of Cosmos 1188 from the then-secret cosmodrome at Plesetsk, north of Moscow. In fact, it is generally believed that many Soviet UFO reports were the result of experimental launches from various secret facilities throughout the continent, and that by labelling these sightings UFOs officials were able to cover up some classified activities.

Another case that seems to fit this category involved a series of objects spotted near Petrozavodsk on September 20, 1977. Soviet media carried many accounts of eyewitness observations of unusual moving lights and other objects in the early morning sky. A disc-shaped, glowing object was seen by pilots of an aircraft near Riga, who were said to have had to make drastic manoeuvres to avoid a collision. A cigar-shaped object was reported to have flown alongside a ball of light that appeared to land in a forest, while a different ball of light was said to have landed near the highway connecting Petrozavodsk and Leningrad. Other reports included sightings of an object with "exhaust pipes" that hovered over towns and villages such as Namayevo, and sightings of UFOs from Western Europe confirmed that something odd had occurred that night in northwestern Russia. Later investigations showed that this incident, too, was likely caused by a rocket launch, this time carrying Cosmos 955 into orbit.

There was even some speculation that UFOs were involved in the Chernobyl nuclear accident on April 26, 1986. It was reported that technicians rushing to the scene of the fire in Unit 4 at 4:15 a.m., saw a brass-coloured spherical object hanging in the sky only about a thousand feet from the reactor. It was moving very slowly, and two red beams of light were shining from it onto the reactor building. After three minutes, the beams of light disappeared and the UFO moved off to the northwest. "Were UFOs to blame for the tragedy?" asked one sensational tabloid.

In January 1985, TASS, the Soviet news agency, made public some details of a strange UFO encounter that had occurred near Minsk. On September 7, 1984, Aeroflot Flight 8352 was flying from Tbilisi to Tallinn at 4:10 a.m. when the second pilot reported seeing a yellow star-like object slightly above and to the right of their heading. As he watched, a thin beam of light shot down from the light source, and the beam then opened up into a broad cone. The witness pointed it out to others on the flight deck and they watched as another cone of light appeared, this time not quite as bright as the original.

The first witness had time to make a sketch of what he was seeing. The ground was illuminated by the beam of light and he could clearly see houses, highways, and trees, despite the hour of night. The beam suddenly turned from the ground to the aircraft, and the crew was dazzled by the intense light directed at them. The source of the light flared outward and became a green cloud that appeared to approach the aircraft at high speed.

The pilot radioed air traffic control in Minsk, and as he did so the object stopped its approach and dropped below the altitude of the plane. It then moved into a position directly opposite them, pacing their progress. It maintained speed and position while the airliner was flying at ten thousand metres (33,000 feet) and eight hundred kilometres (five hundred miles) an hour. The crew could now see that there were individual lights within the cloud that seemed to be moving erratically and flashing off and on. As they watched, the cloud then appeared to take on a solid shape, first developing a tail, then forming a square or rectangular body.

A stewardess came onto the flight deck to say that the passengers wanted to know what the green object flying beside the plane was.

The pilot directed her to tell them it was simply a cloud reflecting the northern lights. He then got confirmation from air traffic control that they could also see flashes of light near the plane, and received word that another airliner was nearby, but its pilot could not see anything at all. Only when the second airliner had approached to within sixteen kilometres (ten miles) did its pilot see the object. He described it exactly as the first crew had. In 1985, the prestigious and conservative Soviet Academy of Sciences issued a statement saying that after investigation, the case had been deemed unusual and that the object was a true UFO.

The most bizarre Russian UFO case on record is certainly that which was spotted on September 27, 1989. The event occurred during a rash of UFO sightings near Voronezh, about two hundred miles south of Moscow. At six-thirty, commuters and schoolchildren were in an area known as the Western Park when they saw a "pink haze" in the sky, like a bonfire seen through mist. As they watched, a silver ball emerged from the mist and came down to Earth, bending treetops as it flew over them. The object was described as shaped like a "banana." As the witnesses looked up, a door or portal opened in its side and a humanoid creature poked its head out then popped back inside. The door closed and the weird craft descended lower into the trees and extended landing gear into the soil. The door opened again and out came several creatures that scrambled down to the ground and began walking towards the onlookers.

At this point, the story gets confusing, with many different details added by different witnesses. Some said that a robot came out of the craft and approached a boy who was screaming in terror. The robot's eyes glowed and the boy was unable to move or make a sound. Another witness said he saw one of the entities aim a gun of some kind at a man who was walking away, and hit him with a beam of light. The man simply disappeared and only reappeared after the UFO left, as if he had never been gone. Other aliens supposedly walked over to an electrical pole and climbed it, but did not expect the high voltage. Reportedly, they immediately caught fire and disappeared in a shower of sparks!

Investigators took soil samples, interviewed witnesses, and videotaped the area while searching for clues. They uncovered many other sightings that residents had been having for months in the same region. Many children claimed that they had seen a variety of alien beings and odd, lighted craft nearby. Soviet news agencies wrote about the sightings for many weeks, carrying stories from a variety of perspectives. They have never been explained. Some people have suggested the sightings were products of children's imaginations, although many adults also reported UFOs in the area.

Curiously, in parallel to the United States' official study of UFO reports, the Soviet Academy of Sciences also prepared an official report on sightings within its country. In 1979, its Institute of Space Research released a study on UFO cases in the USSR, although it was mostly a statistical analysis. It concluded that some of the UFOs may have been the product of "atmospheric optics effects," but added, "the overwhelming majority of cases ... are of a completely different nature." As for the possibility that the UFOs were satellites or terrestrial craft, "the kinematic characteristics exclude the possibility of such an explanation for at least one third of the cases." The report concluded by noting: "Obviously, the question of the nature of the anomalous phenomena still should be considered open."

AUSTRALIA AND OCEANIA

The remarkable encounter of Father Gill and his colleagues in Papua New Guinea has introduced Oceania in our overview of world UFO reports; however, there are many, many other cases that have been recorded in the warm South Pacific and on the continent of Australia that should also be mentioned.

A more recent case from Papua New Guinea took place on November 4, 1999. An object described as two hundred metres (660 feet) long and fifty metres (165 feet) wide was observed by thousands of people in the Gazelle Peninsula of East New Britain. It made a soft puffing noise as it chugged slowly across the night sky. Members of a remote tribe called the Bainingo, who do not have television and other modern influences, claim they saw a large object, glowing like a "red hot stone" and with "lumps on the sides," moving over the mountain range. Other people living near the St. George Channel saw a large object that seemed to have lights circling it moving slowly over the water. It continued on its way until it reached the mountains of New Ireland, which it rose above and passed over.

At Rangulit, a family was sitting on the veranda of their home when they saw the large object fly over their mango trees. It was moving slowly and was "lit up like a shooting star and it had two very bright lights at the tail." According to NUFORC, the witnesses were certain it was not an aircraft. Some people lit torches and chased the object as it flew ponderously along before it headed out over the sea and was lost to sight.

According to ufologist Paul Norman, at around the time the ship *Amelia J* disappeared near Bass Strait off Australia in 1920, unusual lights were reported in the area. And when a search aircraft went out to investigate the lights, it disappeared as well.

Perhaps this was foreshadowing, as in 1978, another aircraft disappeared in association with a UFO, also over Bass Strait. The unfortunate pilot was Frederick Valentich, a young aviator who was planning on picking up some friends at King Island. He dutifully filed a flight plan and checked the weather conditions at the Moorabbin airport office in preparation for his short night flight in his Cessna. His plane fully fuelled, he took off at about 6:20 p.m. for what should have been a trip of less than ninety minutes. During his flight, he was in constant contact with air traffic control in Melbourne.

About halfway through his trip across Bass Strait, he asked the tower if there were any other aircraft near him. He was told there was no known air traffic out there, and he replied that there was "a large aircraft below five thousand feet," above him. He told the air traffic controller that he could see what appeared to be four bright "landing lights," like those of an aircraft, passing about three hundred metres (one thousand feet) over him. He asked the tower about other aircraft again, this time wanting to know if there was any military activity in the area. Again, he was told there was nothing in his area.

At 7:09, he radioed the control tower and reported that the plane was approaching him from due east. The pilot believed that the other craft was "playing some sort of game," and flying over him "at speeds [he] could not identify." Valentich was flying at an altitude of almost 1,400 metres (4,500 feet). When asked by the tower if he could identify the kind of aircraft that he had spotted, he replied, "it's not an aircraft, it is …" without finishing his sentence. Prodded by the tower again, he said that the object was a "long shape," with a green light and was "metallic like" and "shiny on the outside."

As he talked to the tower, Valentich reported that the mysterious craft had become stationary and that his airplane was somehow "orbiting" it. Suddenly, he reported that the object had "just vanished." Looking around, he reported that the same or a similar object was approaching his plane from the southwest, and that his airplane's engine was coughing and sputtering. He told the tower that the strange aircraft was hovering on top of him again, but then abruptly added, "it is hovering and it's not an aircraft." The shocked tower operator heard only a metallic sound before the radio went dead. Valentich was never heard from again.

Despite an extensive search in the Bass Strait, the wreckage of the plane was never found. Many theories for Valentich's disappearance have been proposed, including the possibility that he had become disoriented and was actually seeing the lights of his own aircraft reflecting in the ocean, or that he accidentally flew into the water while flying upside down. Another theory was that Valentich had faked his own death so that he could start his life anew, and is now living in Tasmania. Debunkers have even suggested that he was involved in drug running, and had paid the ultimate price for his illegal activity.

That same year, another UFO case from Australasia made news around the world. This incident took place off the east coast of New Zealand in the early hours of the morning of New Year's Eve, 1978. There had been some UFO sightings off the coast of South Island on December 21, and the tale of Frederick Valentich was still a hot topic in the media.

A television crew had been sent up in a plane to get some video of New Zealand from the air, as the witnesses to the events of December 21 included pilots and radar operators. The cargo plane took off from Wellington late on December 30, and headed for Christchurch carrying newspapers and other goods. Along for the ride with the pilot and co-pilot were reporter Quentin Fogarty, a cameraman, and a sound recording engineer. The plane was flying northeast of South Island just after midnight, when the pilots saw an odd light in the sky. They checked with air traffic control to confirm the sighting, and were told that some intermittent radar echoes had been detected. The plane was flying at about 3,000 metres (10,000 feet) at the time.

Looking towards the ground, Fogarty saw a row of five bright lights that were pulsating and growing in size from a pinpoint to a "balloon." These lights seemed to be near the town of Kaikoura. As he was discussing these lights with the others on board, Wellington air traffic control notified the crew that they had picked up another radar target near the plane. The crew and passengers saw an object with a flashing light. A few minutes later, the tower told the pilots that yet another return was seen, this time directly behind the plane. During the rest of the trip, several other lights and radar returns were seen and detected. Throughout this time, the cameraman recorded the various lights. He was jostled by the others in the cabin and the plane made several turns and banks to see the objects, so the resulting video was very choppy and shaky.

At about 2:15 a.m. the plane headed back to Wellington on the same path. This time, a large radar target was detected by the plane's system only about nineteen kilometres (twelve miles) away. The camera caught images of a "spinning sphere" in a "sort of bell shape," with lines running around its middle. At about 2:50 a.m., two additional bright lights were seen, one of which dropped three hundred metres (a thousand feet) before stopping its descent.

The film shot during this round-trip flight has been analyzed many times by believers and skeptics alike. Depending on which expert you believe, the lights seen by the pilots and news crew could have been Venus, Jupiter, meteors, secret American spy planes, or even the lights from Japanese squid-fishing boats on the ocean.

Before we leave this area of the world, one more case should be mentioned. On August 8, 1993, at about five o'clock, Kelly Cahill and her family were driving from Melbourne to Monbulk; they were near Belgrave when she saw a row of orange lights in a field. As the car passed the field, Cahill had time to see that the lights were on the rim of a disc-shaped object about thirteen metres (forty-five feet) in diameter, that was resting near or just over the ground.

By the time she told her husband what she had seen, the object was already out of sight behind some trees, and he refused to believe it was anything other than an aircraft. They arrived at their destination feeling a bit odd, but they talked with others about the incident and laughed it off. Yet something began bothering Kelly and her husband. She began to vividly recall something much more unusual that had occurred during their trip, and she started having nightmares in which she was visited in their bedroom by strange creatures, one of which was a "soul vampire." Her husband frequently became upset when she told him of such things. (Eventually, their marriage broke down entirely.) Kelly had to be taken to the hospital twice during the next few weeks, once for intense stomach pain and the other for a uterine infection. She also had an odd triangular mark around her navel.

To deal with her nightmares, Kelly began seeing a counsellor. The counsellor helped her relax to the point that she spontaneously recalled another part of her family's experience on the highway. They had been driving farther down the road when a brilliant light appeared up ahead. She told her husband to stop, but he continued driving towards the light, and somehow passed through it. Her next conscious memory was of driving along several kilometres later, as if nothing ever happened. Eventually,

Kelly regained more memories of their experience on the highway, and realized that it was more complex than they had originally remembered.

She now remembered that she had convinced her husband to stop the car and they got out to look at a huge object about forty-five metres (150 feet) in diameter, glowing a soft blue with the orange lights around its upper rim. They walked towards it and saw another car parked there as well. When they got close to the craft, they encountered a two-metre- (seven-foot-) tall creature, black and "void of colour." It had mesmerizing, glowing red eyes and Kelly experienced great fear and dread when it approached. She soon saw several other identical creatures congregating in small groups. She screamed at them to leave her and the people from the other car alone, and she prayed to God to dispel these demonic beings. Suddenly, she and her husband were back in the car, heading for their original destination — but when they arrived, they were about an hour later than they had planned.

Had the story ended there, it would be a rather typical abduction account, but Kelly was determined to find out more about what had happened that night. She contacted a university for advice, and found herself rebuffed and ridiculed. She then located a ufologist who listened to her story and placed an advertisement in a newspaper asking for any witnesses to an event about the same time and date to come forward. The result was unexpected; another family, presumably the one travelling in the car Kelly had seen, came forward with details and descriptions of the exact same object and even drawings of the same tall, black creatures, although they did not have large red eyes.

Two women and one man had been driving near where Cahill and her family encountered the UFO and aliens when they heard an odd noise and fainted. The man, who was driving, lost control of the car and hit a pole. After checking briefly for damage, he continued on. But the two women had conscious memories of being taken on board a strange craft and subjected to a physical examination. Under hypnosis, the man was able to remember parts of his abduction as well. Their combined experiences led ufologists to suggest that this was the first time independent witnesses were found to support an alien abduction.

EUROPE

Some European cases have already been featured in this book, notably the Belgian triangles and the Rendlesham close encounter; however, so many interesting cases have occurred in this region, and so many developments in ufology have originated in Europe, that more time should be spent reviewing events that have taken place there.

The general difference between British and American ufology is that the latter tends to focus on landings, retrievals, and nuts-and-bolts cases. British ufology at one time was called "new wave" because it often looked at the relationship between UFOs and psychic phenomena, ley lines (paths of earth energy), earth lights, and more humanistic aspects. In general, American ufology often considers extraterrestrials as the most probable explanation for unexplained UFO cases, whereas European ufology more often entertains sociological or psychological explanations, and goes even further than its American counterpart to suggest effects beyond the five senses. These general differences have faded somewhat, and there is now more crossover between the two camps, but some subtle differences between the two approaches still exist. It is useful to look at differing perspectives in studying UFO reports in a more thorough way.

European ufological history began before Kenneth Arnold saw his crescent-shaped objects over Washington in the United States in 1947. Starting early in 1946, residents of Scandinavian countries reported seeing strange "ghost rockets" zooming and flashing through the skies. Many of these were fireballs, bolides, and large meteors, but others seemed to be more unusual objects.

Researchers investigating early UFO accounts located an interesting CIA document dated April 9, 1947. It listed several reports of "rockets and guided missiles" seen over Norway and Sweden. It noted a strange object seen flying through the air on July 13, 1946, by workmen in Stockholm. The report said the object was "round, and appeared to be rather small. It sent out a strong blue-green light, but no sound could be heard." The report also mentioned an object spotted by railway workers near Hudiksvall. It made a sound like an outboard motor, and was "a few meters long and with backward-sloping wings flying towards the north at a height of about 150 meters."

Some of the "ghost rockets" flying over Scandinavia were said to have been detected on radar, and there was speculation that they were of Russian origin. The Russian base at Peenemünde could be considered suspect in this regard — but the odd missiles were said to also have mystified the Russians as well. Indeed, even after the British bombed the base in 1943, a V-2 from Peenemünde crashed in Sweden in June 1944 and was appropriated by the British. In December 1944, work on a winged version of the A4 rocket was underway and there was a successful flight on January 24, 1945, reaching an altitude of about eighty kilometres (fifty miles). In May 1945, at the war's end, the Soviet Army occupied the base. At least one historical record noted that even though "Western intelligence" was convinced that the Soviets conducted missile tests from Peenemünde in the late 1940s that produced the Scandinavian ghost rockets, "Russian historical sources available after the downfall of the Soviet Union do not support this belief."

One of the first ufologists to apply reasonable methodology to the study of UFO reports was French researcher Aimé Michel. In 1958, he published a classic work that attempted to quantify sightings of flying saucers by showing that the locations where they appeared seemed to form lines across the French landscape. His detailed analysis, using hundreds of UFO sightings plotted on maps of France, was ingenious and suffered from only one flaw — the alignments were inaccurate, and in some cases, sightings of different qualities were included.

The cases Michel investigated, however, were remarkable in many ways. In fact, he documented several characteristics of the sighting reports that convinced him that there was a real, physical phenomenon at play. One French case in his study took place on September 26, 1954, in the village of Chabeuil. At about four o'clock a woman went walking with her dog in the woods, looking for fresh mushrooms to pick. As they went through the trees, her dog began to bark and howl, and she looked to see what had disturbed it. At the edge of a wheat field bordering the woods was an object that she at first thought was a scarecrow, but she soon saw that it was a "small diving suit, made of translucent plastic material," only about a metre (three feet) tall. The head portion was also translucent, and she could see that a face with two large eyes was staring at her. The being in the diving suit began walking towards her, and, terrified, she screamed and fled back into the trees.

Her dog continued to howl, and she heard many other dogs join in the chorus. She poked her head out of the thicket and saw that the suited creature was gone. Suddenly, a large metallic disc-shaped object rose up out of some nearby trees and flew over the wheat field with a whistling sound, eventually gaining altitude and disappearing into the distance.

The dogs' howling, her scream, and the whistling noise of the craft brought some local townspeople running to the woods to see what was wrong. When they went into the treed spot from which the object seemed to have risen, they found a circular area about three metres (ten feet) in diameter where the bushes had been crushed. Branches of trees surrounding the circle were snapped, leaves were stripped off, and the wheat field had some kind of lines radiating through it. Perhaps this was a forerunner of the British crop formations that would be found decades later.

When the others arrived, the woman was "in a state of nervous collapse." She remained in bed with a high fever for two days following the sighting, and her dog was agitated and nervous for several days as well.

Michel pointed out that this case and two others that were reported on the same day, including one that was actually explained as a flock of starlings, seemed to have occurred in line with one another. He suggested that something was causing people to see unusual objects, whether explained or otherwise along certain lines. Perhaps, he opined, there was something else causing the reports — something that could affect peoples' perceptions of reality.

In June 1965, farmer Maurice Masse was concerned when patches of lavender he grew in his fields for the French perfume industry went missing, and he suspected vandals were at work. At 5:45 a.m. on July 1, 1965, he was sitting on his tractor preparing for the day's work and smoking a cigarette when he heard an odd whistling noise. Military helicopters had landed in his fields before and since he didn't want another one to damage his lavender, he walked towards where the noise was coming from. Instead of a helicopter there was a strange, egg-shaped craft resting on six legs about ninety metres (three hundred feet) away. It was about the size of an automobile and had a small dome on its top. Beside it were two small figures. He initially believed that they were young boys who might have been responsible for vandalizing his lavender, so he walked towards them to accost them. However, as soon as he got near he saw that they were beings just over a metre (four feet) tall in green, tight-fitting coveralls. They had large bald heads, pointed chins, slanted cat-like eyes, and ghastly white skin.

When he was about fifteen to twenty metres (fifty or sixty feet) from the beings, one turned to face him and reached for a small tube that was hanging at its side from a belt. A beam of light shot out and struck Masse. He was suddenly paralyzed, although he could still breathe and watch what was going on. The two creatures talked with one another in low sounds and then they went into the craft through a door that slid open. Soon, the craft rose and vanished, disappearing as if it went through some kind of doorway in the sky.

The paralysis wore off after about fifteen minutes, and Masse walked over to where the craft had been and saw depressions in the lavender where its legs had touched the ground. He went into town and told a café owner what he had seen. The news soon made its way to the local police. The tale was the talk of the town and many people visited with Masse and went to the site. Ufologists eventually investigated and took soil samples, finding only that the spots where the lavender had been affected were hard and highly calcified. Lavender would not grow there for several years.

Following his experience, Masse was very tired for three days, sleeping for over twelve hours each night. He also told investigators that there was some additional aspect of the incident that he did not want to reveal it to anyone. "Nobody will make me tell it," he stated.

Another French UFO case that involved a beam of light occurred on November 1, 1968, in the southern part of the country. The exact location is unknown because the identity of the witness to this sighting has been kept secret, although we know that he was a physician who had served in the Algerian War many years ago. While serving in the war he had the misfortune of stepping on a land mine and received serious wounds, becoming permanently disabled. And only three days before the UFO encounter, he was chopping wood when his axe slipped and he cut his leg, severing a vein. He was bedridden as a result of the accident, and thus was laying down when he was awakened early on the morning of November 1 by the crying of his son.

Dr. X, as he has become known in ufology, struggled out of bed and went to the nursery to see what the baby was babbling about. When he entered the room, he saw the child pointing to the window, where he could see flashes of light coming through the shutters. Assuming the light to be from lightning, and hearing a sound like rushing wind outside and a rattling noise, he thought that a storm was brewing. He went into the kitchen to get a bottle of water for the baby, walked into the living room, then continued upstairs past another window. He poked his head out but could not see what was causing the flashes of light. It did not seem to be lightning. He went back downstairs and opened a set of patio doors that faced the countryside.

Dr. X was surprised to see two cigar-shaped objects hovering over a hill, with columns of bright white light radiating down to the ground. Each object had an antenna on the top and another sticking out the side. They were white on their upper surfaces and red on the lower. He saw that the flashes of light were coming from the top antenna of one of the objects and shooting to the other.

The strange objects slowly moved in his direction and when they were relatively close to the house they seemed to merge and combine to form a single object! The new single craft moved closer, and its beam fell on the house and doorway where Dr. X was standing. There was a loud bang and the object disappeared, leaving behind a white "thread" that flew upwards and vanished into the night sky.

Dr. X was astounded by what he had experienced, and being a scientific man he sat down in the kitchen to write an account of what had occurred. He woke his wife and told her the story. She was surprised — and she pointed out that his leg seemed to be healed because he was no longer limping. Sure enough, the swelling was gone and he could walk normally.

A week later, an odd triangular rash, spreading about fifteen centimetres (six inches) on either side of his navel, appeared on his body. A similar mark appeared on the baby's body a few weeks later. The triangular rashes continued to appear and fade on a regular basis. Perhaps more remarkable is that Dr. X's war injuries seemed to have healed as well. He was checked by other physicians who documented his recovery. French ufologists Aimé Michel and Jacques Vallee interviewed Dr. X and his family at length. He has granted a few interviews to journalists but has insisted on anonymity, and has not sought any monetary gain from his story.

One of the strongest cases on record for the physical existence of UFOs is a sighting that took place at Trans-en-Provence. This sighting was investigated by police, as well as GEPAN, France's official government department involved in studying reports of unidentified flying objects.

On January 8, 1981, at five o'clock, Renato Niccolai, who was at home on sick leave from his work as a technician, was outside his house attending to a water pump when he heard a strange whistling sound. He looked up to see a dull grey disc-shaped object with a ring around it descending from the sky. It eventually landed on a terrace beside his garden about forty-five metres (150 feet) away. Niccolai walked closer to get a better view of the object, and saw that it was more "like two plates glued to each other by the rim, with a central ring some 20 cm [eight inches] wide." The odd craft was relatively small, only about 2.5 metres (eight feet) in diameter and 1.5 metres (five feet) in height, and rested on stubby legs that looked like upside-down buckets. After just four seconds on the ground, the object rose into the air and flew away, disappearing into the east. The entire sighting lasted only about thirty seconds.

Niccolai then walked over to where the craft had rested on the ground and discovered two long skid marks in the soil. When his wife returned from work at about nine o'clock he told her what he had seen. She didn't believe him, probably because he joked with her by saying, "Your cat is back. Extraterrestrials brought him home." It was the next day before she looked at the site. She then told a neighbour, who reported the incident to the police.

Investigators took samples of plants from the affected and unaffected areas a day after the event, then fifteen and forty days later. Critics have found that the samples were not gathered methodically and that errors in the sampling invalidated the process. Despite this, the analysis of the plants within the marks showed "the action of an energy field" or a "beam of pulsed microwaves."

A skeptical French ufologist proposed an explanation for the case that includes all of the reported details. Niccolai's neighbour was an ardent believer in UFOs, so it was suggested that Niccolai concocted a simple hoax in which he made up the sighting and then claimed that the marks in the soil, likely from a terrestrial wheeled vehicle, were from the saucer.

In the 1970s, some British ufologists took up Aimé Michel's mantle and theorized that UFO sightings in Great Britain were related to ancient pathways known as ley lines. They believed that sacred sites were linked through some kind of "earth energy" and "telluric forces." Whether or not there were mysterious energies at work, many British cases are among the most puzzling on record.

On the evening of October 8, 1972, a security guard was on patrol in Oldham, England, when he heard an odd humming sound like a "swarm of bees." He looked up to see a strange object hovering about sixty metres (two hundred) feet over the side of his building. It was about thirty metres (one hundred feet) in diameter, and "almost seemed to completely fill the sky." It had a large "window" in its side, and was glowing with a blue-white light. The object was not casting any shadows or shining any beams of light. Then after about five minutes, it turned upon its edge, and he could see that it was a saucer with a large dome that was also lit up. It then shot into the air without warning, and was lost to sight, all the while making the same humming sound that did not change pitch throughout the sighting.

Ufologist Jenny Randles noted that the object was not seen by anyone else in the area even though it was densely populated, and according to the security guard, the object was very large object. Furthermore, because the guard was paralyzed with fear, he didn't scream or make any noise, which was unfortunate because another person nearby did not see or hear anything. However, the factory cat was terrified by the appearance of the object, presumably because animals are more sensitive to such phenomena than humans, and it hid away for some time following the incident.

At eleven-thirty on the morning of on April 28, 1967, coast guards at Brixham, Devon, reported seeing a large cone-shaped object that they believed was hovering at an altitude of 4,600 metres (fifteen thousand) feet. They watched it through a set of high-powered binoculars mounted on a tripod, and were able to determine that the object seemed to be "revolving." It was "shaped like a cone with the sharp end pointing upward," and appeared to shine as if it was made of glass or metal. Towards the bottom of the object was a small opening like a door, with a white rim that was reflecting sunlight as well. The bottom itself was "crinkled" and "seemed to consist of strips of metal hanging down."

The object drifted slowly northwest over the next hour, rising in altitude. As they watched, an aircraft making a vapour trail approached the object from the northeast, flew above it, then dove and came around to approach it from below. The trail faded, the aircraft disappeared from view, and the object disappeared into clouds. They later learned that no Royal Air Force aircraft was in the area at the time. The British Ministry of Defence suggested that the object was "something like the reflection of car headlights or some sort of meteorological phenomena."

Several months later, on October 26, 1967, another dramatic incident occurred for which the Ministry of Defence had an absurd explanation. Angus Brooks, a retired British intelligence officer and British Airways employee, was walking his dogs one morning near Ringstead Bay, Dorset. A force 8 gale was blowing across the field and making headway difficult. He paused to recover his breath, when his attention was caught by an aerial craft that descended quickly into view. Despite the wind, it slowed to a stop almost half a kilometre (about a quarter of a mile) away and about sixty metres (two hundred feet) in the air. The oddly structured vehicle had a central "chamber" about eight metres (twenty-five feet) in diameter, and four "fuselages" at its front and rear. These cigar-shaped protuberances shifted their position when the object hovered, so that they were evenly spaced around the middle of the craft. Including the four shafts sticking out, the craft measured approximately fifty metres (175 feet) from tip to tip, and seemed to be made of a translucent material. After some time, two of the cigar-shaped appendages shifted again to combine with a third, and the craft ascended into the sky and was lost to sight.

Investigators noted that the object was hovering at a strategic location, centred between an atomic energy station, an underwater weapons base, and a USAF communications base. Checks with the various bases did not show any unusual activity at the time. The witness was interviewed a few months later by officers from the British Ministry of Defence, and in their report, they concluded that what he had seen was a "vitreous floater" in his eyeball. They suggested that perhaps he had fallen asleep while resting and imagined the incident. As the witness himself noted, it would have been nearly impossible to fall asleep while sitting in a strong wind.

On February 16, 1988, at 9:17 p.m., two police officers were patrolling in Willenhall when they saw a large object flying silently overhead. They said it had "red and green lights around its circumference," and that it appeared to be spinning, making it seem as though the lights were flashing on and off. Seven minutes earlier, two different officers had seen the same object over Walsall. Both sightings were reported to the Ministry of Defence, which recorded nearly four hundred UFO reports that year.

The case that seemed to set the pace for British ufology took place on August 13, 1956, over Suffolk. At nine-thirty that evening, a UFO was detected on radar by the USAF base at Bentwaters. The object appeared to be coming from the east over the North Sea at a tremendous speed, as much as 8,000 kilometres (five thousand miles) per hour. Another set of targets was approaching at a relative crawl, about 160 kilometres (one hundred miles) per hour. Because the radar systems were considered in good working order, a T-33 interceptor aircraft already in the air on a training mission was sent to investigate. Since it did not have any airborne radar, it had no way of vectoring to any of the targets, and the pilot could not see anything visually.

About an hour later, another target was detected by Bentwaters radar, this time seen both visually and on the screen. A bright light flew over the base at a high speed and the pilot of a C-47 transport radioed that a lighted object had flown underneath his aircraft. This series of observations spurred other nearby bases to action. Two Venom Night Ranger aircraft from a base at Neatished were sent to intercept the objects, and a pilot had his airborne radar lock on to an object. There are conflicting accounts as to whether the pilots saw anything visually. In addition, the pilot supposedly shot gun-camera film, although it has never been made available. The events of that night have never been explained.

At eleven o'clock on August 13, 1970, in Hadersley, Denmark, a police officer was driving home when a bright light suddenly blocked his path. His car engine quit and the electrical system died. The light was so bright he had difficulty trying to find his radio. The light passed over his car and he felt an intense heat penetrate the vehicle. He could make out that the light was attached to a large grey object, but couldn't see anything beyond that. He judged the object to be about nine metres (thirty feet) in diameter, with two hemispheres on its underside. He got out of his car to watch the object. After five minutes, the light seemed to be pulled into the grey object and it sped away without making a sound. When it was gone, his car started and the radio was again operational. He reported his encounter at the police station, but the other officers would not believe him at first. He stood by his story after considerable questioning, and the other officers decided he must have been telling the truth. This did not sway the air force, which dismissed the observation as the lights of a T-33 jet trainer that had been in the area. The police officer countered by stating that he had also seen the aircraft several minutes later.

A similar encounter took place on May 22, 1979, in Piastów, Poland. Late in the evening a man was walking through a park when he saw three bright lights ahead of him. He looked up and saw that they were shining down from a circular object about three metres (ten feet) in diameter that was hanging in the air above the grassy path. He walked to within three metres (ten feet) of the object and saw that its surface was becoming an array of geometrical shapes, and other lights were flashing on it. It suddenly gave off an intense blue light, and the man felt as if he was being burned, so he ran away. The next morning, he had burns on his face and a bad headache, but had no idea what the object had been.

On March 13, 1982, several teenagers were walking together during the evening in Messel, Germany, At 9:10 p.m., they saw three clusters of lights in the sky. Each cluster was composed of four lights flashing different colours. The first group moved slowly and then stopped in mid-air, while the second group moved slowly through the sky, and the third group of lights flew quickly and disappeared. At about nine-thirty, the teenagers were called to look at something else in the sky. They saw a bright flash like a rotating spotlight; then, a metallic-blue, domed, disc-shaped object appeared over some trees about three hundred metres (a thousand feet) from them.

As the object moved towards them, they could see it was about twelve metres (forty feet) wide, and its dome was segmented with different colours, while inside it a light rotated. Other coloured lights flashed around its rim, and there were four white steady lights on the disc's surface. After a while, the disc started to descend to the ground. It alighted briefly, then took off and flew out of sight. The witnesses called the police to report what they had seen, but when the officers arrived, the object, of course, was gone.

The general rule that only a fraction of all reported UFOs are truly mysterious and unexplainable holds true everywhere in the world. Studies of both classic and modern UFO cases in countries around the globe have shown this to be a characteristic of flying saucer and UFO data as recorded in newspaper accounts, official government records, and ufologists' files. Dedicated researchers in several countries have done exhaustive analyses of cases in their own regions, and these prove that the UFO phenomenon is worldwide.

In the United States, Paul Davenport of the National UFO Reporting Center (NUFORC) and Paul Ferrughelli of the Mutual UFO Network (MUFON) have done extensive work on UFO case data in America. In Canada, Ufology Research of Manitoba has published an annual survey of UFO reports. In Sweden, the Arbetsgruppen För Ufologi, now Archives For UFO Research (AFU) has compiled a massive database of cases in Scandinavia and maintains a huge library of UFO books, magazines, and documents from all around the world. In Italy, Centro Italiano Studi Ufologici does an excellent job of compiling statistics in a very rigorous manner for cases in that country.

One of the most fascinating works to come out of Italy is Maurizio Verga's book, *When Saucers Came to Earth*. It documents in great detail more than one hundred cases in which occupants of flying saucers were observed in conjunction with a landing or an encounter with a strange flying object or light, all between 1912 and 1954. Many of these cases have been written about in other UFO books and publications, but Verga has studied and investigated them thoroughly and has assessed them for their content, reliability, and veracity. Unfortunately, none of the cases were found to be unexplained, but they make for fascinating reading and engage our imaginations.

An example from Verga's work is a case that took place on July 31, 1952. At about 9:15 a.m., Gian Monguzzi and his wife were hiking over the Italian Alps near Scerscen Glacier when they noticed that the sound around them had been dampened; even their voices could not be heard. Suddenly, a disc-shaped craft landed on the glacier only about 230 metres (750 feet) away. It was about eleven metres (thirty-five feet) in diameter, three metres (ten feet) high, and had an antenna on its top. Monguzzi pulled out his camera and took some photos. In a short while a robot-like creature appeared beside the saucer, walking around it as if checking it out. Monguzzi continued to take photos until a few minutes later when the being moved behind the craft and it took off over the mountains.

Monguzzi went to Italian newspaper offices with his story and the photographs, asking millions of lire for the images. His story, accompanied by photos of the saucer and little man framed against the mountains, was printed in many papers and magazines, and was soon was being republished around the world. Investigators eventually determined that Monguzzi had created the entire hoax in a field next to his house, and that he had spun the tale in revenge for being unable to get a job with the newspapers.

It must be emphasized that hoaxes are relatively rare in ufology. Most UFO reports are simply honest misidentifications, but there are still many good unresolved cases on record. The Italian hoax is only given here to highlight the detailed and rigorous investigative work and research that Verga, a dedicated ufologist, does.

Statistically, most UFO reports are simply lights in the night sky. The most dependable recurring "spook light" in the world is in Hessdalen, Norway. For more than one hundred years, the area has been plagued by sightings of an odd bobbing light that moves through its mountainous valleys. Because many expeditions have been undertaken in the area, a number of photographs of the Hessdalen light have been produced.

As an example, one study looked at three specific lights seen in the area on August 6, 7, and 15, 2002. An anomalous light was witnessed by an expedition including astrophysicists and engineers during a project called EMBLA, coordinated by the Institute for Radio Astronomy in Bologna, Italy, and the Ostfold University College in Sarpsborg, Norway. Their goal was to use radio-frequency analyzers and photometric instruments, plus visual observations, to detect the lights. The team of researchers was able to determine, using triangulation, that some of the lights seen were car headlights, whereas others had no explanation.

There is no question that the phenomenon is real, as over the years hundreds of people have witnessed the lights appearing and disappearing over the valley. Rarely has anyone suggested that aliens are responsible, however. The general consensus among ufologists is that the lights are related to seismic activity that frequently is felt in that part of the country. Some proponents of the "Earth Lights" theory imply the lights manifestations of the type of terrestrial energy that creates UFOs elsewhere in the world.

Regardless of their cause, the Hessdalen lights are a strange and fascinating phenomenon that scientists are taking very seriously. Some are studying the lights with complex instrumentation, spectral analyses and triangulation to determine their exact nature, and why they appear so often in the region. Projects and programs involving as many as one hundred people, including researchers and their graduate students, have focused on a methodical examination of the lights. Scientific papers have been published in journals, offering theories as to the lights' origin, and even detailed analysis of particular observations. Speculation centres on the lights being some kind of plasma, but the full explanation for the phenomenon remains elusive.

NORTH AND SOUTH AMERICA

I have already described some UFO cases from North America, but there are many more that are deserving of attention. And others in Central and South America need detailing as well. It is impossible to even list the cases reported in the United States, Canada, and Mexico each year because hundreds if not thousands of reports are recorded in those three countries annually.

The inclusion or omission of notable cases was decided after consultation with other researchers, investigators, and colleagues. How could one pick and choose which UFO cases to focus upon? A truly representative sample would naturally include many misidentifications, as this would accurately reflect UFO sighting characteristics; however, this might not be useful to all readers. Focusing only on unexplained cases seems a logical route; although high-quality and well-investigated cases are relatively rare, they do stir the imagination.

Then again, what is considered unexplained by some people could be banal to others. The series of UFO sightings centring around Gulf Breeze, Florida, is a good example — some ufologists are convinced that the region was visited by extraterrestrials, while others believe the major cases there were nothing more than hoaxes. Ultimately, the same could be said of all the cases in this book.

The prime source for UFO reports in North America (or for that matter, the world) is the National UFO Reporting Center (NUFORC), located in the state of Washington. The centre has been receiving on-line UFO reports since 1974, amassing thousands of cases each year. Its director, Peter Davenport, is a frequent commentator in the media about UFO sightings, and his open and accessible approach does much to advance ufology research. He receives case data from around the world, and is at present the most responsible source for UFO sighting information.

Hundreds of books listing UFO cases in North America have been published since the modern era of UFOs began in the 1940s. Some of these are listed at the back of this book for readers to explore at length. Suffice to say here that each state and province in the Americas has a history of UFO sightings, and that ufologists have documented the reports in several different ways. It is still worthwhile to present a selection of UFO cases that are particularly interesting, or are perhaps under-reported.

At the time this book was written, the Stephenville UFO flap in Texas was underway, and a media frenzy was in full flight, although no investigation report had yet been released, so it cannot be described in detail here. In the midst of all this, some curious cases emerged.

On January 11, 2008, a witness was driving near Denton, Texas, on his way to work at about 6:50 a.m. As he turned east, he saw some bright lights approaching over a dam and thought they were on an aircraft. Having been in the navy, he was familiar with the appearance of aircraft and looked for this object's red and green running lights. He was surprised that no such lights were present, and was further surprised that the object was coming in very low and slow, at only about fifty kilometres (thirty miles) per hour and twenty-seven to forty-five metres away (thirty to fifty yards) away. The strange craft "seemed to be hugging the shoreline, flying at eye level." The witness slowed his car to a crawl and rolled down the window as it passed him. He had a good, long look at the object, which was black and grey in color, delta-shaped, and no bigger than a sedan. Its rear section was rectangular, and there were three large round openings on its side. It made no noise, and there was no visible exhaust. On its upper part was what looked like a metallic canopy. Underneath, there were three white lights that shone brightly and did not blink. He had no explanation for what he had seen. While many of the UFOs reported during 2008 in Texas may have had explanations, the Denton sighting seems not to be explainable as a star, meteor, atmospheric inversion, or stray airliner.

Contrast that report with a more typical sighting that took place elsewhere in Texas on January 14, 2008. Two witnesses looked up to see "a brilliant yellow light, like a star, getting closer to earth." The object was only in view for a few seconds, as it seemed to speed up, spawning a "trail of several little yellow brilliant lights." The object then "appeared to just stop," and "burned out as falling stars may." This sighting has many characteristics of a large meteor, known as a bolide, so it may not be as mysterious as the latter case from Denton.

The following is a selection of other curious cases from North and South America:

One morning in May 1961, at 10:45 a.m., several workers were at the Texaco Oil Refinery in the bay of Santiago de Cuba when one of them noticed an object that looked like a "metallic football" approaching from the northwest. It took up a position directly over the plant, and hovered there for at least fifteen minutes, "rocking to and fro like a falling leaf," before it began moving again and sped off into the distance "in a flash."

A similar kind of rocking motion was observed in May 5, 1958, near Captain Curbelo Naval Air Base at Pan de Azucar, Uruguay. At about 3:40 p.m., a pilot was flying a Piper Cub airplane when a bright "top-like" object flew towards him on what seemed to be a collision course. It fortunately stopped when it was just over a mile away and rocked twice, in a balancing motion, then zoomed away towards the sea at "fantastic speed," leaving a thin vapour trail. When the object was near the plane, it gave off such intense heat that the pilot had to open the plane's windows and take off his jacket.

Uruguay was also where a dog died apparently as a result of a close encounter with a UFO in 1977. The dramatic incident occurred on a large ranch south of the city of Salto. A farm family and their ranch hands had seen unusual moving lights throughout the month of February, but on the eighteenth at around four o'clock in the morning, something more sinister came by. As the farmers were milking the cows, all the lights on the farm suddenly went out and a bright glow appeared near the barn. The owner of the farm ran towards the source of the glow, thinking the barn might be on fire. His watchdog, a large black-and-brown police dog, was excited and ran with him to investigate.

The farmer saw a "fire disc," that looked like two plates facing one another moving with a "rocking motion" across the barnyard about eighteen metres (sixty feet) above the trees, breaking some branches as it progressed. The livestock were greatly agitated, "going crazy, running everywhere." The strange craft finally came to a stop about six metres (twenty feet) above the ground and next to a water tank, where it shone a bright light around the entire yard. The watchdog ran towards the object but stopped in its tracks, sat down and began howling as if in pain. The farmer walked almost underneath the craft, and got a good look at it. It had beams of light like lightning or small wings on either side, and was radiating intense heat. The farmer felt "electric shocks" all over his body and he was unable to move. After several minutes, the object moved away and eventually headed over a forest and out of sight.

The electric generator started up again when the object was gone, but its wires were "burned out." The dog was lethargic throughout the next few days and on the third day it was found dead in the yard. An autopsy report noted that the dog's blood vessels had ruptured and that he had been bleeding internally. The farmer's own arm became very red after the encounter, and investigators told him that that he might have been burned by "radiation."

The Falcon Lake case in Canada in 1967 also involved "radiation." On May 20, 1967, an amateur prospector was in the rugged swamp and bush in eastern Manitoba and had just stopped to have lunch at 12:15 p.m. He was examining a quartz vein when he saw two disc-shaped objects flying overhead, one of which dropped down and appeared to land on a large, flat rock near him. He watched it for thirty minutes, and made a sketch of the object. Waves of warm air radiated from the craft, and he could smell sulfur and hear the whirring of a fast electric motor. A brilliant purple light flooded out of slit-like openings in the upper part of the craft.

Suddenly, a door opened in the side of the craft and the prospector could see smaller lights shining out of the opening. He slunk closer and heard two human-like voices coming from inside. Thinking it was an American secret test vehicle, he called out, "Okay, Yankee boys, having trouble? Come on out." The voices stopped when he said this. He walked up to the open doorway, where he could see lights on some sort of panel, flashing in a random sequence.

He touched the side of the craft, and found it was so hot it literally melted his rubberized glove. The door suddenly shut, and the craft rotated until an exhaust vent was right in front of him. Sure enough, a blast of hot gas hit him in the chest and the saucer took off and flew away, leaving him literally smouldering.

He managed to stagger, dizzy and injured, out of the bush and back to civilization. Doctors examined his second-degree burns, and investigators interviewed him about the object. Royal Canadian Mounted Police and Canadian Air Force officials went back to the area with him to look for the site when he had recovered enough to travel, but no sign of the incident was found in the dense forest. It was only some months later, when he visited the area again with ufologists, that the site was located. Charred leaves, twigs, parts of his clothing and, amazingly, radioactive pieces of metal were discovered at the site, prompting government officials to consider restricting travel into the area because of a possible danger to the public. Although the Condon Committee, which studied UFO reports for the United States Air Force, listed this dramatic case as "unexplained," noting that if the case "were physically real, it would show the existence of alien flying vehicles in our environment," some debunkers simply consider it a complicated hoax.

An earlier Canadian case that has received little attention took place on April 16, 1953, near Chatham, New Brunswick. At 3:34 p.m., an airline pilot formerly with the air force was flying at 9,000 feet with his co-pilot on a routine flight when they saw a "disc-like" metallic object approaching from directly in front of them, but flying about 450 metres (1,500 feet) below their altitude. It was estimated to be about five to eight kilometres (three to five miles) away when they first saw it. It approached at about 150 knots and "passed beneath and behind" their plane. At its closest point, they could see it was definitely not an aircraft, and was about eight metres (twenty-five feet) in diameter, leaving no trail or exhaust.

The report filed with Project Second Storey, the Canadian government's official UFO study, read: "Both observers are quite definite in stating that the object was NOT a balloon. The object passed nearly over Chatham but has not been reported by any other witnesses." The file noted that in the "interrogator's opinion," the statement was "very reliable."

Far to the south, in Peru, aircraft had strange encounters with unusual aerial objects in 1980. According to American Defense Intelligence Agency documents, on the morning of May 9, a group of Peruvian Air Force officers were at Mariano Melgar Air Base at La Joya, Peru, when they saw a round UFO "hovering near the airfield." A jet was ordered into the air to intercept the invader, and the pilot reported that he successfully closed in and even "fired upon it at very close range without causing any apparent damage." When he brought the plane around to make a second pass, the UFO simply flew away at high speed. The next morning, before sunrise, another UFO was seen, this time in the form of a light, and another jet was sent up; however, the object didn't stick around for the dogfight this time.

Ufologist Timothy Good discovered other American Defense Intelligence Agency files that consisted entirely of clippings about UFOs from South American newspapers. These included the story of two experienced Argentinian airline pilots who were flying over Punta Arenas when they saw a UFO that ran on June 8, 1968, and another from July 13, 1968, about a UFO that landed at an air force base at Tandil. On July 26, 1968, a Buenos Aires newspaper carried an account of how five policemen in Olavarria tried to "capture and later shoot three crew members of [a] UFO."

Mexico has a long history of UFO sightings; many significant cases have occurred during the past few decades, including videos and photographs of strange flying objects. One of the most popular and well-documented sightings was captured on infrared video on March 5, 2004, over the state of Chiapas in southern Mexico. A military aircraft of SEDNA, the Mexican Secretariat of Defense, was flying at about 3,400 metres (eleven thousand feet), patrolling the skies for drug smugglers, using an infrared camera designed to detect illegal flights. But instead of drug smugglers, the infrared video camera picked up a group of eleven objects that could not be identified, and which were not seen in regular light. This isn't all that unusual, as the brilliant glare of the sun can make distant objects very difficult to see; in fact, that is exactly why the military planes are equipped with such devices.

"We are not alone! This is so weird," one pilot said while he and the other members of the crew were watching the objects on the infrared monitor. The radar operator later said he had felt afraid because they were "facing something that had never happened before." The captain of the crew told an investigator that he believed "'they' could feel we were pursuing them."

During the observation, the plane's radar detected two objects, although ground radar did not show anything in that area. Furthermore, the direction of the radar returns did not match where the infrared images were; later investigation showed that the radar returns lined up with a highway underneath the plane, on which numerous trucks and other vehicles passed.

The Mexican government gave the video to Jaime Maussan, a popular Mexican broadcaster and ufologist who has frequently been in media regarding UFOs and other esoteric subjects. On May 11, 2004, he held a news conference during which he showed the video and had various experts discussing it. Almost immediately, debunkers leapt to the fore, and offered a multitude of contradictory and nonsensical explanations for the images, including weather balloons, high-altitude plasmas, meteors, and ball lightning. It was not until Alejandro Franz, a Mexican ufologist, did a more thorough analysis of the video that the real explanation was made clear — the lights were actually flares on oil wells burning in the Gulf of Mexico, a fact that was verified by later flights.

The flames on the oil wells seemed to be objects flying in the sky because of the angle of the camera, the passing of the clouds, and the movement of the aircraft itself. This explanation wasn't embraced immediately, but once the evidence was presented for everyone to examine and verify, ufologists agreed that in this case, the mystery was solved.

Another well-witnessed UFO over Mexico occurred on July 11, 1991, during a total solar eclipse. Astronomers from all over the world flocked to a band of totality stretching from Baja, California, through Mexico City and beyond for a few minutes of observation. None of them reported seeing anything unusual, but hundreds of lay observers (members of the general public), said that they saw and took photos and videos of a strange object near the obscured sun. The object was in view only a matter of minutes before and after totality. Videotapes showed only a bright object in the sky, that in some cases left a trail as it moved jerkily. Reports claimed that the UFO was seen by people throughout Mexico City, although again it must be noted that no astronomer in the area saw the object, which according to some witnesses looked "metallic."

Astronomers pointed out that during the eclipse, both Jupiter and Venus were east of the sun's disc and shone brightly during the short period of darkness. An examination of photos and videos taken of the UFO during the eclipse confirmed that the sources of light seen before, during and after totality could have simply been planets that became visible because of the sun's brief disappearance.

Not everyone agrees with this explanation. In his book *Confirmation*, abduction researcher Whitley Strieber argues that the objects that appear on the videotapes could not have been Venus. According to his recreation of the conditions at the time of the eclipse, Venus would not have looked like the object in the Mexican videos does. Public opinion following the airing of the videos almost universally supported the view that the UFO observed was not a planet. Furthermore, UFO sightings continued during the days and weeks following the eclipse. The entire state of Puebla was inundated with reports of strange flying lights in the night sky, some of which flashed and remained in place for long periods of time, and others that zipped throughout the air.

Since this time, a number of videos showing apparent flying saucers hovering and moving over cities and towns have been shown on Mexican television. Some of these are obvious fakes, while others show considerably more skill at digital manipulation. Still others do not have easily accessible explanations.

Mexico City had previous UFO sightings that caused some concern. On September 16, 1965, for example, traffic jams occurred throughout the city as people stopped to look at several "glowing objects" seen manoeuvring in the sky. During one evening close to this date, at about seven-thirty, twelve people watched two "huge luminous things with intermittent flashing lights" dancing near the dome and turrets of the Fine Arts Palace before they "took off straight up."

A very strange and alarming incident is said to have occurred on November 4, 1957, at Fort Itaipu, Brazil. Several sources allege that at about two o'clock in the morning, two guards were on duty when they saw what they thought was a star exploding over their heads. They were surprised to realize that what they had seen was actually the rapid descent of a bright orange object from over three hundred metres (1,000 feet) to just forty-five metres (150 feet), where it stopped not far from them.

The guards reported hearing a humming noise as it approached and became aware of an increase in heat. The heat intensified and the men felt that their bodies were on fire, causing them to scream in pain. A power failure across the entire base happened at that moment, confusing the personnel even more. When the lights came on a short while later, other soldiers saw a light moving away from the area. The guards had serious burns and needed to be hospitalized for their injuries. The case has not been closed, according to some accounts.

As unusual as it is, the strange case of these guards is not mentioned in a major work about UFOs in Brazil, written by South American ufologist Irene Granchi. However, she documents many cases of UFOs and encounters with aliens that test the imagination. One of the earliest cases that she notes occurred in 1930, in an area southwest of Rio de Janeiro called Jacarepagua, before it was developed. One night, a couple was asleep in their small cottage, situated in a large expanse of primitive grassland. They were awakened to light streaming into their bedroom through the slats in the blinds, a very unusual thing because there were no other people living near them, and no roads or railroads close by. When they opened the window to look out, they were shocked to see what they described as "a white rounded object with two monstrous 'eyes'" and a "leg" or column coming down from it. The "eyes" were square, brick-shaped holes in its body. They likened it to a man-made "ghost" constructed to frighten them for some reason. The husband took out his pistol and fired several shots in its direction, but the object was unaffected.

The object crossed the lawn in front of them, moving slowly up and down as if it was "walking." It then rose up and headed for a dam some distance away, but paused and rotated back to "look" at the couple several more times before it was lost in the distance. The next day, the wife broke out in a rash of some kind, but it cleared up after a few days. Another apparent physical effect was that the grass on their lawn had turned from a lush green to a dead grey.

On August 14, 1965, a man was driving from Itabira to Belo Horizonte in the state of Minas Gerais, Brazil. At around eight o'clock, he saw a glow in the distance beside the road, and puzzled over what it was because there were no houses or buildings there. When he got close enough, he stopped his car and turned off his lights to get a better look at the glow. He saw a bright white patch shaped like a "trapezoid," and he decided to get out and walk closer to see what it was. When he was only about thirty metres (one hundred) feet from it, he "felt the presence" of a huge disc-shaped object at least ninety metres (three hundred feet) in diameter and fifteen metres (fifty feet) tall, hovering motionless only a metre (three feet) above the pavement. He could see a dome of some sort on top, but he did not see any windows or other openings or protuberances.

The object was completely black and making no sound. It was visible only because of the bright light streaming from its underside. The man watched in awe for several minutes until the object began moving slowly away from the road and down into a depression that led to a field and corral. The witness noted the bright light that it shone on the ground was so intense, "one could have seen an insect creeping there." When the disc was about 450 metres (1,500 feet) away, the beam of light decreased in diameter and began rising until it was at the height of the road again. It rose up more quickly and disappeared into the sky.

The witness noted: "I was under the impression that there were beings aboard it though I cannot explain what gave me this impression." He wrote: "After it was lost from sight, I went on standing there for some time, motionless, before I decided to proceed on my journey."

Far to the west and much more recently, a tour group staying at a hotel in Banos, Ecuador, on April 26, 2003, saw a strange procession of lights in the night sky over the city. At about seven o'clock, they looked out from their balcony and saw "two small balls in the sky," that were reddish-yellow in colour and looked like spheres of lava. They were each zipping independently about the night sky, bobbing and weaving. One descended at high speed down into a valley and then zoomed back up into the air.

Across the valley was a mountain from which flashed something like sheet lightning. Then, a third ball rose into the sky and began performing the same aerial manoeuvres as the first two. There was a flash from behind the mountain, and a fourth ball of reddish light joined the antics. Then, the first three balls flew to one side, formed a triangle, and remained in place.

According to reports from NUFORC a flash came again, and a fifth light rose up into the air, but instead of dancing around the sky, it flew directly across the valley, over the witnesses' hotel, and went behind another mountain and out of sight. The group watched the lights' movements for thirty more minutes and then went off to a scheduled dinner at a restaurant. When they returned, the sky had clouded over and the lights were obscured from view.

Some might believe this sighting was caused by earthquake lights, a natural phenomenon created when stress fractures inside the Earth release energy that may be visible as light in certain circumstances. However, most cases of earthquake lights do not involve numerous balls like those described here, and they tend to be more directly associated with seismic events, which were not in evidence on that evening. Arch-skeptic Philip Klass might have suggested the lights were ball lightning formed during an approaching thunderstorm, but that poorly understood natural phenomenon is hardly an explanation in its own right.

Sightings throughout North and South America continue to be reported nearly every day of the year. The record of UFOs in our terrestrial environment grows each year.

Africa

UFOs have also been sighted over Africa, from Egypt to South Africa, and from Madagascar to the Ivory Coast.

In July 1975, in what was then Rhodesia, a flurry of UFO activity had many residents concerned. In Salisbury, a couple watched an odd orange light remain in a stationary position near their home for six minutes on July 4. Two days later another couple saw a similar object. At 8:15 p.m. they were driving near Karoi and saw an orange object "with a jagged tail and pointed front." When they stopped the car to get a better look, the object stopped moving as well. Although such behaviour is typical of a star or planet, the light in this case began moving downward rapidly and vanished below the trees in a matter of minutes, thus ruling out an astronomical body.

On the evening of July 26, near Macheke, a man was walking around the side of his house when a bright white beam of light struck him and threw him to the ground. It appeared to be coming from a source about twelve metres (forty feet) away and about the height of nearby power lines. He tried to get up and out of the path of the beam, but found that he was paralyzed and could not move at all. On the ground, he could see the light and the beam reflecting in a window. He blacked out and when he came to, the light and beam were gone and he could move again, although he was stiff and sore. He went inside his house and found that his fire had gone out, indicating he had been unconscious for more than an hour.

One of the most remarkable African UFO cases took place in the same country after it had been renamed Zimbabwe. On September 16, 1994, teachers at the Ariel School in Ruwa, not far from Harare, were having a morning meeting while their sixty-two students between the ages of five and twelve played in the schoolyard. A young boy ran into the school "tuck shop" (snack bar) where he told the adult there that something had landed in the schoolyard, and that a "little man" was running around with the children. Since the adult thought that the boy was simply being mischievous, she did not go outside to look herself.

Illustration by Jennifer Wang

On September 16, 1994, children playing in their schoolyard encountered strange creatures with long black hair that emerged from objects that landed near them.

The children later explained to their teachers, parents, and investigators that they had been playing games when they observed as many as five unusual craft flying through the sky and ducking in and around the electrical power lines. Eventually they landed in some brush next to the schoolyard, about a hundred metres (350 feet) away from the students. As they watched, two small humanoid creatures dressed in black emerged from one of the objects and walked towards the children. The entities had long black hair, large staring eyes, no noses at all, but slit-like mouths, and they walked in a stilted manner.

The children said that the creatures came up to them and "spoke" to them without using their mouths, through a kind of telepathy. Some children were given warnings about pollution, others were told that the Earth was going to be destroyed, and still others were informed that humans were too technologically advanced. After a while, the creatures went back to the craft and according to the children, the objects "just went."

The headmaster of the school had all the children draw pictures of what they had seen. The case was investigated locally by renowned ufologist Cynthia Hind. Later, abduction researcher Dr. John Mack travelled to Zimbabwe from America and spent several days interviewing and counselling the children.

On August 28, 1966, a mysterious object was seen flying over Pretoria, South Africa. At about four o'clock, a police officer was notified of the UFO and managed to shoot some film of the craft, which was disc-shaped with a dome on top and flashing lights on its surface. The dispatcher notified other officers, who drove off in pursuit, and even the police helicopter was sent up to chase it. The helicopter pilot, who was also a police superintendent, said that he chased the craft for some time and was baffled by its undulating course. A police car chased the object for about a hundred kilometres (sixty miles) until the officers reached the town of Cullinan, where they broke off their pursuit.

On July 22, 1985, a similar pursuit took place, although this one was by military personnel. At 5:45 p.m., two Zimbabwe Air Force jets were scrambled from Thornhill Air Base in response to UFO reports from Bulawayo and other towns in the western part of the country. The object was observed by airport personnel and also tracked on radar. It was described as disc-shaped with a cone on top, and it was shining so brightly in the afternoon sun that it was difficult to look at directly.

"This was no ordinary UFO," an air marshal was recorded as saying. "It was no illusion, no deception, no imagination." When the jets arrived over the city, they found the UFO at an altitude of 2,100 metres (seven thousand feet) but it immediately shot upwards to 21,000 metres (seventy thousand feet) in only a minute. The jets pursued the object to about 9,000 metres (thirty thousand feet), then broke off their chase. The object was briefly seen again near the ground, before it flew off across the horizon at high speed and was lost to sight. When asked to comment on the incident, the Director General of Air Operations said, "We believe implicitly that the unexplained UFOs are from some civilization beyond our planet."

Elsewhere in Africa, UFOs had been reported for some time. On June 30, 1948, the ship *Llandovery Castle* left Kenya bound for Cape Town. At eleven o'clock on the night of July 1, it was going through the Straits of Madagascar when the lookout and some passengers saw a light high in the sky heading in their direction. As they watched, it descended until it was only about fifteen metres (fifty feet) above the water, and began travelling alongside the ship. As it flew, it shone a beam of light like a searchlight down onto the water; then, the beam and its lights were extinguished. The crew and passengers of the ship were then able to see that the object was a cigar-shaped metallic craft, with its rear section truncated. It did not have any windows or portholes, and seemed to be three hundred metres (a thousand feet) in length! It kept pace with the ship for approximately a minute, then it ascended to an altitude of about three hundred metres (a thousand feet). Flames came out of its tail section and it shot forward, moving quickly out of sight.

Only a few years later, another ship had a similar encounter on the other side of the continent. A cargo ship was anchored at Port Gentil, Gabon, on June 1, 1952, when at 2:40 a.m. the first mate notified the master seaman that a luminous object was passing directly overhead. He said he had watched it come from the shore, stop, turn, and continue on its course out to sea, and make another erratic move as it flew near the ship. The master held up his binoculars and saw a bright, "phosphorescent

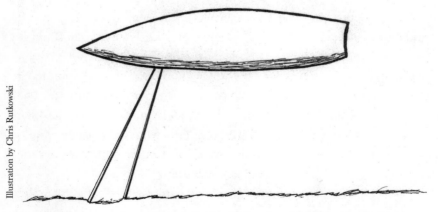

Illustration by Chris Rutkowski

In 1948, the crew of an ocean vessel in the Straits of Madagascar saw a cigar-shaped object playing a searchlight upon the water.

orange light, circular in shape and moving at great speed in a seemingly straight-line course." He followed the light for three minutes as it headed out to sea and was lost to sight. He confirmed that there were no planes in the air near there at the time.

Far to the north, but only a handful of weeks later on July 15, 1952, two bakers in Boukanefis, Algeria, were outside their shop at eleven o'clock when they saw an object shaped like a "plate," flying through the sky and giving off a greenish smoke. It kept a constant course as it headed south across the desert and out of sight. That year, UFOs were reported in many towns across Algeria and Oran, including Lamorciere, Mostaganem, Algiers, and Marrakech, and far to the south in the Belgian Congo near its uranium mines.

The next several cases are from e-mails sent by witnesses to the NUFORC website. The availability of such information speaks volumes about the importance of an international and accessible site where people can file reports, even if they are anonymous.

On November 10, 2005, at six-thirty, a man in Accra, Ghana, happened to look outside his window and saw a bright, round, orange fireball moving overhead at a high altitude. As he watched, it quickly changed form to a cigar shape, and bright emerald or fluorescent green light glowed out from its sides. It left no visible trail, and it flew off to the south towards the ocean, travelling out of sight within about five seconds.

On Christmas 2005, at eight o'clock in the evening, as many as one hundred miners were gathered in an open area near Taparko in Burkina Faso, for a Christmas dinner. Suddenly, the mine manager looked up in the sky and saw a group of lights in a triangular formation. He pointed it out to the other miners and they all watched it for at least a minute. The object travelled not much faster than a jet, but its lights were not flashing and no noise was heard. The miners wondered what the object was, and using the Internet, one of them discovered that many others around the world had reported seeing triangular formations of lights.

On March 22, 2006, at 9:15 p.m., two witnesses at Port el Kantoui, Tunisia, reported seeing a rod-shaped object about eighteen to twenty-one metres (sixty or seventy feet) in the air, at about the same height as their hotel. It was estimated to be about one to two metres (four to six feet) in length, with dim lights running along its underside. The object appeared to be travelling towards the observers at about eighty kilometres (fifty miles) per hour, without making a sound.

At about midnight on June 9, 2002, an amateur astronomer in M'bour, Senegal, was observing the sky over the ocean when he thought he saw a satellite almost overhead moving slowly and steadily from north to south. He watched it for about thirty seconds as it traversed the sky, stopped moving for a second, moved erratically, and then took off to the southwest very rapidly. The witness noted that he spends much time observing the sky with binoculars and telescopes, and is familiar with astronomical phenomena and satellites. He was certain that the object he observed that night was unusual.

On January 31, 2000, the Egyptian newspaper *Al-Ahram* published an article by noted author Mohamed Salmawy about several UFOs that had been seen over Cairo. On January 25, 2000, three witnesses were driving on the Mouneib Bridge from Cairo to Giza, when they saw objects they described as glowing, neon "frankfurters" floating in the sky over the pyramids. Salmawy saw either the same or similar objects that same night while flying from Italy to Egypt as his plane approached Cairo. At around eleven-thirty, he saw a bright light like a "big light bulb" that he could later distinguish was a "rectangular shape flying just above the ground."

THE ARCTIC AND ANTARCTIC

If UFOs are seen throughout the world, it shouldn't come as any great surprise that even the North and South polar regions have had reported sightings.

As noted earlier, the American Defense Intelligence Agency has received information on events in many areas across the globe, and some of this data is related to observations of unusual aerial phenomena. In June 1965, British, Argentine, and Chilean personnel stationed on

Deception Island in Antarctica reported seeing odd coloured lights moving over their base for periods of up to thirty minutes. On July 3, 1965, at 7:20 p.m., nine scientists and technicians at Aquirre Cerda, the Chilean Antarctic base, watched a stationary light move from east to west in the sky, low on the horizon. It had a "solid appearance like a celestial body," and flew on a "trajectory with oscillations." The light eventually disappeared into the clouds.

Twenty minutes later, seven personnel saw another object, this time oval-shaped, with intensity brighter than a first magnitude star. They watched it for more than an hour — it was stationary sometimes, and would then move "above the stratus," all the while flashing different colours. It too was low to the horizon, and was 335 degrees in azimuth (in the northwest), and estimated to be about eight to sixteen kilometres (five to ten miles) away. While it was in sight, instruments on board an Argentine Navy ship were affected by some kind of magnetic field.

In an official report, the officers insisted that the object was not a hallucination and that the testimonies of the personnel were valid. The commander of the Chilean base stated: "It is rash to say that we all saw a flying saucer, like those in science fiction. But nevertheless it was something real, an object traveling at a staggering speed." He concluded: "As far as I am concerned it is a celestial object that I am unable to identify. That it could be an aircraft constructed on this Earth, I do not believe possible."

It would be so easy to dismiss this case as refracted observations of a star or planet, despite the scientists' testimony; yet, one wonders why scientists trained in their fields, especially meteorologists like those who saw the lights at the base, were unable to reduce their observations to sightings of common astronomical objects. Surely someone on board a long-term oceanic mission would have been familiar enough with the night sky from hours of skywatching that the possibility that the object was a star or planet would have occurred to him or her?

An astronomical explanation was immediately suggested in a more recent case. On May 15, 1994, a technician at McMurdo Station in Antarctica was with two others repairing a runway at one o'clock, when a brilliant green fireball streaked across the sky. There was no sonic boom, indicating it was at a very high altitude. In this case, the witnesses were fairly certain the UFO was actually an IFO, likely a bright chunk of cometary debris entering the Earth's atmosphere over the South Pole.

The sparse population near the Earth's poles means that few UFOs are reported at those latitudes. However, the number of cases from near these latitudes suggest that UFOs are not afraid of the cold.

The following report comes from the files of Ufology Research of Manitoba (UFOROM): On January 18, 2007, United Airlines Flight 829 departed Chicago for Hong Kong, travelling at high altitude over Canada's North. At a point beyond the eighty-first parallel, somewhere over the Arctic ice pack, the pilots saw "a flaming ball" pass their airliner on a shallow but flat trajectory. As it passed them, it "was dropping wreckage." The object dropped into the clouds and was lost to sight. As this object was likely a large meteor or a bolide, somewhere on the ice there is a meteorite waiting to be found.

THE
UNEXPLAINED

In 2007, documentary filmmaker Paul Kimball produced *Best Evidence: Top 10 UFO Sightings*, which aired on several science-fiction television networks. He asked various ufologists around the world, including this author, for their suggestions on which UFO cases were "best" according to their own criteria. Using these lists, Kimball came up with ten cases that seemed to be endorsed most often by ufologists.

Number ten on Kimball's list is a historical account of strange lights and objects seen by many residents of Nuremburg on April 4, 1561 — almost 450 years ago. Records of the event suggest that a veritable "invasion" by a plethora of lighted objects created fear and trembling among peasants and lords alike. Of course, what was actually seen is beyond our reach at this time, as the verification of any details is impossible.

Number nine is a curious series of photographs taken by astronauts Alan Bean, Owen Garriott, and Jack Lousma on September 20, 1973. They were well into their stay in space when they observed and photographed an oddly shaped object that was estimated to be as much as three hundred metres (one thousand feet) in diameter. NASA has so far been unable to identify the object, but it has been implied that the object was simply a stray chunk of a rocket booster or shielding from a previous space mission of the United States or Soviet Union. Nevertheless, it remains as an unidentified orbiting object, a UOO.

The Yukon case of December 1996 mentioned earlier in this book is ranked at number eight on the list. As noted, it is the well-witnessed, well-investigated case of a large unexplained object seen by independent witnesses separated by time and distance.

Number seven is an incident that occurred on March 16, 1967, at Malmstrom Air Force Base near Lewiston, Montana. A UFO was reported directly over one of the E-Flight missile silos. Then, at 8:45 a.m., an alarm sounded and each one of the Minuteman missiles suddenly indicated a no-go status. Military witnesses admitted that when the unidentified lights were seen in the area of the base, power interruptions occurred, and the launch capability of the silos was completely disabled. If that wasn't of grave concern to the United States Air Force, it should have been. There was never a satisfactory official explanation for the events that night. In fact, the only way that the event was replicated was through sending a string electromagnetic pulse from an outside source through the shielded missile system.

The Shag Harbour UFO crash on October 4, 1967, was ranked number six in Kimball's presentation. Eyewitnesses, including pilots of a DC-8 airliner and several Royal Canadian Mounted Police officers, saw a glowing object fall from the sky into the Atlantic Ocean off the coast of Nova Scotia. Witnesses on a ship off the coast had seen objects on radar and in the sky, and watched as a red light flew from its position on the horizon to a point directly over their vessel before it headed out to sea. Rescue vessels found a bed of luminous green foam on the surface where the object went down. It was also never satisfactorily explained. Ufologists Don Ledger and Chris Styles uncovered a series of official government documents that showed an investigation of the reports had taken place and that an "underwater search" may have been conducted by American or Canadian Navy teams. Rumours circulated in the area that military divers had been in the region for some time and that "something" was taken out of the water. Was this a crashed UFO or a secret underwater navy exercise to recover a spy satellite instrument package that had fallen off course? Perhaps the navy was in the sea off the Canadian coast setting up sonar nets for submarine defense. Or perhaps it was something else entirely.

Number five is a little-known UFO sighting by a very capable and reputable observer. On December 16, 1953, Kelly Johnson, one of the developers of the infamous U2 spyplane, reported seeing an anomalous object while at his ranch near Agoura, California. At around five o'clock, he and his wife watched a dark, saucer-shaped object hanging low in the sky. It remained stationary for several minutes, but then began to move away from them, and against the direction of movement of the clouds. He guessed that it was about sixty metres (two hundred feet) in length, but could not reconcile it as any known aircraft. He maintained it was mysterious, and was not a conventional vehicle. In addition, two of Johnson's test pilots also observed the same object while flying near Long Beach, California. Skeptics have argued that pilots are not perfect observers and frequently make errors of observation, but one would hope that their observational skills would at least allow them to tell the difference between a conventional aircraft and something else.

A photographic UFO case, in McMinnville, Oregon, that has been debated since it was reported in 1950 sits at number four. On June 8 of that year, Paul Trent and his wife watched a dark, hat-shaped object fly over their property, and some clear photos were taken. Skeptics and believers have traded insults about the case for more than fifty years, focusing on shadows on buildings in the foreground, the density of the image on the negative, and so forth. There's no question that something was captured on film and, if the witnesses were truthful, an unidentified flying object did pass over a small farm that day.

The Rendlesham Forest incidents are listed as number three on the Kimball's list, and as we have seen, this case too has been embroiled in controversy. Did an object or objects land in the English countryside in December 1980?

The 1976 Iranian Air Force UFO encounter is considered number two on the list, even though it has been dismissed by skeptics as a series of radar malfunctions and misinterpretations by witnesses.

Finally, the best UFO case on record is the encounter of an American crew of an RB-47 aircraft on July 17, 1957, over the continental United States. Their plane was followed by an unidentified object that was apparently tracked by radar on the ground, as well as on-board instrumentation. The argument for the high quality of this case is based in part on the fact that all personnel were highly qualified and highly trained, yet were unable to solve the mystery of their pursuer. The Condon Committee, which studied UFO reports for the United States Air Force, made the following statement about the case: "If the report is accurate, it describes an unusual, intriguing, and puzzling phenomenon, which, in the absence of additional information, must be listed as unidentified." However, the committee director also stated, "it may be assumed that radar 'chaff' and a temperature inversion may have been factors in the incident."

This is contradicted later in the same study, when three hypotheses for the sighting are offered: a radio-optical mirage of another plane seen through an inversion layer in the atmosphere; anomalous propagation echoes on the radar screens; or a light on the ground that was mistaken for a flying object. The analysis concludes: "There are many unexplained aspects to this sighting, however, and a solution such as given above, although possible, does not seem highly probable … From a propagation standpoint, this sighting must be tentatively classified as unknown."

Cases included on this list do not necessarily prove that aliens are invading the Earth. In fact, some of them may be explainable by diligent researchers. It is difficult to select a group of cases as being the "best" because there are so many factors and unknown quantities that affect the outcome of investigations. Not all ufologists adhere to strict methodology, and there is no guarantee that consistent investigative standards and techniques were used in all cases.

The truth is that if you were looking for proof that aliens were visiting Earth, even one good observation of an unexplained craft under apparent intelligent control would be proof enough.

UFOS
FROM A TO Z

UFOLOGY IS MORE THAN JUST UFO REPORTS. IT encompasses the entire UFO phenomenon, from books to magazines, from conventions to TV shows, from government documents to blogs, and from fans to debunkers.

I found myself drawn into the field by accident — I was an astronomy student in university when I answered the department phone one day and had a conversation with a person who said she had seen a UFO the night before. Since I had been taught by my professor that UFOs didn't exist, I was simply going to tell the caller that she was mistaken, but her persistence and pleading with me to help her understand what she had seen gave me pause. I was puzzled as to why an intelligent person would think that a conventional or prosaic object in the sky was something out of the ordinary.

Curious, I arranged to meet with the witness on her farm about an hour outside the city. I drove there and spent a fascinating afternoon listening to not only her story, but also to the stories of neighbours and friends who had heard of the visit of an "astronomer from the city," and dropped in to meet with me as well. While I was sure I could explain many of the sightings, some did not seem to have simple explanations and I wondered what they could have been.

When I got back into the city, I was asked about what I had heard, and then was requested to give a short talk about the reports to a few people in the department. I was asked to write a short article about the sightings and it was published in a small local publication. Not long after that I was invited to present the cases at a formal colloquium. The hall was packed with the largest crowd the organizers had ever seen. The public wanted to know what was being seen in the skies over rural Manitoba.

That was in 1975. More than thirty years later, the public still wants to know about UFOs. People seem to have an insatiable appetite for stories about possible sightings of extraterrestrial spacecraft, even though the cases themselves are not probative in this regard.

I am fascinated with the UFO phenomenon as a whole. I've attended UFO conventions, publicly debated the topic of UFOs (from both pro and contrary viewpoints), gone on UFO sighting watches, and driven for long hours to meet with witnesses of odd lights in the sky. I've sat in sterile RCMP offices paging through official UFO files, and spoken with pilots who swore they had seen objects that were not fireballs or balloons. I have sat on the other side of a two-way mirror as an alien abductee was regressed by a clinical hypnotist. I've even had an air force officer walk into my office and tell me he thought he had been abducted by aliens — but couldn't possibly talk to any other officer about it.

What drives people to believe that they have seen alien spacecraft or had encounters with extraterrestrials? Is it a matter of wish fulfillment? Self-expression? A longing for something more than the banality or painful reality of our lives? Could it be that, just possibly, aliens are visiting Earth?

I'm often asked if I have seen a UFO myself. After all, that would be a logical explanation for the root of my fascination and involvement with ufology research. But no, I've never seen anything that to me was truly mysterious. Oh, I have made some curious observations, like the time I was with one of two groups of UFO hunters, separated by a few miles, in a field one night in 1976. Everyone in two groups watched what seemed to be a saucer-shaped light rise up out of a field on the horizon and move away ... but an airport was located in that direction. And on another occasion, I was with an atmospheric physicist and some photographers determined to get images of a "light at the end of the road" that had been reported in a particular area for years. But weren't the lights we saw and photographed only distant automobile headlights?

I wasn't there in 1967 when Stephan Michalak encountered a flying saucer near Falcon Lake in Canada, getting second-degree burns in the process. I was not aboard the plane with Kenneth Arnold in 1947 when he saw the first "official" flying saucers, that turned out not to be saucers. I wasn't with the loggers in Arizona when Travis Walton was zapped by a UFO and disappeared for several days. I don't know what they saw, exactly, but I'm curious to know what was seen and experienced by these individuals.

I feel the same way about people who report their sightings to me today. I want to know what they have seen. If, from their descriptions, I can explain their sightings, I use the opportunity to tell them about astronomical phenomena such as conjunctions, bolides, and scintillation. If I can't, their sightings provide the opportunity for me to learn about their experiences, and assume the role of Sam Spade or Sherlock Holmes to solve the puzzle of the observation.

In previous books, I have written about the statistical probability of life on other worlds. Astronomers are generally convinced that intelligent civilizations exist elsewhere in the universe, but few are willing to postulate that some of these may be traversing the galaxy and possibly visiting Earth. I don't see the incontrovertible proof that aliens are here, but as *The X-Files* mantra goes: "The Truth is Out There." Unfortunately, I'm stuck down here.

ABDUCTIONS

Although we now know that some people have extensive histories of abduction encounters dating back to when they were children, the abduction phenomenon began with the publication of books in the 1980s, such as *Communion* by Whitley Strieber and *Intruders* by Budd Hopkins. After this time, alien abductions were accepted into ufology on a broader scale than ever before, and the general public became keenly interested in the concept of aliens invading bedrooms, snatching drivers from their vehicles on lonely patches of road, and having mystical knowledge imparted to them by omnipotent space beings.

Ufologists specializing in abductions began appearing on television talk shows to discuss their theories, and *OMNI* magazine even conducted a readers' survey to find out how many people had their own such experiences. The results seemed to indicate that a significant percentage of the population believed that they had an abduction experience. The stories ranged from visitations in witnesses' homes to the actual transporting of witnesses to places that are literally out of this world.

Some abduction ufologists have compiled lists of attitudes, feelings, sensations, and memories that they believe indicate that a person might have been abducted by aliens, but may be unaware of it. The scientists' questions are very general, and answering "yes" to these questions does not necessarily mean that a person has been abducted by aliens. Their questions include:

- Have you had missing or lost time of any length, especially one hour or more?
- Have you seen balls of light or flashes of light in your home or other locations?
- Do you have a memory of flying through the air which you do not feel was a dream?
- Have you had dreams of UFOs, beams of light, or alien beings?
- Have had a UFO sighting or sightings in your life?
- Do you have a cosmic awareness, an interest in ecology,

environment, vegetarianism or are very socially conscious?

- Do you have a strong sense of having a mission or important task to perform, without knowing where this compulsion came from?
- Have you ever awoken in the middle of the night, startled?

Since nearly everyone could answer "yes" to some of these questions, the list is not useful in indicating that someone has had a UFO abduction experience; however, an individual who answers affirmatively to all of the questions may believe in UFOs, or be predisposed to a belief in alien abductions.

The first alleged UFO abduction that was studied in great detail was the case of Barney and Betty Hill, which took place 1961 as the couple drove home from a vacation in Canada. There has been a great deal published about this significant case, which is discussed earlier in this book. Several years earlier, of course, Antonio Villas-Boas had his own sexual encounter with an alien in Brazil, although his case received much less public attention and scrutiny. The remarkable case of Travis Walton was also discussed here; his disappearance after being zapped with a beam from a hovering saucer was turned into a Hollywood movie and spawned much speculation.

The Hills, Villas-Boas, and Walton all encountered relatively human-like aliens, but a different kind of creature was blamed for an incident in Pascagoula, Mississippi, in 1973. Charles Hickson and Calvin Parker were out fishing very late at night when a large UFO appeared behind them. Out of it came silver robots that floated towards the two men and grabbed them with pincer-like hands, and took them on board the saucer. The men were given examinations by unusual mechanical devices, then released.

Sandra Larson, her daughter, and a friend were driving to Bismarck, North Dakota, one morning in 1975 when they had a classic abduction experience. After seeing a UFO approach their car, they all had apparent memory lapses and suddenly found themselves sitting in their car off the road. Under hypnosis, Sandra provided a detailed description of her abduction by alien creatures, and her medical probing on an alien operating table inside the UFO. When an alien device was focused on her head, she felt as though her entire brain had been removed.

These are only a few of the many cases that have been written up in books and magazines over the past few decades. In several volumes, Whitley Strieber described his own series of abduction experiences, and his work and that of others has served to popularize the phenomenon. In 1994, Pulitzer Prize-winning author Dr. John Mack, a Harvard psychiatrist, published the landmark book *Abductions*, in which he laid out his thesis that aliens are abducting humans for purposes unknown, and that it has been going on for many, many years.

Mack interviewed hundreds of abductees at length over the course of his research. He debated skeptics on TV and at conferences, often gaining the upper hand because of his prowess at using logical arguments and his knowledge of ufology, something that most debunkers did not have because they had not done much or any research on the subject. In some cases they had simply dismissed the possibility without much careful thought. Mack died in 2004 in a tragic accident, cutting short what would have been a decidedly interesting lifetime of publishing in this field.

Mack was one of many participants in a scientific conference on alien abductions held at MIT in June 1992. The meeting laid the groundwork for investigation and research in this field. Diverse aspects of the phenomenon were discussed, including the use of hypnosis, case studies, and the development of clear and consistent methodology that would allow the scientific community to better appreciate the work that was being done. The conference was most noted, perhaps, for the discussion of a code of ethics for abduction investigators. The code would guide practitioners so that, like researchers in other psychosocial fields, they would "above all, do no harm" in the course of their investigations. In fact, not long after the conference, such a code was drafted and offered to ufologists, but few have formally endorsed the document. Other similar codes of behaviour among ufologists have been drafted, but without a formal regulating and monitoring body, they are not enforceable. At the conference, Dr. Stuart Appelle of psychology at the State University of New York, noted in unfortunate understatement that, "many investigators in ufology are not acting professionally."

During the past few decades, hundreds of people have come forward with claims of their own abductions, and investigators are trying to deal with this new aspect of ufology as best they can. Although some psychologists are convinced that abductions are a psychological reaction to personal problems, others, especially those who have studied a large number of such cases, do not believe that the abduction phenomenon can be so easily resolved.

There is no consensus as to what really happens during an abduction experience. Some researchers insist that witnesses are actually encountering alien beings, while others suggest that an abduction experience is nothing more than a very vivid dream. Even if they are dreams, the traumas associated with these experiences seem to indicate that the witnesses/victims are having particularly strange psychological reactions to something in their lives or their environment. Some skeptics have argued that abductees have some kind of psychological condition that makes them prone to fantasies, and prompts them to think in abnormal ways. Standard or specialized psychological testing on abductees does not usually show such abnormalities.

One example is that of an abductee who had been counselled by John Mack and gave a presentation at the MIT conference. His psychological tests showed that he was "highly functioning, alert, focused, intelligent, well-spoken and without visible anxiety." The results indicated "the absence of psychopathology," with no sign of "psychosis of major affective disorder." So if most abductees are diagnosed as otherwise normal by psychologists, then what explanation for their experiences is there?

Regardless of the reality of abduction experiences, it is obvious that something unusual is being reported, and should be studied in detail. A number of decades ago, UFO investigators would often ignore reports of creatures associated with sightings of flying saucers. This was because the observation of aliens was deemed too bizarre, even for UFO enthusiasts who already faced negative reactions as a result of biased news stories that poked fun at UFO witnesses. Over the years, however, the idea that such entities may be associated with UFOs has become more widely accepted, and more attention is given to such cases. Statistically, very few UFO reports have associated entities, although when considering the hundreds of thousands of UFO cases now on record, the number of entity cases is not insignificant. Even in Canada, creatures have occasionally been reported with UFOs, though such cases are definitely rare. British ufologist Jenny Randles has suggested that, "it is perfectly possible to consider that UFOs and abductions are two separate phenomena linked by an accident of social context."

Over the past few years, there has been strong public interest in abduction stories, and many ufologists view them as perhaps the next step beyond mere contact with aliens. If we are under observation by extraterrestrials, then the infrequent examination of a human guinea pig is a plausible scenario. Unfortunately, there has never been any incontestable physical evidence to support any claims of such contact, leading to the basic problem of the acceptance of UFOs by the scientific community.

Until verifiable proof of alien visitation is available to the populace, we are left with a volume of cases that suggest that space entities are in our midst, and with a fascinating body of stories that are said to be true tales of alien encounters. Skeptics insist that these events are imaginary, but to witnesses or victims of the strange phenomena, they are as real as anything else in life.

We should also make a distinction between abductees and contactees. The former are UFO witnesses who believe they have had a contact experience with alien beings, though their recall of the event may be partially obscured. Sometimes, hypnosis is used to enhance recall of the event, though skeptics contest its use in abduction regressions. Contactees, in slight contrast, believe that not only have they had a contact experience, but they feel compelled to tell the world of their meetings with aliens. Often, contactees say they were instructed by the aliens to warn their fellow earthlings of the consequences of their ignorant habits, such as war, pollution, and secularity. Abductees generally do not have such missions, and in fact shy away from public exposure to the point where they request anonymity at all costs.

Unfortunately, the line between abductees and contactees has become blurred in recent years. More and more abductees come away from their experiences believing that they have been chosen to spread the word, or directed to make changes in their lives. Some, like Richard Dreyfuss's character in the movie *Close Encounters of the Third Kind*, become obsessed with the UFO phenomenon, spending an inordinate amount of time trying to discover more about aliens and UFOs, by reading books and attending conferences, and proselytizing.

An example of a contactee is a woman I shall call V. In 1977 she came to me and explained that she had intimate knowledge of aliens and their spacecraft, as she spoke to the Space Brothers twice a week. ("Space Brothers" being the term often used by contactees to describe benevolent aliens who resemble humans but are vastly advanced both technologically and spiritually.) She began her story by stating: "I died when I was six years old, but I rose up again on the third day. I soon found that I could talk to the insects and animals." V went on to describe how she felt she was psychically gifted. Her contact with benevolent space beings had begun at an early age, when the creatures took her to other planets and even inside the Earth through holes in the North and South Poles.

In the 1970s, her car was "teleported" by aliens while she was on a long road trip, which resulted in a period of missing time. There were "burn marks" (that looked to me like rust) left on her car after the experience. In eastern Canada, she had a large following in a church-like congregation, and she held religious ceremonies in fields where "scout ships" had landed. She lauded the benevolent Space Brothers for their omnipotence and mystical revelations. Her followers even built a pyramid in the middle of a field, sitting inside so that spiritual energy could be better focused upon them during meditation. V also claimed that using the power invested in her through the aliens, she healed the sick, and caused the blind to see and the lame to walk.

Following a talk on January 26, 1988, by ufologist Stanton Friedman at a university, a shy man asked him and I to meet later so he could talk about some UFO experiences he had had. When we did meet, he related what we might call a classic abduction experience, or a visit by some sort of entity to his home. There was of course no physical evidence to support the experience he claims to have had, but he was sure that it did happen, and he seemed to have had a history of such experiences throughout his life. He rarely talked with his friends or family about the incidents, and was worried about their reactions should his story ever become public knowledge.

The most vivid of his memories originated from a night in the middle of November 1987. He was in his bedroom preparing to go to sleep. He had been thinking about the day's events, and meditating. He got into bed with the lights out, and lay on his back drifting off to sleep. After a while, he became aware of a presence in his room that seemed to be in the vicinity of his closet. Almost simultaneously, he felt a peculiar tingling sensation in his body. He was surprised to realize that he was paralyzed and unable to move in any way, except to rotate his eyes. He felt that the presence was somehow responsible and that it was approaching his bed.

Although he couldn't recall seeing the entity in its entirety, he did have the distinct recollection of seeing a face not more than a foot in front of his eyes. He drew this face without much difficulty, depicting a cherubic character with skin folds, slit-like eyes, and a thin mouth, that was wearing some sort of tight-fitting helmet. He also felt that something had touched his mind, and that images of things he had seen in his life were brought to the surface of his mind and taken from him. He remembered feeling or sensing that whatever was doing this to him was also reassuring him that it meant no harm and that it only wanted certain things from his memory. After a while, the flashes from his past ceased, the entity seemed to withdraw, and sensation once again returned to his body. He admitted he was extremely disturbed by this incident.

This was only the most recent in a series of strange events throughout his life. He had experienced similar paralytic episodes before, each associated with some out-of-body flight. On one occasion he had seen a UFO radiating pulses of light as if it were signalling to him. One winter night, he felt as though he had been dragged out of his bedroom through a glass window, drawn physically into a UFO that had been hovering over a field.

In conjunction with a clinical psychologist that I consulted as part of my own investigations, I worked with this man over the next several years. Later, I was contacted by other abductees who knew I was a ufologist, and who hoped I would help them understand the memories of their own experiences. There was such a demand for a sympathetic ear that I even assisted with the creation of an abductee support group where like-minded individuals could share their abduction experiences, and seek advice and recommendations for professional help. I could see how a trained psychologist or psychiatrist like John Mack could devote his entire practice to helping abductees.

My question to myself was, "What is it that is happening to abductees?" I also knew that such support groups can be detrimental to individuals, so I encouraged them to seek physicians and clinicians who could help them overcome their anxieties, depression, and confusion. The other problem with support groups is that contagion between abductees can cause them to change their stories so that any investigation of a single case by a researcher becomes more difficult.

Common to many published accounts of alleged UFO abductions is the hypnosis of the abductees, which is used to regress them to the time of the incident in order to uncover suppressed or hidden facts. Sometimes details of medical examinations on board spacecraft are revealed, or trips with beings from other planets. From a psychological standpoint, hypnotic regressions are sometimes useful as therapy to uncover suppressed feelings or remove mental blocks. Some ufologists use hypnotic regressions to penetrate witnesses' memories of their experiences, which may have been deliberately clouded by their antagonists. Skeptics note that hypnosis cannot determine the truth of any memory, but instead allow a person's own beliefs to come through, whether they are true or not. That is, if a person believes he or she has been on board a UFO, even if they were not, then that story will still be told under hypnosis. Hypnosis cannot be used to accurately distinguish between fact and fantasy.

In a previous work, I described a condition that I labelled Alien Abduction Syndrome, in which certain people believe they have been contacted by aliens. It could be that there are a number of factors that cause this belief: dissatisfaction with life; stress; domestic problems; family problems; peer pressure; rape trauma; chemical imbalances; or child abuse. There may be other factors, especially since Mack and others insist that abductees do not, in general, have any obvious psychopathology, though I have found many who do. It is only through further serious study by researchers not bent on debunking alien abductions or proving their reality, that we will make progress on this subject.

Belief

"Do you believe in UFOs?"

This is a question I often am asked by both reporters and acquaintances. It's the most common question asked of people interested in the subject of aliens and UFOs.

The problem is that the question makes no sense. What is it that those who ask the question want to know?

If I believe in UFOs, I must be of the opinion that UFOs are things that are true or real. But what are UFOs? Alien spaceships? Hoaxes? Hallucinations? If I think that UFOs are nothing more than figments of peoples' imaginations, they are nonetheless things that I believe in.

It is more likely that the question these curious people actually want answered is, "Do you believe that UFOs are real?" However, this question is actually more difficult to interpret. What is "real"? A hoax? A misidentified aircraft? Those are certainly real, but that's not what we're being asked about, is it?

"Do you believe that UFOs are alien spaceships?" is another problematic question. Is the question asking if all reported UFOs are alien spaceships? If so, then the answer must be no, because many reported UFOs turn out to be explained as stars, airplanes, and fireballs

Ultimately, the question that is probably meant to be asked is, "Do you believe that some UFOs are alien spaceships?" A yes or no answer can be given, depending on whether or not we think the Earth is being visited by extraterrestrials.

What if we ask, "Do you believe in life elsewhere in the universe?" This has no bearing on UFOs at all; this is a matter of personal faith, and something that cannot be supported or proven scientifically at this time. Most scientists would answer yes to this question, since prevailing theories about the evolution of stars and planets suggest that life should be a natural consequence of long-term development. The nature of this life would vary in the minds of people being asked — one person's idea of life might be a green-skinned alien, whereas another, perhaps a scientist, might consider bacteria or viruses to be life. Obviously, the difference between these two views of life has a bearing on what the ultimate question should be.

"Do you believe that there is intelligent life elsewhere in the universe?" is another possible question. Again, this could also be answered "yes" by most people, including scientists, since we are not asking anything about how far away this life might be, or the degree of its intelligence. Is a bee intelligent? A puppy? Would it make a difference to us if the alien "puppy" were on a planet in our solar system or in the Andromeda Galaxy?

What we really want to find out by asking such a question is if we believe that intelligent life elsewhere in the universe is advanced enough to develop a civilization like ours here on Earth. Apart from the easy joke about how we hope it's more civilized than ours, the intelligent life would have to be very intelligent indeed, far beyond viruses, bees, and puppies. This life would have to have systems of knowledge, commerce, exploration, and biological health.

Still, an extraterrestrial civilization that resembles ours might not have a particular interest in travelling to other star systems. Humans have no physical means of efficient transport that would allow such a journey, or the ability to finance it. It's possible that another similar civilization might not have these same values or obstacles, but they may have other reasons for not wanting to go trekking between the stars.

Alright, another question: "Do you believe that intelligent life similar to ours and with a civilization similar to ours exists elsewhere in the universe?" It's also easy to answer this question in the affirmative.

The universe is big. Very big. In fact, most people have no concept of the vastness of space. Astronomers do, because they routinely make measurements and calculations with numbers that are, well, astronomical.

The rest of us, well, we need some perspective.

Many of us made models of things when we were children — model aircraft, cars, and boats. Some of us played with dolls and built dollhouses, even to scale. It's easier to put things into perspective when we look at models of very large things, instead of the actual enormous objects.

So, let's make a model of the universe. Not the entire thing, but perhaps just a small part that we know fairly well. Imagine that our sun is the size of a typical poppy seed bagel. Using this scale the Earth, our home, is the size of a poppy seed.

We see the sun in the sky every day, and have no real idea of how big it is. It looks the size of a basketball to some people, although what does this mean?

Witnesses often provide similar descriptions of the UFOs they have seen, such as, "It was the size of a beach ball." I know that a beach ball is only about a foot in diameter — that's a very small UFO, isn't it? The witness usually means that the UFO looked as large as a beach ball would appear if it were held not far away. In other words, the UFO had the *angular diameter* of a beach ball. But how far away was the UFO? Two feet? Ten feet? Twenty? The distance is vitally important when using such an analogy.

Early in my UFO report investigation career, a UFO witness told me that the object she had seen was the size of a beach ball. When I asked her how far away she thought the object had been, she replied, "Oh, about three or four miles away." I made the mistake of telling her that it would be impossible to see such an object at that distance, and she became furious that "scientists never believe us UFO witnesses."

What was painfully obvious to me was frustrating to the witness. The angular diameter of a beach ball at a distance of three miles is so small that it is essentially invisible to the eye. There's no way she could have seen it clearly. She probably meant that she saw a light in the sky that she estimated to be the angular size of a beach ball at a relatively small distance from her, possibly fifty feet. She then juxtaposed the observed object with her impression of a nearby beach ball, and that was what she thought was the UFO. She did not have the ability to describe accurately her impression of what she was seeing, so she compared her observations to a previously viewed beach ball.

This situation didn't have as much to do with belief as it did perception, although the two are related. Often, our beliefs shape how we perceive things. If I believe that alien spaceships are flying in the skies overhead, and I see lights I cannot explain in the night sky, I will consider them to be part of an alien spacecraft, rather than an airplane. If I believe that the chair I'm sitting on is sturdy, I have faith that my weight will not cause it to fall apart. If I believe that there is no possibility that aliens exist and might be able to travel between the stars, then any discussion about that possibility is completely pointless.

Contact

Part and parcel of the UFO phenomenon is the idea that aliens exist elsewhere in the universe; not only that they exist, but that they are capable and have a desire to travel across the vast distances of space and come to Earth. But space is very, very big, and astronomy is a science that deals with very big numbers.

Remember that poppy seed bagel? Well, if the sun was the bagel and was held in your hand, and the Earth was a poppy seed, it would be many feet away and practically invisible.

But let's get a bit wider in our world view. Let's make the sun a bit smaller. Imagine that it is the size of a pea held in the palm of your hand. On this scale, the Earth is invisible, but would be across the room. Where would the next nearest pea be? — that is, where, using this scale model of size and distance in the universe, would the next nearest star be located? In front of your home, a block away? Downtown?

If our star, the sun, was as small as a pea in your hand, the next nearest pea would be several hundred miles away. That's how vast the space between stars is, and how far away we are from even the *nearest* one. However, the nearest star may not harbour life. In fact, statistics tell us that intelligent life and extraterrestrial civilizations may be relatively rare in our universe. Some astronomers believe that we are completely unique in our solar system, although most think that there are other civilizations out there, somewhere.

Most readers will have grown up with science-fiction TV shows such as *Star Trek* and movies like *Star Wars*, in which interstellar travel is commonplace and apparently simple. We live in the "Steven Spielberg generation," in which science-fiction concepts are accepted as real, or at least probable. But while present-day science is making advances in these areas, we're still a long way from even sending manned spacecraft to other planets within our own local solar system. The fastest space vehicle launched from Earth to date will take thousands of years to reach the distance of even the nearest star.

It's possible for us to build spacecraft today that could reach a planet orbiting a nearby star within the lifetime of an astronaut on board.

Einstein showed that if a spacecraft were moving fast enough, time on board would slow down, although to an observer on Earth, time would pass normally and it would seem that the spaceship was gone a very long time, perhaps many decades. The astronaut on board would age at a much slower rate, and reach the destination in only a handful of years.

This is still a long way from "warp factor three," but it shows that space travel is possible even with our present technology. But here's the single fact that could change science fiction into science fact — not all stars are the same.

The Milky Way has about 100 billion stars. Some are hotter than our sun, while others are cooler. Some are larger, and some are smaller. Some are younger, and some are older. In fact, some stars are much older, perhaps millions of years older. This means that some stars with planets that can support life have had much longer to nurture and advance that life into highly evolved and technological civilizations. It is reasonable to think that some of these civilizations may have advanced so far technologically that they have discovered a way to travel between the stars, like in *Star Trek,* or at least have lifespans that allow for long journeys between stars. Maybe they have found ways to use sleep chambers to prevent aging on long voyages.

At any rate, the possibility that some alien civilizations are much more advanced than we are is very good. If so, perhaps they have visited the Earth during our history or are doing so now. Just because we have no incontrovertible evidence they are doing so does not prove they are not. By definition, aliens will think and act in alien ways, beyond our comprehension and understanding. Maybe we simply cannot detect their existence because of some peculiar characteristic of their spacecraft.

Let's suppose that they are here, and that they have decided to make themselves known. If you were an alien, where would you land first? To which individual or group of people would you announce your presence? Would you break in on our television broadcast bands on all channels and frequencies and bring greetings? In what language? How would you be able to convey your intentions?

Let's be blunt — it is possible that the aliens' intentions are not benevolent and they actually are here to conquer us and enslave us. So who speaks for Earth? The President of the United States? The President of Russia? In terms of population, wouldn't the political leader of China be the logical choice since he directs the largest number of humans? What about the Pope? The Dalai Lama? Perhaps it should be someone whose words and image reach more people every day, such as Oprah Winfrey or Anderson Cooper? Perhaps the richest person on Earth would be our leader, such as Bill Gates or Warren Buffet. It's not an easy choice.

There's an anecdotal story about debunker Donald Menzel, who at one time was a member of the National Academy of Sciences, based in the United States. He did not think much of UFOs and ridiculed ufology and ufologists whenever possible. His arrogance is legendary. When asked why he knew that aliens were not visiting Earth, he is reported to have replied: "If aliens were wanting to make contact with Earth, they would certainly know to contact the National Academy of Sciences, the most prominent scientific panel studying the problem of intelligent life in the universe. And if so, since I am directly involved with these studies, I would be among the first to know. Since I am not aware of such contact, then they obviously are not here."

Similarly, famed science popularizer Carl Sagan believed that life probably existed elsewhere in the universe, but ridiculed witnesses of UFOs whenever he had the opportunity. To him, scientists were heroes who battled foes who harboured irrational thoughts, and anything that conflicted with established scientific doctrine was "pseudoscience." Yet he tackled the issue of aliens and UFOs from time to time. In his novel *Contact*, published in 1985, scientists are the first to decipher a message from space and make contact with extraterrestrials, although in the novel (which was later turned into a movie), there is some doubt as to whether the contact really occurred. The main character waxes philosophical about the meaning of contact, and it is described in terms of a quasi-religious event.

(My wife, an ardent fan of Sagan, has insisted that I note how his last book, *The Demon-Haunted World: Science as a Candle in the Dark*, was perhaps his best. In it, he wrote about how, even through its faults, science is "all that stands between us and the enveloping darkness" of irrational thinking and misguided mysticism.)

Ufologist Stanton Friedman also addresses these concerns in his writings and presentations on the implications of contact. He believes that actual contact will almost certainly devastate the world's economy, herald a new era in religion, and probably destroy political territorialism. If contact with aliens was formally announced, there would be a profound shift as people began to view themselves as Terrans, rather than as belonging to a particular country. Friedman notes:

> The younger generation, which, unlike me, was never alive when there wasn't a space program, would push for a new view of ourselves as "Earthlings" instead of as Americans, Canadians, Greeks, Peruvians, etc. Many would think that would be great. But I know of no government on Earth that wants its citizens to owe their primary allegiance to the planet (where it belongs) instead of to individual national governments. Nationalism is the only game in town. I believe that alien visitors — they may be our landlords, for all we know — think of us as earthlings even though, because of our military traffic, they would be well aware of different ruling groups in different places.

If aliens wished to contact us, they might choose to do so in a way that would seem illogical to us, or at least unexpected. Contact may have occurred hundreds or thousands of years ago, or may not come for another millennium. It's very possible that aliens might not wish to contact us at all.

DEBUNKING

What constitutes proof of alien visitation? Isn't eyewitness testimony enough? When it comes to the subject of UFOs, the general population seems to be polarized. Some people accept the possibility that aliens are visiting Earth, and others simply refuse to even consider it. The words used to reject the possibility of UFOs being alien spacecraft show the topic is infused with extreme passion. Debunkers describe this notion as balderdash, preposterous, or even dangerous. This in itself is strange, because some normally calm, objective people become agitated and vehement when the subject is broached.

Scientists are particularly prone to polarization on this topic. Whereas they are usually meticulous and exact when it comes to laboratory measurements and reserved when it comes to speaking about advances in their field of interest, the topic of UFOs often spurs scientists to make out-of-character statements. Most zoologists wouldn't think of offering a scientific opinion about a cosmological theory. A physicist wouldn't be able to comment on the reasons that certain bird species are waning in the subarctic. If a particular topic is outside of a scientist's area of interest, he or she obviously hasn't studied the data in enough detail to comment. But ask about UFOs, and a scientist from any discipline will give his or her opinion. Usually, this opinion is skeptical, and probably favours debunking.

Scientific methodology forbids jumping to conclusions without detailed study of the facts, yet this is what happens in the battle between science and ufology. Scientists who know better make pronouncements about the non-existence of UFOs without having read any books or journals on the subject.

This usually happens because in the process of becoming scientists, scholars learn ways in which to reason and assess knowledge. In effect, they learn how to learn. They learn to look at the world in a way that is critical and analytical. Technically, scientists are in a good position to judge the merit of any theory or proposal, in any discipline; however, scientists are not immune to biases. Scientists are people just like anyone else, with predilections and prejudices, and laudable talents as well as character flaws. Some are even prideful.

UFOs pose a serious problem to scientists. Ufology, despite its efforts to quantify UFO research, does not qualify as a science by itself. Certainly, one can use scientific methodology to study the subject of UFOs, but ufology is no more a science than is a study of beat poetry, matchbook covers, or web logs.

Unfortunately, scientists are often called upon to give opinions on UFO reports or some aspect of the phenomenon. Because they generally have not had any experience in the subject, their answers can be trite or scoffing, and they are usually ill-informed. Early in my own study of the UFO phenomenon, I had the opportunity to attend a lecture by an eminent scientist from the National Research Council of Canada, a government-funded body that oversees and generates much of the scientific research in the country. During his presentation, he responded to questions regarding a then-current UFO case, namely that of a multiple UFO sighting where several silver bowl-shaped objects were seen taking off from a farmer's field, leaving behind swirled patches in the long grass.

This scientist, who had made his view that UFOs were nonsense abundantly clear to media and to conference attendees, calmly stated that the formations in the grass were undoubtedly caused by fairy ring mushrooms. This was many years before crop circles became a popular topic of sensationalist tabloids, and the formations in the field were then considered landing traces by UFO buffs. The scientist's statement floored me. I was shocked that such a learned individual with self-professed expertise in the UFO phenomenon would have thought that fairy rings could possibly be an explanation in this case. What's more, he admitted that he had not investigated the report, nor visited the location first-hand.

The problem with his explanation is that such formations do not appear overnight. In fact, they take years and many seasons of growth to achieve a size comparable to the swirled patches found in the field. They are created when a spore from a mushroom lands on a patch of grass, usually a lawn. The mushroom sprouts, grows, and then releases its own spores in a burst that sends them out in a circle. These take root, grow, and continue the growth of the circular patch of dead grass until it is a few feet in diameter. Some get to be quite large.

This swirled patch wasn't on a lawn, but in very tall grass, which wasn't dead, but was flattened in a large patch several feet in diameter. Mycologists I have since spoken with have said that fairy rings simply couldn't have formed in such a field, yet an expert UFO debunker, a scientist whose credentials would otherwise have qualified him to give presentations to scientific panels on a variety of subjects, gave completely wrong information to a roomful of scientists who laughed along with him as he pooh-poohed the entire notion of UFOs. It was exactly what they wanted to hear.

Now, before I am lambasted by skeptics for attacking one of their own (but I'm sure I will be, anyway), I must say that I have been called a skeptic more often than a believer. In fact, hard-core UFO believers find my views highly skeptical. Debunkers, on the other hand, have attacked my writings on ufological topics as being far too generous and credulous. After more than thirty years of research and investigation into many aspects of the UFO phenomenon, I believe I can see its weaknesses and problems, but I also see that debunkers who are overzealous cause self-inflicted wounds. I consider myself an open-minded skeptic; however, one of my favourite observations is that it is wise to have an open mind, but not so open that your brains fall out. I've seen a lot of grey matter on the sidewalks, from both believers and skeptics.

To debunk means to present evidence showing the foolishness of someone or something. Curiously, although most debunkers are scientists, debunking is not a scientific procedure. Rational argument is the normal way for scientists to disagree and present differing theories, usually through a series of papers published in peer-reviewed journals. As a rule, name-calling and character assassination are not found in the pages of scientific journals, although there have been notable exceptions when very unprofessional conduct by scientists has been observed on certain issues. These have included debates on continental drift, cold fusion, N-rays, and most recently, global warming.

The subject of UFOs has been categorized as paranormal by debunkers, placing it in the same group with astrology, ESP, ghosts, Bigfoot, the Loch Ness Monster, cattle mutilations, and faith healing. The term "paranormal" means something that is outside the range of "normal" human experience and explanation, and can be applied to "anything that comes within the range of human imagination and is thought to be 'incredible.'" I would add, "by mainstream science" to the end of that definition.

Prominent skeptic Paul Kurtz, a profound disbeliever in UFOs, pointed out that since "the boundaries of human knowledge are constantly expanding ... what was unknowable yesterday may become scientifically explicable the next." He noted that the DNA helix, black holes, and quarks could not have been considered paranormal, implying that they were somehow different from other things skeptics consider to be in that category, yet one hundred years ago, the idea of a black hole was complete nonsense and would certainly have been considered paranormal. Two hundred years ago, seeing the image of a distant person in a small box would have been paranormal, as would laser pointers, cellphones, and iPods. Why, these would all have all been considered some kind of magic, and certainly inappropriate for scientists to ponder. Galileo was put to death for heresy.

I have always been amazed that that the subject of UFOs elicits such highly emotional debate from both debunkers and believers. Few people seem capable of holding a middle ground. Most people either believe in or disbelieve the existence of UFOs, opposing views that do not actually mean anything, as we have seen. Why is this so? There does not seem to be any other topic that can inflame people as quickly as UFOs.

I would offer that the reason UFOs are such a contentious issue is that there's a lot riding on it. If aliens really are visiting Earth, then the scientific community has been totally wrong and governments around the world have probably been lying to their citizens. The amount of evidence needed to create an overwhelming upset of this kind would be enormous, and only the proverbial landing on the White House lawn would be enough to tip the scales. It is no wonder that such an all-or-nothing long shot arouses such passion.

Debunking is a completely expected response by scientists to such an important issue, especially one that attracts many people unversed in science. Many scientists advocate on behalf of ufology, but they are in the minority; the majority of those in the scientific community do not hold ufology in high regard.

Science continues to develop new ways of looking at, dealing with, and understanding our world. Its methodologies have helped achieve the high level of civilization we have today. We depend on science for energy, food, and survival. Debunking is part of the scientific process, whether we like it or not.

EVIDENCE

What constitutes evidence? To answer this broad question, let's look at a specific example that we encounter when considering UFOs: What evidence is there that aliens are visiting Earth?

The answer, which will surprise some people, is that there is plenty of evidence. The catch is that the evidence may not be incontrovertible, and it may not be convincing.

Eyewitness testimony by witnesses of unusual aerial craft is evidence that something real is occurring. Plane-spotters stationed on Pacific islands during the Second World War were put there specifically to report their sightings of enemy aircraft to the American Navy. Their eyewitness testimony was used to plot Japanese activity and thus help the Americans understand troop movements. They were, in effect, reporting unidentified flying objects, which were later resolved and explained as military aircraft.

Today, when pilots, air traffic controllers, or military personnel report seeing unusual aerial craft, their testimony should also be taken seriously. In fact, such reports are mandatory, as dictated by government and military directives. The Canadian Department of National Defence has made one such directive regarding the actions of all pilots in Canadian airspace. In documents relating to Communications Instructions for Reporting Vital Intelligence Sightings (CIRVIS), both civilians and military personnel are instructed that: "CIRVIS reports should be made immediately upon a vital intelligence sighting of any airborne, waterborne and ground objects or activities which appear to be hostile, suspicious, unidentified or engaged in illegal smuggling activity." The document listed the following examples as events that require CIRVIS reports: unidentified flying objects; submarines or warships which are not Canadian or American; violent explosions; and unexplained or unusual activity in polar regions, abandoned airstrips or other remote, sparsely populated areas.

In other words, it is considered in the best interests of everyone to report UFO sightings, and these sightings are certainly of interest to the Department of National Defence. Similar directives exist in the United States, and there is no reason to believe that such policies are not in effect in other countries around the world.

Sightings of unidentified flying objects alone are not proof that alien spaceships are visiting Earth. They could under some circumstances be considered circumstantial evidence, but not proof. Extreme manoeuvrability of observed aerial objects beyond conventional aircraft is evidence of a superior technology, but not proof. Abductees' descriptions of encounters with aliens that look inhuman and seem to possess advanced technology may be added as evidence, but are also not proof.

I once asked a physicist colleague what he felt would constitute proof that aliens were visiting Earth. He replied that only a sample of an alien artifact with a different radioisotope ratio than a terrestrial object would constitute proof. Anything manufactured elsewhere in our galaxy would be made of materials with slightly different traces of radioactive atoms than anything from Earth. Arch-skeptic Philip Klass used to complain that abductees and contactees never emerged from a flying saucer with so much as a towel or an ashtray from the Mars Hilton. In effect, we need something that's not from around here to demonstrate that aliens have visited Earth. I would charge that even if such an item was found or recovered from a purported UFO landing, it would be suspect.

Flying Saucers

At two o'clock on the afternoon of June 24, 1947, Kenneth Arnold finished work as a fire control engineer at the Central Air Service in Chehalis, Washington. He took off from the Chehalis Airport in his own Callair aircraft for a short trip to Yakima, but decided to assist in the search for a marine transport plane that had gone down somewhere near Mount Rainier, not far away.

He flew around the area, looking down into the numerous rocky crags and ridges, then turned and began flying east towards Yakima at an altitude of about 2,800 metres (9,200 feet). He noted that the sky was "crystal clear," and that it was a perfect day for flying. He also noted a DC-4 was in the air about twenty-four kilometres (fifteen miles) away from him, but at a much higher altitude.

Suddenly, a bright flash attracted Arnold's attention. He looked around for the source and eventually saw nine "peculiar" aircraft flying south at about the same altitude as his plane. He noted they were flying towards the mountain very quickly, and he thought they were jets. The flashes recurred as the strange aircraft occasionally dipped and slightly adjusted their flight paths, catching the bright sun.

Initially, Arnold couldn't tell what kind of aircraft they were because they were very far away, but as they drew nearer the mountain he could see them against the snow. He was surprised to see that they didn't have tails or stabilizers like jets. Using the clock on his dash, he timed how long it took them to pass a distant reference point, and calculated their speed. They were indeed going very fast — as fast or faster than some military planes.

To make sure that he was not seeing a mirage or reflection, Arnold opened the cockpit window and watched the objects through the clear, high air. After almost three minutes, the formation of odd objects passed behind a distant ridge of mountains out of sight. But Arnold had got a good enough look at the objects as they wobbled in flight that he could determine they were roughly disc-shaped, with a missing chord at their trailing edges that made them look like chubby crescents.

When Arnold landed at Yakima, he told his story to some ground crew there. A helicopter pilot told Arnold the discs were probably just a flight of guided missiles from a nearby military base. Arnold then flew to Pendleton, Oregon, but wasn't aware that someone from the Yakima Airport had called ahead to let them know a pilot on his way there had seen some very unusual objects. Pendleton was in the midst of hosting an air show, and when Arnold landed there, many people wanted to hear his story.

Although he had been told by some skeptics that the objects he had seen were guided missiles, Arnold was certain he had witnessed something more unusual. The next day he went to Pendleton's newspaper office to speak with reporters. The result was a wire service news story written by reporter Bill Bequette:

> Pendleton, Ore., June 25 (AP) — Nine bright saucer-like objects flying at "incredible speed" at 10,000 feet altitude were reported here today by Kenneth Arnold, Boise, Idaho, pilot who said he could not hazard a guess as to what they were.
>
> Arnold, a United States Forest Service employee engaged in searching for a missing plane, said he sighted the mysterious objects yesterday at 3 p.m. They were flying between Mount Rainier and Mount Adams, in Washington State, he said, and appeared to weave in and out of formation. Arnold said he clocked and estimated their speed at 1200 miles an hour.

Although Bequette is sometimes credited with being the first person to coin the term "flying saucer," that term does not actually appear in his story. It is likely that as the wire story went out to newspapers across the continent, headline writers created the phrase from a quick reading of the news copy. The result was that many newspapers carried the Bequette story under a headline that contained the now-familiar term "flying saucer," even though neither Arnold nor Bequette actually called the objects that.

Several explanations for Arnold's sighting have been put forth over the years by skeptics and debunkers, all of which are inadequate. One example is the theory suggested in 1977 by Harvard University astronomer Dr. Donald Menzel, who proposed that the discs Arnold observed were actually raindrops on the Callair's windows. This, of course, makes no sense when Arnold's own testimony is read, as he clearly indicates he had thought of such a possibility himself and opened the window to rule this it out. Why a trained scientist would make such a suggestion in light of the facts of the case is remarkable; it is certain that Menzel would not have proposed a theory in his area of specialty that was not based on observations.

A more reasonable explanation for Arnold's sighting is that he saw a group of secret military test vehicles, perhaps missiles with their fins and/or ailerons rendered invisible by the bright sunlight reflecting off their surfaces. However, no evidence that would support this contention has emerged through any investigation of the case.

We are left with a sighting of nine saucer-like objects that sparked the popular imagination and impressed the image of flying saucers indelibly on our collective memories. The term "saucer" is rarely used to describe sighted objects in official UFO reports.

For example, according to the 2007 Canadian UFO Survey, which looked at 836 reported UFO sightings across Canada that year, the most common term used in a witness's description of a UFO was "point source," or "starlike object." These terms were used in about 46 percent of the cases in which a description of the shape of the observed object was available. The next most common shape was "irregular" (such as "diamond, "ribbon" or "ring"), at 9 percent. The term "flying saucer" or "disc-shaped" object was used in only slightly under 6 percent of the reports. The number of UFOs of each shape that were reported in the 2007 Canadian UFO Survey are as follows:

Ball/Globe/Round/Orb/Sphere	76
Boomerang/Crescent/Chevron/"V"/"U"	14
Cigar/Cylinder	43
Fireball	67
Disk/Saucer	43
Irregular	104
Oval/Egg/Elliptical	22
Point Source or Star-like Object	382
Triangle	51

If we were to make some assumptions about the nature of the objects seen, these terms could be complementary. What if most UFOs were, in fact, shaped like saucers? At a distance, at night, if they were glowing or illuminated somehow, they would appear as distant lights. Therefore, these star-like objects could also be saucers. Kenneth Arnold originally thought the objects he saw were thin missiles when they were seen edge-on; only as they pitched and yawed and banked could he see their disc shapes. So could cigar-shaped objects also be saucers seen edge-on? If so, we could add them to the disc-shaped category as well. Similarly, oval objects could easily be saucers seen at oblique angles. If we combine the categories in this manner, the percentage of flying saucers thus increases to more than 14 percent of the total for 2007.

A minority of cases describe sightings of "boomerang" or "triangle-shaped" objects, but to diehards who like to think of UFOs as flying saucers, the shape analysis offers some encouragement. This exercise is clearly an overgeneralization. There are many cases on record of objects shaped like spheres seen at relatively close range, and they are very probably ball-shaped. Cases of "orbs" would fall into this category. Also, distant star-like objects are often just that — stars and planets that are not saucer-shaped, either.

The shape of a perceived object depends on many factors, such as the witness's visual acuity, the angle of viewing, the distance of viewing, and the witness's own biases and descriptive abilities. Nevertheless, in combination with other case data such as duration, experienced investigators consider shape to be a good clue towards a UFO's possible explanation.

GOVERNMENT

What does the government really know about UFOs?

A CNN poll in 1997, on the fiftieth anniversary of the Roswell crash, found that 80 percent of Americans thought their government was engaged in a cover-up, "hiding knowledge of the existence of extraterrestrial life forms." Supposedly, the government has been secretly studying the situation for decades, knowing full well that the aliens are here. Some conspiracy theorists are certain that the government is even in possession of crashed flying saucers (debris or intact) and their dead (or otherwise) alien pilots as well. Ufologist Stanton Friedman even calls the cover-up a "Cosmic Watergate."

Suspicion of government is not a new phenomenon, but the degree to which this is pervasive in society is alarming. UFOs are perhaps the ultimate government conspiracy, and the TV series *The X-Files* played into these fears and suspicions well. Writers for the show admitted that they got many of their ideas for episodes from stories about UFOs in the news and in magazines, so the show reflected much of what the public believes about official interest in the subject.

A cynic could point out that a conspiracy as complex and long-lasting as the cover-up of a crashed flying saucer could only be accomplished by a polished, resourceful, efficient, and competent organization, none of which are adjectives that are used by the general public to describe their government. The reality is that government officials have successfully covered up many secrets, including the Manhattan Project and the Corona program. The former involved the creation of the first nuclear bomb literally under the noses of students at Columbia University and in downtown New York City, employing a total of more than 100,000 people, while the latter was a spy satellite that regularly dropped its package of film to Earth for retrieval by military aircraft.

It is also known that each year the United States Congress passes billion-dollar budgets for so-called "black projects," for which their are no paper trails, detailed listings, or accountability. This implies that there are many things about which the public is blissfully ignorant. UFOs may or may not be one of them.

In the United States, official investigations began immediately following Kenneth Arnold's sighting of a group of flying saucers over Mount Rainer in 1947. Army Air Force Intelligence and the FBI co-operated to look into selected cases that they thought were deserving of attention, under two premises — that the objects seen were astronomical bodies, or were enemy aircraft. After all, this was only a few years after the end of the war. After only a few weeks of study, they concluded that flying saucers were not imaginary and that "something is really flying around."

Another study, this time by Air Materiel Command, also found that reported flying saucers were not imaginary and that, apparently, physical objects were being seen by reputable observers. This led to a recommendation that an official air force project called Project Sign be set up in 1947 to investigate reports. It was established at Wright-Patterson Air Force Base in Ohio.

Officially, Project Sign reached no definitive conclusion regarding flying saucer reports, although it considered the possibility that they were alien spacecraft. Among the reasons it dismissed this idea was that, at the time, all the flying saucer reports it studied were from the United States, and it did not seem reasonable that aliens would single out one country. A now-infamous "Estimate of the Situation," which was described as an interim analysis of reports studied under Project Sign, was allegedly released in late 1948. It concluded that flying saucers were extraterrestrial; however, when this analysis reached the Pentagon, it was supposedly rejected and destroyed so that we have only anecdotal evidence of its conclusions. The project did recommend further investigations and collection of data, so although Project Sign itself ceased to exist, its worked carried on under the name Project Grudge, which reflected the attitude under which it was operating. Ufologist Barry Greenwood notes that when the project name was changed, "former Sign personnel who favored UFOs were reassigned to other duties and replaced with more critical staffers."

Grudge laboured for several years. Its final report concluded that UFOs were a combination of misinterpretations, mass hysteria, hoaxes, and hallucinations. An examination of the Project Grudge data shows that about 32 percent of reports were astronomical objects, 33 percent were hoaxes or had insufficient information for analysis, and 12 percent were weather balloons. But the remaining 23 percent were listed as "unknown," and not hallucinations or mass hysteria, so one wonders what these cases might have been.

One case from the Project Grudge collection took place on November 16, 1949, near the University of Mississippi. At 9:15 a.m., a cigar-shaped object estimated to be about fifteen metres (fifty feet) long was seen by five witnesses travelling between Oxford and Batesville, Mississippi. The object was flying at about sixty metres (two hundred) feet through the clear blue sky, at a leisurely pace of only about fifty kilometres (thirty miles) per hour. All five witnesses agreed on the shape and size of the object, and said that it looked like "a beam of light that stayed level" as it flew. As it passed by, the object "gave off an exhaust that had the appearance of phosphorus." Investigations did not explain the object as an aircraft or weather balloon. Since the thing they had seen certainly wasn't an astronomical object, it was placed in the hoax category, which seems unlikely given the number of witnesses.

A clearer case in which a very similar object was seen took place only two days later, on November 18, 1949, at Raceland, Louisiana. At nine-thirty in the morning, five different witnesses observed a shiny, aluminum-like object "similar to [the] fuselage of aircraft, without protruding appendages of any type." It was thought to be larger than a cargo aircraft, and did not seem to be a dirigible or blimp. It flew straight before making two successive ninety-degree turns and heading towards the northwest and out of sight. The Grudge report on the case noted: "Investigation failed to establish the identity of unconventional aircraft sighted at Raceland, Louisiana." This sounds like the case was unexplained, rather than a misidentification or hoax.

According to USAF Captain Edward Ruppelt, the first director of Project Blue Book, which was Project Grudge's successor, the Grudge investigations were incomplete and inadequate. However, Edward Condon, director of the USAF-sponsored Condon Committee which studied Blue Book cases in detail, the Grudge reports were "too vague for interpretation and … if anything, the Air Force investigators gave them more attention than they deserved." The two cases cited here do not seem vague at all, and one wonders what criteria were used by Condon and Ruppelt to make their judgments. In any event, Project Grudge was suspended in December 1949, but flying saucer reports continued to be investigated by the Air Technical Intelligence Center (ATIC) "as part of regular intelligence activities."

In October 1951, Project Grudge was dusted off following a sighting of an unidentified object over a military base in New Jersey, and renamed Project Blue Book in March 1952 under Ruppelt's direction. It continued under various directors until December 1969, when an order to shut it down resulted in its complete termination in January 1970. A factor that contributed to its cessation was the conclusion of the Condon Committee, which noted "nothing has come from the study of UFOs ... that has added to scientific knowledge," and that "further extensive study of UFOs probably cannot be justified." It found that, in general, all UFO reports had conventional explanations, and that the media was responsible for distorting facts and encouraging the public's whimsy.

Despite this, the actual Condon Committee report raises many interesting questions. In fact, one contributed chapter on psychological aspects of UFO reports concludes by stating that the suggestion that UFOs are psychological aberrations "raises more questions than it answers." Its author asked, "Why do some persons who see an UFO regard it as simply an unidentified aerial phenomenon, while others are sure it is a 'space vehicle'?" He added: "The answers to such questions must await future research." Of course, this chapter was included in a large work that concluded that there should be *no* further research.

Project Blue Book collected a total of 12,618 UFO reports between 1952 and 1969. Of these, 701 or just over 5 percent of the total were unexplained. It is important to note that these unknowns were not a "residue" as they have been labelled by some researchers, as there was also a Blue Book category for cases with "insufficient data." In fact, the unknowns were labelled "unidentified" if they could not be explained as myriad other things, including astronomical objects, such as meteors, stars, and planets; aircraft; balloons; satellites; hoaxes; missiles; rockets; reflections; flares; fireworks; mirages; inversions; searchlights; clouds; contrails; radar chaff; or birds. This list of possible misidentified objects seems quite exhaustive, and if there was sufficient data to rule out all of these, then one wonders what could have been observed.

Many people accept the conclusions of the Condon Committee and Project Blue Book that there is nothing worthwhile in the collection of UFO reports. One mandate of Blue Book was to assess whether or not UFOs posed any threat to national security, and it concluded that they do not. The Condon report was endorsed by the National Academy of Sciences, and the scientific community has accepted the study as the definitive answer to the UFO question.

Critics of the Condon Committee have charged that it only looked at fifty-six cases, and that some of these cases were not explained so much as dismissed. Critics of Blue Book have said it was little more than a public relations exercise, and contend that the really good cases were not sent to Blue Book investigators at all. They also believe that the cases that were sent in were not handled well. According to a Condon Committee investigator who visited the office of Project Blue Book, "public reports of UFO sightings were not investigated seriously by a great number of the 'UFO Officers,' one officer being so designated at each air base."

The way in which the public was informed about official UFO investigations was a concern. Air Force Regulation 200-2, released in August 1954, set the tone for dealing with the public on the subject: "In response to local inquiries, it is permissible to inform news media representatives on [UFOs] when the object is positively identified as a familiar object ... For those objects which are not explainable, only the fact that ATIC will analyze the data is worthy of release." In other words, if a sighting was explained, the news media would be told, but any unexplained objects would not be described.

This approach makes perfect sense since it would be embarrassing and awkward for the USAF to admit that it could not explain the UFOs seen overhead by American citizens. It also makes sense that such a policy continues in some form today. It is this closed attitude that causes confusion when air force spokespersons are asked to comment on particular UFO cases, sometimes making the government appear foolish. The question is whether the government is covering up the truth, or is simply at a loss to explain what is really going on.

Another insight into how UFOs were being viewed within the American government and military came through, of all things, a

Canadian electrical engineering project. Wilbert Brockhouse Smith was a prominent electrical engineer with the Canadian Department of Transport. During the Second World War, he was involved in Canada's wartime monitoring service, and after the war he was responsible for the creation of a chain of ionospheric measurement stations in Canada. Smith's expertise was in radio-wave propagation and geomagnetism, and he became convinced that the Earth's magnetic field could be harnessed and used as some form of propulsion system. He chanced upon some books about flying saucers that said they were speculated to fly using some kind of magnetic propulsion. His curiosity led him to investigate some flying saucer sightings in the 1950s. Through his contacts within the Canadian Government, he was able to ask questions directly about flying saucer research through the Canadian Embassy in Washington, D.C.

Smith met with Dr. Robert Sarbacher, former dean of Georgia Tech's graduate school and a consultant to the United States government, and asked him directly if flying saucers were real. Sarbacher replied, "Yes, they exist," and added that, "it's pretty certain they didn't originate on the earth." Furthermore, Sarbacher told Smith that UFOs were "classified two points higher even than the H-bomb" in terms of secrecy.

Sarbacher did not offer any proof that this was so, but Smith was convinced that the information was correct. In November 1950, Smith sent a memo to the controller of telecommunications at the Department of Transport, informing him that, "the existence of a different technology is borne out by the investigations which are being carried out at the present time in relation to flying saucers." He also passed along Sarbacher's information about UFOs, noting that flying saucers exist, and that "the entire matter is considered by the United States authorities to be of tremendous significance."

Ufologists later found documents that supported Sarbacher's credentials and claims. In fact, some diligent researchers found documents that seem to show that there exists a mysterious group known as MJ-12 (or Majestic Twelve) within the United States government. This group of scientists and military personnel oversees UFO investigations, and may be responsible for the cover-up of everything from UFO case investigations to the actual crash of a saucer at Roswell in 1947.

Another possibility is that the story of a UFO crash is just a subterfuge, and that the U.S. military is using the public's fascination with UFOs to conceal their secret aircraft experiments. Because many people still ridicule UFO witnesses, and the scientific community generally scoffs at UFO reports, the experiments can even be conducted in the open, without fear of observation.

Governments in other countries have investigated UFO reports to one degree or another over the past several decades. Besides the United States, Canada, Great Britain, France, Belgium, Sweden, Brazil, Mexico, Spain, and the Soviet Union have all done some studies on the subject.

In France, the French Space Agency CNES created a unit in 1977 to investigate unidentified aerospace phenomena (UAP). Originally called GEPAN (Groupe d'Étude des Phénomènes Aérospatiaux Nonidentifiés), it was later renamed SEPRA (Service d'Expertise des Phénomènes de Rentrée Atmosphérique, then Service d'Expertise des Phénomènes Rares Aérospatiaux). Finally in 2005 the unit was renamed GEIPAN (Groupe d'Études et d'Informations sur les Phénomènes Aérospatiaux Nonidentifiés). The French Gendarmerie is directed to send UFO reports it receives to GEIPAN, which maintains a large database of cases. GEIPAN can also use the technical expertise and resources of CNES to investigate any physical trace cases. In March 2007, GEIPAN made its UFO archives available on-line. The quality of their investigations has been heavily criticized by the French skeptics.

COMETA was a French non-profit UFO investigation organization made up of officers and officials from the armed forces and the aerospace industry, most of whom were former members of IHEDN, a high-level French defence think tank. In 1999, it produced the COMETA Report on UFOs and their possible implications for defence in France, but the report was not actually endorsed by the French government. The report drew largely on the research of GEPAN and SEPRA.

By the early 1950s the United Kingdom's Air Ministry was involved in the investigation of UFO reports; however, it has always claimed that its UFO files from before the mid-1960s were destroyed because the ministry did not take the cases very seriously. In his detailed work *Above Top Secret*, Timothy Good found evidence that investigations were conducted and that interest existed at the highest levels. Even Sir Winston Churchill asked his staff about the various reports of flying saucers he had heard in the news, and was told that there wasn't anything to them at all. In the early 1950s, the Deputy Directorate of Intelligence of the Air Ministry noted that as many as 10 percent of all the flying saucer reports they investigated were from qualified observers and "carried conviction," and were unexplained.

Former intelligence officers in the British Armed Forces have since gone on record to state that yes, secret UFO investigations were done within the ministry, in secure sites such as "Room 801," which supposedly contained a file on more than ten thousand cases. Later, the Ministry of Defence took over the responsibility for UFO sightings, although they also denied that they had found any evidence of a phenomenon that merited concern. Ufologist Nick Pope, former "UFO Desk" officer in the Secretariat (Air Staff) for the Ministry of Defence in the early 1990s, has documented the way in which reports were handled within the office. After working there for several years, his conclusion is that "some UFO sightings are probably extraterrestrial in origin."

In 2006, the Ministry of Defence released details of a UFO study called Project Condign. It was a secret investigation of UFO cases briefly conducted within the ministry that concluded that many sightings could be explained as glowing plasma, a natural but poorly understood phenomenon. Condign has been greatly maligned because its conclusion is at odds with many other similar studies, but it does show that the British government has been taking the subject seriously for some time, enough to have at least one officer spend time studying cases in detail.

As it stands today, UFO sightings continue to be reported to the Ministry of Defence, but their official policy remains that UFOs are of no significant interest; however, the ministry now makes UFO reports they receive as information available on-line. The following information appears on the Ministry of Defence website:

> During a policy review in 1996 into the handling of Unidentified Aerial Phenomena sighting reports received by the Ministry of Defence, a study was undertaken to determine the potential value, if any, of such reports

to Defence Intelligence. Consistent with Ministry of Defence policy, the available data was studied principally to ascertain whether there is any evidence of a threat to the UK, and secondly, should the opportunity arise, to identify any potential military technologies of interest.

The Ministry of Defence has released this report in response to a Freedom of Information request and we are pleased to now make it available to a wider audience via the MOD Freedom of Information Publication Scheme.

In Australia, UFOs are officially known as Unidentified Aerials Sightings (UAS). The Royal Australian Air Force used to investigate sightings, but this was terminated "after careful examination of the factual data" showed it "did not warrant the continued allocation of resources by the RAAF." Current Australian policy is to refer UFO witnesses to local police or civilian UFO organizations.

In January 1992, the Spanish government started declassifying UFO files after having sealed its records following a leak in the 1970s of information regarding its official investigation of UFOs. Based on this information, journalist J. J. Benitez published a Spanish-language book in 1976 about secret Spanish UFO investigations by the government. Following the clampdown, it took years of lobbying by ufologists Vicente-Juan Ballester Olmos and Joan Plata to ensure the release of more official documents. The Spanish Air Force seems now to be co-operating with ufologists by releasing files about more cases.

Most governments of larger countries around the world have conducted at least some simple studies of UFOs, although the policies and procedures have varied. Their conclusions are, with some exceptions, classified information, but many files are slowly being released to the public under freedom of information or access to information requests. For the most part, the official conclusions follow those of the United States government: studies of UFO reports have found that most have simple explanations, and that the few that are unexplained are not worth bothering about.

Most countries have policies to refer UFO witnesses and inquiries to local police or authorities, but it is not government policy to waste valuable budgetary resources on UFO investigations. With wars, global warming, energy crises, and domestic problems, spending even a small amount of a departmental budget on UFOs would be viewed by opposition parties as foolish and would be very politically incorrect.

Hoaxes

While books about UFOs tend to focus on unexplained cases, the fact that some UFO reports turn out to be spurious cannot be completely ignored. However, the number of reports that turn out to be hoaxes is much smaller than skeptics would suggest. In fact, known hoaxes comprise such a small percentage of UFO data that their effect on UFO data analysis is practically insignificant.

In the U.S. Air Force's analyses of unidentified flying object reports collected as part of Project Blue Book between 1953 and 1964, a total of 6,817 cases were examined. Of these, 237 were listed as "unexplained," while 226 fell into a category labelled "Hoaxes, Hallucinations, Unreliable Reports and Psychological Causes." These 226 accounted for about 3 percent of the total number of cases studied, and hoaxes comprised only a part of this set. I would suggest that hoaxes are the explanation for less than 1 percent of all UFO reports, based on my investigations and research of UFO report databases.

One reason we can be sure of this is because other explanations for UFO reports are adequate. We know, for example, that when a witness reports seeing a star-like object, it is almost certain that he or she did not make up a fictitious story about seeing a star-like UFO, but that the witness observed an actual star or planet. In most cases, a check of star charts and sky maps can help identify stars or planets that were actually in the sky at the time of the sighting, and which may have been observed as star-like UFOs.

I can think of only a handful of hoax cases that have come to my attention in the investigation of UFO reports in Canada during the past thirty years. One that stands out was an incident in which two men constructed a homemade balloon out of a garbage bag and lightweight material, attached a railroad flare to it with some twine, and filled the bag with acetylene. They then set the balloon aloft over a city and waited for the reaction of the populace. The balloon rose silently with the flare burning brightly, then the bag caught fire and the acetylene exploded with a blinding flash and a loud explosion high in the air.

The balloon/flare was initially seen by numerous people, but when it exploded the noise shook the entire area, and the fireworks-like display that followed was seen by many more. What made the prank into something more serious was that the balloon had been launched directly into the path of airline approach vectors for a nearby international airport. Police investigation, hundreds of UFO witnesses, and some tips led to the arrest of the men.

This case was similar to an actual experiment conducted by the U.S. Air Force in 1964 over Clearwater, Florida. The idea was to learn how independent witnesses describe an initially unidentified aerial object, which would allow witnesses' observational capabilities to be evaluated. Flares were dropped over the city and the air force sent out a release asking for letters from people who may have seen the lights.

Out of eighty-one witnesses who responded, only three reported seeing the flares as well as the airplane's regulation running lights. The others saw only the red flares. All witnesses correctly described a line of lights, and many also reported seeing an aircraft, but only two thought that the lights could be flares. Only one of the witnesses alluded to the possibility that the lights may have been alien spacecraft.

These cases establish the fact that witnesses reporting UFOs are seeing real objects, with generally good observational capabilities. This tells us that when UFOs are reported, there is likely something in the sky to precipitate the sighting; in other words, it wasn't made up.

This does not mean that UFO hoaxes don't come around every now and then. In March 2005, hoaxers sent out e-mail messages to thousands of recipients, encouraging them to report an identical fake UFO sighting to official reporting agencies and UFO groups:

Posted: Thu Mar 03, 2005
Subject: Ssshhh! What I am about to tell you is a secret. Do not tell anyone.

On Saturday, March 19, many people on the internet will hoax the world with the biggest mass UFO sighting in years. The craft will zoom around the United States and the world. What will they see?

A craft with 4 lights, 2 of which blinked several colors. They will then report their sighting as happening at APPROXIMATELY (not exactly) the appropriate time, and that's it....

Report the sighting to the National UFO Reporting center. [The phone number was given in the original e-mail.]

Do not post this information online. Only share it with 'real life' friends.

Sure enough, the National UFO Reporting Center in the United States received reports from people throughout North America. Cases were also reported to investigative groups in Canada, and I personally received a handful of reports. Not having heard about the planned hoax beforehand, I did find it odd that I received cases that seemed to confirm or support one another, but were scattered across the country in different time zones. The sightings were reported as having taken place at very similar local times.

When follow-up e-mails were sent out, no one replied, and it soon became evident that something fishy was going on. The hoax was uncovered in a short time and ufologists began sorting through the phony reports. In retrospect, it was an interesting experiment in viral communication. To the possible chagrin of skeptics, investigators did not initially accept the reports as real and laud a major new UFO wave. Separately, the hoax UFO reports could have been added to a UFO sightings list or database, and assigned "insufficient information" labels, but individually the cases might have been considered valid UFO reports.

Ironically, it was the fact that so many nearly identical reports were made that alerted UFO investigators to the prank.

In late 1989, UFO investigators and researchers in Canada and the United States received a package of documents through the mail from a mysterious "Deep Throat." These papers described the crash of a UFO that had occurred at Carp, Ontario, near Ottawa, and included a photograph of an alien standing in some shrubbery. The absurdity of the information contained in the material made it particularly easy to dismiss it as nonsense. It included snippets of rumours about secret government and military operations, splicing together stories about the crash of a flying saucer, underground bases, clandestine laboratories, and advanced technological weaponry, all within a few dozen miles of the capital of Canada. The text was mostly paranoid "New World Order" ramblings, like the information disseminated by civilian militia groups and semi-terrorist operations.

Canadian investigators, although certain the papers were hoaxes, nevertheless decided to trace their origin in the hope light could be shed on the perpetrators. With some detective work, one was able to locate the "crash site," and even some apparent witnesses.

One witness claimed that on November 4, 1989, she saw an intense, bright light pass overhead, and move south towards a swamp at the far end of the field behind her home. Another woman had been scared by a very bright light that shone through her bathroom window, and had heard the sound of helicopters overhead. A few talked of dogs and cattle being "disturbed." But with these few exceptions, most people in the region could not recall anything unusual happening that night.

Investigators examined the field and swamp indicated on the map, but could not find any sign of a massive recovery effort with heavy equipment to retrieve the crashed saucer. Other UFO investigators visited the area too, and all concluded that the whole affair was likely a hoax.

Almost two years later, the Carp case resurfaced with even more bizarre twists. In 1991, more secret documents were sent to several ufologists, all postmarked in Ottawa. There were partially censored documents that looked similar to blacked-out UFO-related government papers uncovered by retrieval experts such as Stanton Friedman, who documented an apparent government cover-up of information about UFOs. These Carp documents described how China, assisted by aliens for some undetermined reason, was preparing for war against the United States. The documents boasted: "America will be crippled; power grids, tanks, missiles, cars, antennas, phone lines will stop," but said that the "ELITE will survive WW3" in "installations under mile-thick Canadian-shield granite." The documents went on to say that the American government had built large underground installations in the Carp area, where secret research was being done.

The package of materials included cryptic notes signed by someone calling himself Guardian, and a map and sketch of alien activity near Ottawa between 1970 and 1991, using Masonic symbols and identification guides for different alien craft. There was also a black-and-white photograph of an alien standing in some tall grass and a Polaroid photograph of a UFO hovering over a road. Some packages contained copies of a videotape that showed what was alleged to be an alien craft on the ground. Although the packages of materials had the earmarks of an elaborate hoax, some UFO investigators thought there might have been a genuine UFO landing.

In May 1992, a group of ufologists met in Carlton, Ontario, to make an expedition to examine the landing area identified on the Guardian's map. They quickly found a location where something unusual had been occurring. There was an abandoned farmhouse with signs reading "Do Not Enter" and "DND Killing Fields," with drawings of tanks, helicopters, and weapons on it. DND is the acronym for the Canadian Department of National Defence. The farmhouse was also riddled with bullet holes. It was thought that the area was being used for war games.

The ufologists located a witness who told them of many strange UFO sightings over the years, and suspicious military activity in the area. One of the sketches of the UFOs she drew exactly matched one of the UFOs on the "alien craft spotting chart" that Guardian had sent to the ufologists. The witness's story and account did not seem believable to the investigators because of some inconsistencies. They also discovered that a local man was an avid UFO buff and referred to himself as Guardian.

Finally, some burned patches and a burned-out vehicle were found in a nearby field, leading the investigators to conclude that flares and fireworks had been set up to make a pickup truck look as if it were a hovering craft when the scene was videotaped. Despite the investigators' publication of their detailed report and conclusions, the Carp case has continued to be debated and discussed, and the video has been promoted and shown on TV programs as one of the best UFO videos of a hovering saucer. An exposé of the hoax was posted on the Virtually Strange Network, a major UFO discussion list.

INVESTIGATION

UFO investigation is a lost art. At one time there were hundreds of UFO investigators across North America and around the world, but investigating reports of UFOs has become less and less important to those interested in the subject.

During the heyday of their popularity, flying saucer clubs sprang up in practically every city and town, often competing for attention and membership. Although in the beginning you could join simply by paying dues, later groups had prospective members fill out questionnaires and take short exams to gain entry into a club's elite.

Some UFO groups, such as the Midwest UFO Network (later the Mutual UFO Network or MUFON), and the British UFO Research Association (BUFORA) published actual manuals for field investigators. These contained detailed instructions on how to gather information, approach and get accurate testimony from witnesses, take soil samples, and talk with police and airport personnel. Some manuals contained sample case reports, guides to writing effective and informative reports, rules for winnowing out misidentifications, filing procedures, and even standards for investigators to follow. Codes of ethics were also adopted, and bona fide investigators had to sign a series of documents before being admitted into some groups.

At one time, every state and province in North America had

directors of investigations representing at least one UFO group, with myriad county and regional associates. Often, rival groups actively competed for UFO witnesses' statements, and local battles occasionally erupted between members of major groups such as MUFON, the Aerial Phenomena Research Organization (APRO), and the National Investigations Committee on Aerial Phenomena (NICAP).

In the United States, the Center for UFO Studies (CUFOS), founded by astronomer Dr. J. Allen Hynek, kept its field investigators informed of the latest happenings through its *Center Investigators' Quarterly (CIQ)*. It was a resource for the hundreds of local investigators around the United States who often had such good relationships with local police that sheriff's offices in many counties had a CUFOS sticker (with a toll-free phone number) on their dispatch desks. A sighting reported to police would often be passed along to a keen investigator in a matter of hours, if not minutes, contributing to a quick response and investigation as UFO flaps developed.

Most developed countries around the world also had at least a few UFO groups. Great Britain, for example, had many small groups, including the British Flying Saucer Bureau, the Irish UFO Research Centre, and the Federation for UFO Research, in addition to the aforementioned BUFORA.

Most groups, no matter where they were based, existed almost exclusively for the private investigation of UFO sightings. It was their primary raison d'etre. Why? In one sense, the answer may be as simple as "because they're there." Polls have shown that about 10 percent of all North Americans believe they have seen a UFO. There have not been comparable polls in many other countries around the world, but in both developed and developing countries, it is thought that the percentage of the population that has seen a UFO is significant. Given the population data available, this implies a very large number of UFO reports.

If UFOs are trivial and non-existent, as some claim, then one might ask why such a large percentage of the population is labouring under the delusion of seeing things that are not there. If, on the other hand, UFOs represent a real phenomenon, the data should be examined for insight into its nature. In either situation, it can be argued that UFO reports merit serious scientific attention.

In general, the public equates UFOs with alien visitation; however, there is no incontrovertible proof that this connection exists. In order to determine if there might be signs of extraterrestrial contact, investigation, and research on the actual characteristics of UFO reports is needed. Do the reports really bear out such a linkage? What, exactly, are people seeing and reporting as UFOs? Are they seeing classic flying saucers, like those portrayed in movies and television shows? Are there really well-documented and well-witnessed UFO reports, with no explanation as to their nature? Given the general perception that aliens exist and are present in our solar system, and that the answers to these questions may already exist in popular culture, for example, the showing of television ads with aliens selling soft drinks or shows with alien characters, a thorough examination of actual UFO reports would go far to provide necessary insight into the phenomenon. That's why case investigation is so important.

Many writers and readers on the subject of UFOs focus on speculation about the aliens' method of travel, their abductions of humans, their messages for humankind, and their ultimate meaning, proceeding on the basis of assumptions, theories, and individual anecdotal accounts. Many books about UFO abductions give the impression that this aspect of the UFO phenomenon constitutes most of ufology. This is certainly not the case; UFO research begins with the investigation of UFO reports. It is through later collection and study that researchers theorize about the phenomenon and eventually write papers and books speculating about UFO origins, including possible evidence of alien contact. Abduction cases actually comprise a very tiny fraction of the bulk of UFO data. The "bread and butter" of UFO research lies not in fanciful discourse about aliens' genetic manipulation of humans, but in what UFO witnesses actually see and report. This point cannot be overemphasized. It is the collection and analysis of UFO reports that provides the data upon which studies of UFOs can be reasonably based. In effect, this is the empirical data for research in this field. If one wants to know what people really are seeing in the skies, the answer lies within these reports.

Many individuals, associations, clubs, and groups claim to investigate UFO reports. A few solicit reports from the general public. Comparatively few actually participate in any kind of information-sharing or data-gathering for scientific programs. Some are primarily interest groups based in museums, planetariums, church basements, or individuals' homes, that essentially do *nothing* with the sighting reports they receive. Because there is no way to enforce standards in UFO report investigations, the quality of case investigations varies considerably between groups and across provinces.

Quantitative studies are difficult because subjective evaluations and differences in investigative techniques do not allow precise comparisons. Empirical data requested by UFO researchers and investigators includes basic information such as the date and time of the sighting, its duration, and the number of witnesses and their location. These facts, which are not subjective, can be used in scientific studies before interpretation.

Studies of UFO data routinely include reports of meteors, fireballs, and other conventional objects. In many instances, observers fail to recognize stars, aircraft, and bolides, and therefore report them as UFOs. Witnesses often report watching stationary flashing lights low on the horizon for hours, without ever concluding that they are observing a star or planet.

Intense investigation and a determined effort to explain UFO reports used to be of extreme importance to UFO clubs and groups. Training manuals were very thorough, giving members instruction in astronomy, optics, psychology, and aeronautics. Although this is far from the case now, some UFO investigators spent many hours sorting IFOs from UFOs. Historically, analyses of UFO data such as the American projects Grudge, Sign, and Blue Book all included raw UFO data that was later resolved into categories of UFOs and IFOs. Sometimes, observed objects are quickly assigned a particular IFO explanation even though later investigation suggests such an explanation was unwarranted. The reverse is also true.

The issue of including IFOs in studies of UFO data is an important one. One could argue that once a sighting is explained, it has no reason to be considered as a UFO report; however, this overlooks the fact that the IFO was originally reported as a UFO and is indeed valid data. It may not be evidence of extraterrestrial visitation, but as UFO data, it is quite useful. It must be remembered that all major previous studies of UFOs examined UFO reports with the intent to explain a certain percentage of cases. These cases were the IFOs — definitely part of the UFO report legacy.

IFOs are problematic in that they are not interesting to most ufologists. In fact, some UFO investigators readily admit they do not record details about UFO reports that seem as if they can be easily explained as ordinary objects. This may be a serious error. The UFO witness may be conscientiously reporting an object that is mysterious to him or her — the exact definition of a UFO. Therefore, even late-night, anonymous telephone calls that are obviously reports of airplanes or planets should be rightly logged as UFO reports. It seems reasonable that all UFO reports be included in statistical databases and in studies on the phenomenon, regardless of the fact that they will later be reclassified as IFOs. The fact that most UFO reports can be explained and reclassified as IFOs attests to the reality of the objects seen. UFO reports reflect real events. When a UFO is reported, a real object that was not just a product of a witness's imagination has been seen.

By the time of the millennium, most major groups had folded or evolved into sources of information only. Most monthly newsletters have become quarterlies or biannuals, or have ceased completely. Field investigators are few and far between. It's much easier to type a few messages on-line and get instant feedback from a witness many miles away. And because physical trace cases are very rare these days, in-person investigation seems almost a waste of time. This is an unfortunate situation, since UFO sightings remain the basis and foundation of ufology. Inadequately investigated sightings can only undermine serious UFO research.

Typically, a UFO sighting today is not reported to police, airport personnel, the FBI, USAF, or civilian UFO investigators. Instead, a witness simply searches for an on-line UFO group and fills out an electronic report form. The case information is then posted to a readable (although not always searchable) database that can be viewed on a web page, usually with names and contact information removed to protect privacy. Sometimes, webmasters of these virtual UFO groups do some basic follow-up with the witnesses by phone or e-mail, and podcasts are produced of conversations with witnesses and made available for downloading.

This is not the same as investigation, and that is why I would suggest that UFO investigation, at least in the form that was so effectively practiced during the development of ufology, no longer exists.

J. Allen Hynek

Josef Allen Hynek is known as the Father of Ufology, or the Grandfather, depending on your generation.

Hynek was born in 1910 in Chicago. In 1935, he earned his PhD in astronomy from Yerkes Observatory. He became professor of astronomy and director of McMillin Observatory at Ohio State University. In 1948, he was asked by the USAF to be a consultant on Project Sign, the first official government/military study on flying saucers. It was Hynek's job to examine reports of unidentified flying objects and evaluate them in terms of astronomical phenomena such as stars, fireballs, and meteors. This was serendipitous or perhaps prophetic, as in 1956 he joined fellow astronomer Fred Whipple at the Smithsonian Astrophysical Observatory to work on a project to track satellites. Hynek was in charge of a major observing program called Operation Moonwatch, using cameras to search and detect satellites and other objects in space. He later taught at Northwestern University in Chicago and conducted basic research into binary stars.

Hynek successfully explained about 80 percent of the UFO reports presented to him through Project Sign; however, after his retirement from the air force's UFO study, he wrote a book called *The Hynek UFO Report*, in which he essentially recanted many of his explanations. He stated that he had been under pressure to explain all the cases given to him, even when there did not seem to be a reasonable conventional explanation. Hynek viewed some of the cases labelled "Insufficient Information" as intellectual "cop-outs," because there was enough information to determine that the sighted objects were not aircraft, stars, or meteors, yet the assessors were pressured to assign explanations to them anyway.

Hynek was in the perfect position to study and research UFO reports. He had access to official report data. He was a trained astronomer and knew a great deal about astronomical objects that might be mistaken as UFOs. He was a scientist and could therefore apply scientific methodology to the study of UFO reports. He could speak with authority to other scientists about the actual nature of UFO investigation, on a peer-to-peer level.

Hynek had a calm, considered approach to ufology. He knew very well the ridicule afforded UFO witnesses by the media and debunkers, and fought hard to obtain respect for the subject. In doing so, he had to contend with both ends of the belief spectrum — skeptics and fanatics — and he often alienated himself from one or the other, depending on the situation.

I first met Hynek in 1976, when he came to Canada as part of a speaking tour, and to help create local UFO groups that could be affiliated with the Center for UFO Studies that he founded in the United States in 1973. Because of his scientific background, his visit attracted the attention of many scientists at universities in my area, and a meeting to decide on how best to organize a scientific study group was held following one of his talks. Not having a scientific degree at that time, I had been invited along with several other keen and active lay investigators by the scientific community to observe, but not participate in the creation of the group. It wasn't surprising that this planned scientific study group got bogged down by technicalities, bylaws, and worry about protecting reputations, and did not actually get to the point of investigating any UFO sightings.

Hynek, realizing the difficulty of getting tenured scientists to commit to spending time and effort on a project outside their field of expertise, especially one that involved an unorthodox and taboo subject, asked me after the meeting to initiate what was originally called the Manitoba Centre for UFO Studies.

After several years of working in conjunction with Hynek's centre in Chicago, I founded Ufology Research of Manitoba (UFOROM), inviting into a loose consortium several of my associates who had been active in the investigation and research of local UFO cases. Throughout the years, I have worked closely with CUFOS, responding to inquiries, submitting case reports, and supporting the centre's work.

I've done this out of a respect for and loyalty to Hynek. When in town, he sometimes came to my home for a visit, and we had frank and honest conversations about the nature of ufology. I was taking my undergraduate courses in astronomy at the time I met him in 1976, and I learned a great deal about astronomy from him; however, I learned a great deal more from him about the nature of scientific inquiry and methodology.

While at a TV station being interviewed about a local flap of UFO sightings in Canada, he and I were shown a film clip of a nocturnal light UFO that had been taken not long before his arrival. The film showed a small, featureless red light bobbing and weaving against a black night sky. I remember his on-air comment distinctly: "That is certainly the best film of a nocturnal light I have seen." It was perfectly scientific, succinct, and careful. It did not endorse or debunk the film in any way, and left it entirely open to speculation by believers and skeptics alike.

An anecdotal story about Hynek at the Center for UFO Studies in Chicago also demonstrates Hynek's careful nature. He answered the phone and spoke with a woman who told him at length and in detail about her numerous encounters with aliens. She went on and on for almost an hour, describing dozens of different kinds of aliens, from lizard-like creatures to pale-skinned humanoids. She detailed which planets they were from, their culture, their motives, and their various messages for mankind. At then end of the diatribe, she asked him what he thought of her knowledge of alien races. He replied, simply, "I can't dispute anything you've told me."

For the 1979 total eclipse of the sun in Canada, Hynek travelled to Manitoba with his family on a winter vacation. Many other scientists accompanied his family and me to a small, isolated resort where we spent a weekend relaxing and preparing to observe the celestial event. He and I had several opportunities to talk about things, and one conversation was particularly interesting.

We were in his room in the lodge, sitting in some overstuffed chairs looking out though a large window across a snow-covered meadow. Our discussion ranged between recent UFO cases and some astronomical advances, when he suddenly became distracted and stopped in mid-sentence, staring out at the snowy montage. After several moments had elapsed, he said, "You know, Chris, if a UFO landed just outside our window in the meadow there, you and I could never talk about it. No one would believe us, of all people, because of our history of studying the phenomenon." And then he resumed our discussion.

I always wondered what he meant by that.

Hynek appeared on many TV shows about UFOs and related subjects, and was even a consultant for Steven Spielberg's classic movie *Close Encounters of the Third Kind*. In deference to Hynek's position and influence in ufology, Spielberg allowed him to appear in the movie in a cameo role towards the end of the film. He later told me that much of what he was filmed for wasn't used. He explained that in one cut scene, young girls dressed in alien costumes gathered around him as if in curiosity, one even taking his trademark pipe and toying with it.

One of Hynek's most bizarre TV appearances was on a Canadian show about psychic phenomena. It was a kind of quiz show where clairvoyants, astrologers, palmists, and other seers were challenged to identify a mystery guest hidden from view, asking questions based on the impressions they received about him or her. Hynek had been flown into the city secretly for the show, so I was surprised to hear he was in town when I was called after the show to drive him back from the television station. He explained that security had been tight to ensure no collusion was possible so that the psychics had no way of knowing the identity of the mystery guest in advance.

I was startled to learn that a clairvoyant had guessed that Hynek was the mystery guest. I was impressed by the show when it aired. Somehow, by simply holding Hynek's watch, she began intoning, "I'm sensing something about space ... about stars ... about communicating with other beings ... this must belong to a famous UFO investigator ... it must be Allen Hynek!"

When we next met, I asked him about the incident. He laughed and rolled up his sleeve, then took off his watch. He handed it to me. Etched into the back of the watch was an inscription from his wife: "To Allen Hynek, with love from Mimi."

Hynek died in 1986 from a brain tumour. No single individual has replaced him as a spokesman and advocate of the UFO phenomenon.

KLASS, PHILIP J.

Philip Julian Klass was born in 1919 and raised in the American Midwest. His post-secondary education in the field of electrical engineering, led to work at General Electric in aviation electronics. He later became a writer for the trade magazine *Aviation Week*, which later became *Aviation Week and Space Technology*.

When a series of UFO sightings were reported near Exeter, New Hampshire, in 1965, Klass's knowledge of electrical plasmas suggested to him that glowing lights seen near power lines might be explained as highly charged plasmas. Furthermore, he reasoned that they could theoretically be capable of interfering with automobiles' electrical systems, something often associated with UFO sightings. He published his theory in *Aviation Week*, which set the tone for scientists' debunking of UFO reports based on a science-based theories of cause and effect. In later writings, he went even further, implying that plasmas could be used to explain many other kinds of UFO reports, including close encounters, daylight discs, and even abductions.

The plasma theory did not hold up to scrutiny by experts in the field and was eventually rejected by physicists. Many cases suggested to be plasmas seemed to have simpler explanations, and for some the plasma explanation did not seem tenable. Undaunted, Klass quietly de-emphasized the plasma explanation for UFO reports, and instead focused more on misperceptions, optical illusions, and hoaxes. He became known for his mocking attacks on the gullibility of UFO witnesses and ufologists, ferreting out embarrassing quotes, misquotes, and trivial information that undermined the credibility of his targets. Although this made him largely unpopular among ufologists in general, he actually helped refine the investigative methodology of UFO researchers by forcing them to ask harder questions than they normally would, thus uncovering disturbing problems with some UFO witnesses' testimony and details of UFO reports.

He was often described as an "arch-skeptic" because he was so opposed to any possibility of UFOs being real. Klass's belligerence to explain UFO sightings in any way possible led to some false allegations that angered ufologists and undermined his own credibility. When a pilot and his plane disappeared in 1978 off the coast of Australia following a mid-flight encounter with a UFO, Klass suggested that the missing man had vanished because of a failed drug smuggling venture, despite the fact that there was no evidence of this at all. One of the tenets of skeptics' arguments against the reality of UFOs as alien spacecraft is "extraordinary claims require extraordinary evidence;" in this case, Klass offered no evidence for his claim, thus violating his own rule.

My own interactions with Klass were few, but one conversation involved a similar claim. In 1974, farmer Edwin Fuhr in Saskatchewan was swathing his field when he saw a metallic sheen on an object on the ground nearby. He climbed on his tractor for a better look and saw a total of five upside-down, bowl-shaped objects, each about three metres (ten feet) across, all spinning rapidly in place. As he watched, they rose one by one into the air and flew away, leaving behind odd swirled patterns in the grass.

The case was investigated by the Royal Canadian Mounted Police, as well as the Center for UFO Studies. The RCMP noted that Fuhr was very shaken by the experience, and could find no evidence that the markings on the ground were the result of a hoax. In fact, in his report an RCMP officer stated: "I believe that he saw something and I don't see why he would exaggerate what he saw. There is no way this is a hoax." He added: "People who know him ... all believe that he did see something out there."

Despite this, debunkers were convinced that a hoax was involved somehow and were searching for a possible break in the case. When I had the opportunity to talk with Klass in 1995, he told me that he had received a letter from a church pastor in Fuhr's hometown expressing concern over the case. Klass claimed that the pastor implied that Fuhr had a somewhat tarnished reputation in the community, contradicting previous testimony. This was enough for Klass to label the case as a hoax perpetrated by an unscrupulous local prankster, even thought Fuhr did not benefit monetarily from the incident and did not seem to have any motive.

Klass was so convinced that UFOs were nothing but hoaxes or misperceptions, that in 1966 he offer to pay ten thousand dollars to anyone offering proof of the existence of UFOs as alien spacecraft. He publicly made the offer on many occasions. His conditions, although seemingly straightforward, were stringent enough that his money was guaranteed safe.

His first condition was that any crashed alien spacecraft or major piece of an alien spacecraft must be verified as such by the National Academy of Sciences of the United States (NAS). Given the historical reluctance of the NAS to make revolutionary scientific statements this would seem a very remote possibility — debate over a piece of an alleged alien spaceship could last for decades. And, if an alien ship were found intact, would it have necessarily crashed?

His second condition was that the NAS would have to state that the Earth has been visited during the twentieth century by extraterrestrial spacecraft. This, of course, would rule out historical visits, which would be statistically more likely than a present one — given that many hundreds of years of terrestrial history are in the past, it is more likely that we have been visited long ago than it is that we are being visited just this year. It is difficult to conceive of any scientific proof that would cause the NAS to make such an announcement and fulfill this condition, other than the outright landing of a UFO on the White House lawn.

The third possible condition would be the live appearance of an extraterrestrial being at a meeting of the United Nations General Assembly or on a national television broadcast. This is reminiscent of the exhibition of the alien, Klaatu, and his robot, Gort, to humans in the movie *The Day the Earth Stood Still*, and may not reflect how aliens would want to make themselves known to us, if they did at all.

In short, Klass's conditions would be met only if aliens wanted to make themselves known in an Earth-style, formal ambassadorial presentation. This also assumes that aliens would behave in a logical, human manner, with human motives and ways of approaching colonization and encountering new life forms.

No UFO investigator or researcher, including sensational UFO writer Frank Edwards, noted investigator John Fuller, nuclear physicist Stanton T. Friedman, and noted UFO proponent J. Allen Hynek, ever took Klass up on his offer.

Although Klass was considered a thorn in the side of ufologists, anecdotal stories exist of his civil and even amicable relationships with some UFO proponents. He told me that he considered me a good investigator, but said that I believed "too many UFO nuts."

As a parting shot to ufologists and UFO buffs, Klass cast the following "UFO curse" upon all those who believe UFOs are real:

> To ufologists who publicly criticize me ... or who even think unkind thoughts about me in private, I do hereby leave and bequeath: THE UFO CURSE: No matter how long you live, you will never know any more about UFOs than you know today. You will never know any more about what UFOs really are, or where they come from. You will never know any more about what the U.S. Government really knows about UFOs than you know today. As you lie on your own deathbed you will be as mystified about UFOs as you are today. And you will remember this curse.
>
> Signed, Philip J. Klass

The curse was completely in character for the cantankerous anti-ufologist, who will be remembered as a debunker's debunker. He was the epitome of the staunch "refusenik," whom Stanton Friedman quoted when he said, "Don't bother me with the facts, my mind is already made up."

Philip Klass died in 2005 at the age of eighty-five.

Little Green Men

In popular culture, aliens are green. In the cartoons, Fred Flintstone's nemesis from outer space was the green-skinned Great Gazoo. Superman fought alongside the green-skinned Martian Manhunter in the Justice League. And, while Marvin the Martian seemed to have black skin when confronting Bugs Bunny, his companion, K-9, was green, as were his Instant Martians.

And poor Mr. Spock. His green blood gave him such a ghastly pallor.

Some ufology historians note that the term "little green men" was an amalgam of popular images that originated in the novel *The Green Man* by Harold Sherman, published in the science-fiction pulp magazine *Amazing Stories*, October 1946. (The sequel, *The Green Man Returns*, was published in the same pulp in December 1947.) Sherman was a science-fiction author (and later, a psychic researcher) who wrote about the visit of a green-skinned alien to Earth. His alien had powers that were later reflected in UFO reports, such as a ray that could stop cars, and his usual transport was a saucer-shaped craft. Because flying saucers conjured up images of aliens, which were denizens of popular culture represented by pulp magazines in the 1940s, the link between what was in the news and what was in the public mind was made. And it stuck.

Pulp magazines continued to portray aliens as green, as more was written on the subject. The pulp *Flying Saucers From Other Worlds*, which had been a science-fiction magazine simply called *Other Worlds* before the flying saucer craze caught on, published a variety of stories with green aliens as the protagonists. One was "I Found A Little Green Man," by Ron Ormond, published in August 1957.

In 1979, Sherman's *Green Man* novels were reprinted together as a set. In the foreword to the collection, the editor noted:

> Because Sherman had described his leading character, Numar, as green-complexioned, when sightings of UFOs began to take place, "little green men" became a part of the literature. This is still true today — Space People are often reported as "green in color."

The only trouble with this attribution is that "Space People" are rarely, if ever, reported by witnesses to be green-skinned. The most publicized alien encounter of the past sixty years was the Betty and Barney Hill abduction by aliens in 1961, and the Hills noted their captors' skin was grey, not green.

Noted ufologist Jerome Clark pointed this out in an on-line UFO discussion in 2007:

> I doubt that the Harold Sherman story had much to do with it. In those days, science fiction fans comprised a fairly small subculture. I know that from personal experience, when I read SF enthusiastically in the latter '50s and early '60s. Sherman's *Green Man* drew its inspiration from a well-known fertility god in ancient British folklore.
>
> Some years ago debunkers fell all over themselves to prove that Bill Brazel (or somebody) was lying when he was said to have made an oblique reference to bodies at Roswell, allegedly insisting that they "weren't green." A huge discussion followed, during which it was clearly established that the phrase "little green man" was in popular usage in 1947 and well before. A check just now on a newspaper archive to which I subscribe finds references to "little green man" as early as 1911 and "little green men" in 1908. At one time some researcher (others may recall the specifics) found a Martian little green man as a recurring character in a turn-of-the-last-century comic strip. The original little green men were elfin figures of fairy tradition.

Clark's note about elfin figures also brings to mind images of leprechauns, who traditionally wear green suits. Furthermore, green is the most often cited as the preferred colour of fairies in European legends. In his PhD thesis on UFOs and folklore, Peter Rojcewicz noted that, "nearly all the fairy tribes of Britain and Ireland ... dress in green." Even in Shakespeare's time, fairies or the "wee folk" were known to be of a particular colour, as Mrs. Page describes in Act IV, Scene IV of *The Merry Wives of Windsor*: "We'll dress like urchins, ouphs and fairies, green and white." As for more contemporary citations, as Clark notes, a story in the *Kennebec Journal*, published in Augusta, Maine, in 1908, was the first reference to "little green men" as beings from another planet.

So, if small green figures have been part of our culture for centuries, why has the term "little green men" been adopted by popular culture as the archetypal alien from another planet? This is especially confounding since UFO witnesses and abductees almost always report that the aliens they observed or confronted were grey-skinned or had normal human skin tones.

MUTILATIONS OF CATTLE

One of the most persistent issues regarding UFOs and alien contact is that of cattle mutilations. Even though most reported cattle mutilations have no associated UFO activity, many people believe that aliens, or perhaps a clandestine government agency, are involved in the killing and vivisection of cows and bulls across North America.

In the early 1970s, ranchers in the American Midwest reported that cattle were mysteriously dying in growing numbers. Supposedly, there was never any obvious cause of death, and most strangely, certain organs seemed to have been removed from the animals with surgical precision. Teats, rectal areas, sex organs, lips, and tongues were often missing when the cows were discovered, leading ranchers to believe that some person (or group of people) was deliberately killing and mutilating cattle for nefarious purposes.

In most cases, however, mutilations were not examined by reputable veterinary pathologists but by amateur investigators, including UFO buffs. The UFO connection arose because of a number of UFO cases in which animals disappeared or were otherwise reported killed. In 1970, for example, a book on UFOs and cattle mutilations noted (without a reference): "In Barcelos, Brazil, 15 children, seven pigs and two cows vanished from a farm during a UFO flap." In March 1977, UFOs described as white lights were seen to hover and land on the ground near Everett, Washington. The same night, a steer was found mutilated. A veterinarian stated, "it was not predators," and said that he "could not duplicate the mutilation with any instruments."

A more typical case was that which occurred on a small farm near Elsberry, Missouri, in 1978. Six cows were discovered dead on the property, with their eyes, ears, tongues, and sex organs cut out as if with a sharp knife. No blood could be found around the animals, suggesting it had all been drained away by whoever had perpetrated the atrocity. The animals were discovered inside a fenced pasture and police could not find any evidence of intruders. According to farmers, coyotes and buzzards, which are normally attracted to carcasses, would not go near the dead cattle.

On June 8, 1978, Elsberry farmer Forrest Gladney found a dead, mutilated calf on his farm, and the following night he witnessed a large, glowing orange UFO, "as big as the Moon," over the same field. On June 16, a bright red light was observed soundlessly flying in an arc over another farm, and the next day a mutilated calf was discovered in that field.

Police sometimes found evidence suggesting satanic cults or individuals were connected with the mutilations, including stone altars and the bodies of smaller animals, such as rabbits and weasels, all drained of blood. Some laboratory analysis did detect unusual drugs in the bodies of some mutilated cattle, leading some investigators to believe a complex, secret nationwide mutilation project was underway; however, investigators could find no hard evidence of a large conspiracy, satanic or otherwise.

Officials within the government both encouraged and stymied investigations of mutilations. There was a growing outcry from ranchers about the perceived epidemic of "mutes." For example, in Colorado in August 1975, Senator Floyd Haskell sent a letter to the FBI asking them to investigate, and noting that "ranchers are arming themselves to protect their livestock, as well as their families and themselves … Clearly something must be done before someone gets hurt."

Surprisingly, the FBI said no. A letter in reply to Haskell came from none other than Clarence M. Kelley, the director of the FBI:

The information set forth in your letter regarding the mutilation of cattle in Colorado and several other western states and the reported use of an unidentified helicopter by those individuals responsible has been carefully reviewed. I regret to inform you that these actions do not constitute a violation of Federal law coming within the FBI's investigative jurisdiction.

Many people found it odd that the FBI did not find any reason to investigate or act on an official request from an elected official regarding suspicious activity, or on the reported arming of civilian vigilante groups. This led some to believe that there was an official cover-up in effect, and possibly even some secret activities on the part of the FBI itself. This spread paranoia and rumours throughout the United States, leading to a widespread belief that the government was using black helicopters to snatch cattle from farms for secret experiments and operations. This may have been a catalyst for science fiction stories, movies, and TV shows such as *The X-Files*.

In my own experience as a UFO investigator, I have had only two cattle mutilation cases, and only one involved UFOs. That one took place in the late 1970s near Teulon, Manitoba, and involved a cow that had been found in a field after it had been missing for several days. A bright light had been seen near the field about the time it was missing. When I visited the farm and was shown the cow carcass, it was already badly decomposed. The farmer thought that predators "had been at it," but he did not think they had caused the cow's death. Not having experience in veterinary pathology, I sought out a regional agricultural representative who said they would be investigating the case, but they were under the impression that dogs, wolves, or coyotes were responsible.

The other case, which took place in 1980, was somewhat more curious, although it had no direct link to UFOs. I had been told about it simply because of the alleged connection between UFOs and mutes, according to sensational tabloids. A dead male calf was found on June 10, 1980, in an alfalfa field along with the rest of its herd. The left ear, scrotum, testicles, anus, and tail had been cut and removed. There were also two cuts or incisions on its left flank. There were no marks on the ground to indicate how any perpetrator may have done the mutilation.

I spoke with a veterinary pathologist with the provincial Department of Agriculture, who told me he had performed an autopsy on the animal soon after the farmer brought it into his laboratory. The pathologist determined that the calf had died of peritonitis and that it had been mutilated after its death.

As for the mutilations, a regional veterinarian explained that the parts removed were "an unusual collection of coincidences," and that predators seemed an unlikely explanation. The mutilation occurred in a very conservative farming community and there had not been any publicity or media reports about mutes to encourage pranksters. Nevertheless, he noted there were many predators in the area, including coyotes, foxes, cougars, and even the occasional bear.

A year earlier, the RCMP had responded to a farmer's report of a mutilated calf found on his property near Tofield, Alberta, at the end of September 1979. In this case, the veterinarian had performed a post-mortem exam of the animal at the farm, in situ. This calf had much more extensive injuries. While its anus and scrotal area had been excised like other mutes, the pathologist found "massive contusions" on its body, broken ribs, large bruising, cervical dislocation, and other damage, including the odd fact that the bladder was missing. He noted "some scavenger damage in the pelvis was present but was not extensive."

After his examination, the veterinarian made the following statement:

> In my opinion this animal was struck on the right side by a large object, probably a vehicle, with sufficient force that the animal's neck was dislocated at the level of cervical vertebra C5 or C6, resulting in its death. The removal of the anal area and scrotum and section of penis was done with a sharp instrument, probably a knife. Since the urinary bladder is [difficult to locate within a large animal], it is my opinion that whoever removed it must have some knowledge of the anatomy of the area. In my opinion, the removal of the portions described previously was definitely done by human

hands immediately after the death of the animal, using,
I believe, a knife.

In other words, evidence was found to suggest that, as in many other cases throughout North America, humans were behind the mutilation. But why? One science fiction scenario has government mutilators killing cows as part of a program to monitor how certain toxic chemicals have been absorbed into flora and fauna. In effect, it's part of an experiment upon living tissue in the environment, perhaps (according to conspiracy theorists) biological warfare agents.

Contradictory and more cautious views have been offered by other veterinary experts. A major paper published in the *Canadian Veterinary Journal* in 1989, for example, insisted that mutes were only caused by predators. A provincial veterinary pathologist examined several animals whose owners believed they were mutes. His conclusion was that in all cases, "the parts reported missing from mutilated cattle are the same as those known to be removed by scavengers, primarily coyotes and birds, in the early stages of scavenging a carcass. Jagged edges and tooth marks were found in all laboratory-examined animals."

To this day, the debate rages on. One of the foremost experts on mutes is Fern Belzil, an Alberta rancher who has travelled throughout North America to talk with farmers, examine mutilated cattle, and try to solve the mystery. In his opinion, predators cannot be held responsible for the mutes. Some kind of human intervention is involved, whether it is by satanic cultists, government agents, or something more benign.

I had long ago proposed a simple, but admittedly cruel experiment that might have shed light on the cattle mutilation phenomenon. If a healthy calf was tethered to a sturdy tree or pole and left by itself, eventually it would die naturally or be killed by a mutilator or predator. In any case, its carcass could be examined for marks and damage that would show how predation or mutilation occurs over time. The animal's body would have to be watched carefully throughout the process. We would either get a baseline study of natural predation that could be compared with other mutes, or possibly, we would catch the night mutilators in the act.

Or maybe even the aliens.

News Media

Journalists know that a good UFO story can attract readers or viewers. This is because of the public's fascination with the subject of aliens and flying saucers, and the belief that "the truth is out there."

There is some motivation, then, for reporters to take interest in sightings of UFOs. The last story of a TV newscast is often reserved for something light, like the birth of a tiger cub at the zoo, a man who has created the largest ball of twine in the country — or a UFO report. In newspapers, UFO stories are often used as fillers in columns next to car dealership ads.

At one time, however, flying saucer stories were front-page news.

Ufologist Stanton Friedman has written extensively on the evidence for crashed flying saucers and the cover-up by military officials and the government. He has found that newspaper coverage of the story that a crashed flying saucer had been recovered near Roswell, New Mexico, on July 7, 1947, differed between western and eastern parts of the continent. Only the evening newspapers in the western United States carried details of a press release sent at noon from an air force base in New Mexico, which advised editors that debris from a flying saucer had been recovered by the military.

A few hours later, according to Friedman, the air force hastily called a news conference to cover up the event and inform reporters the "saucer" was nothing more than pieces of a balloon. The news conference was too late for the evening papers on the west coast to cover, but editors of morning newspapers on the east coast had time to prepare stories based on the later information. Californians, therefore, read stories that evening about a recovered flying saucer, while New Yorkers read about a balloon the next morning.

Friedman recommended that other UFO researchers examine microfilm of North American newspapers to see the difference for themselves. When they did, Friedman's hypothesis was proved correct. In fact, on the night the Roswell saucer story emerged, North Americans were being treated to numerous and widely separated sightings of flying saucers.

On Monday, July 7, 1947, a headline on the front page of Canadian papers read: "Mystery of the Flying Discs Deepens." The story recounted a sighting of six metallic saucers shining in the sun as they flew over Montreal, Quebec, in the afternoon. A trapper in Saskatchewan reported seeing a mysterious object that he was convinced was a meteor, crash into the ground. Another object was seen at Port Hope, Ontario, by a railway employee, who said it had a slight reddish tinge and was not a shooting star.

Newspapers quoted experts who were quick to offer their opinions, although they varied greatly. In Syracuse, New York, psychiatrist Dr. Harry Steckel discounted the element of mass hallucination in connection with the reports. "They have been seen by too many people in too many different places to be dismissed so lightly," he said in a radio broadcast. A noted astronomer believed that "Some kind of flying device, still on the secret list, is definitely being tested somewhere on the continent ... One or two reports suggest meteors, but that is not the answer. Experimentation, that's it."

In Winnipeg, Manitoba, two competing newspapers tried to one-up each other in their coverage of the flying discs. While both sponsored saucer-spotting parties on top of downtown buildings, one paper's slant was decidedly cynical. It enlisted the services of a "Prof. Roberts" to set up a "flying saucer observation station," equipped with binoculars and a canteen of "barley water," on the roof of a building.

The general theme of ridicule by news media continues today, more than sixty years later. And who can blame reporters for not knowing who to believe or which expert to interview? Ufologists don't speak with one voice, and they certainly vary in terms of approach, credentials, beliefs, and credibility. There are no universities offering degree programs in UFO investigation, nor is ufological research a part of any accredited curriculum.

This means that anyone can claim to be a ufologist or UFO investigator and get media attention for doing so. Media do not care whether the UFO expert they are interviewing has a PhD in astronomy or is wearing a tinfoil hat to keep aliens from reading his mind. In the new media era of infotainment, if a story gets ratings and generates interest, it's news.

Another aspect of media with regard to UFOs is the generation of reports through news coverage. This is a version of the chicken-and-egg problem; do people report UFOs because they see or read about UFOs in the media, or do media produce stories about UFOs because people are reporting them? There is no question that running a news story about UFOs will cause some people to report their sightings. Many witnesses do not know where to find someone who will be sympathetic to their experiences. A news story identifying a witness or an expert provides such an outlet for a person to open up and tell his or her own story.

But here's the catch: someone who comes forward with his or her own UFO sighting because of encouragement received from a news story about current UFO reports may not necessarily report a recent experience. In fact, my experience as a UFO investigator is that news stories about recent UFO sightings usually prompt people to come forward with older sightings, because they finally feel comfortable doing so. True, some witnesses to recent sightings will come forward as well, but in most cases, sightings from weeks, months, years, and even decades ago will come to light.

Ufologists have learned to use media to get their message out. One of the most successful talk-radio programs has been *Coast to Coast* with Art Bell. Bell began broadcasting his unique mixture of news and editorials on psychics, aliens, and conspiracy theories in 1989, in an all-night format designed for insomniacs. He had a huge following through syndication in most major North American centres, with a listening audience estimated to be in the tens of millions. His guests included ufologists like Stanton Friedman, Linda Moulton Howe, and Whitley Strieber, with whom he co-authored a work on dramatic world upheaval. Jeff Rense has almost as large a following as Bell. His website, rense.com, is highly popular, and his radio show is heard by millions each week.

Both radio shows are way off the beaten track when it comes to mainstream media, yet their audiences persist and their approaches seem to fill a void. Mainstream media appear to be content to ignore the subject of UFOs entirely, unless there's a need to inject some humour into an otherwise dry and depressing newscast featuring battlefield atrocities half a world away. And it's so easy for reporters to find a tinfoil-hat-wearing person who exemplifies what debunkers want all ufologists to be.

Yet, occasionally, reporters do their jobs. At the beginning of 2008, just as the American presidential campaign was getting into gear, media were looking for quirky angles to focus on instead of the usual political rhetoric emanating from the candidates' public relations machines. It was brought to national attention that Dennis Kucinich had once reported seeing a UFO in 1982, and had even told Shirley MacLaine about it. He, of course was branded a lunatic for making such an admission, even though polls have shown that at least 10 percent of the American population believe they have seen a UFO. As voting demographics go, this in itself would be a good thing under normal circumstances. But biased media (and they are all that, admittedly) used the ridicule factor to make Kucinich appear foolish.

That is, until reporter Michael Phillips of *The Wall Street Journal* decided to look deeper and actually investigate the story. There seems to have been something to Kucinich's report, which surprised some people. One media watchdog criticized *The Wall Street Journal* for wasting valuable column inches on something as silly as a UFO report. But at least one media analyst found their attack unreasonable:

> So the ink isn't even dry on *The Wall Street Journal*'s 1A story Wednesday providing additional eyewitness details on Dennis Kucinich's 1982 UFO sighting when Editor & Publisher takes its first shot. Sensing a rogue and cheapening shift in the wind at the hands of new WSJ owner Rupert Murdoch, E&P asks: 'Was there really any pressing need to cover Dennis Kucinch's old, and much laughed over, UFO encounter, especially with him about to poll about 1% of the vote in Iowa?'
>
> Phillips' reporting stands out not because he sensationalized it, but because the guy played it straight. The traditional formula for covering UFO stories like this is to place a phone call to the Committee for Skeptical Inquiry or some other expert who wasn't there to explain why Kucinich and others saw Venus or swamp gas instead. That's considered "balance."

The analyst points out that the newspaper industry is in big trouble, with sagging readership that could be traceable to an out-of-touch conservative editorial policy.

> But it's the WSJ that draws arched eyebrows for trying to buck a trend. It decides to cover a UFO story the way it might also report a murder — by talking to witnesses and, without judgment, letting the facts speak for themselves. And to think: the editors could've used that space to run another analysis of the presidential race in Iowa.

The Strentz study, an early study on news media and its relationship to UFOs, was published in 1970. Thousands of newspaper clippings about UFOs from across North America were examined in great detail and analyzed for their content and editorial bias. It concluded that "extensive press coverage has caused widespread public awareness of flying saucers, or UFOs."

This is an obvious fact: people learned about sightings of UFOs primarily from reading about them in newspapers. Newspapers are more readily available than magazines, more frequent and more timely. Television news coverage of UFO sightings was very rare, comparatively.

Another of the study's findings was that: "Press coverage of UFOs has encouraged and maintained periodic waves of UFO reports by focusing public attention upon the subject and combining previously unrelated and isolated UFO reports." As UFO reports were covered by newspapers, more people were encouraged to come forward with their own sightings, which in turn were covered by the newspapers, and so on. This resulted in two other effects: press coverage lowered barriers against the reporting of UFOs, and the willingness to print UFO reports made the press more vulnerable to hoaxes and less critical of the sightings it reported on.

The third finding was that "Media played a major role in creating and sustaining interest in UFOs, but it was not solely responsible for the existence of the phenomenon."

In other words, there was a real phenomenon that was occurring beyond the media coverage itself. Other findings of this study were:

UFO news coverage is primarily local in nature.

This may not be true today, as the Internet has significantly improved communication within the global village. But in the 1950s and 1960s, local news stations often protected their sources and exclusively carried UFO stories themselves. And of what relevance would a sighting eight hundred kilometres away be to a local witness?

Press coverage relies on inexpert witness testimony and rarely includes commentary from police or other officials.

My own observations indicate that present-day media coverage almost always includes an expert of some kind, even if the individual has no personal experience with the subject. This would include an astronomer from a local college who is asked about a nearby UFO sighting even though he or she has not visited the site, interviewed the witness, or studied relevant, serious published materials about the UFO phenomenon.

Although the U.S. Air Force UFO study (the Condon Report) is generally depicted as thorough, scientific, and meriting public confidence, the inquiry actually did not exhibit any of those characteristics.

The study wondered why a one-room office at Wright-Patterson Air Force Base was investigating reports of UFOs around the world, when NORAD was far better equipped to handle it. It also viewed the air force study as little more than a public relations exercise.

The large amount of ridicule in regards to UFOs was reflected in media coverage, and media failed to distinguish between nonsensical flying saucer stories and those which merited study.

This is still true today, as sensational UFO stories are more likely to attract media attention and get coverage, especially during TV sweeps weeks. Meanwhile, serious research projects to study UFO cases receive less coverage. The media cannot be faulted, however, as there is no obvious authority to help determine which stories are worth covering in the press.

The study concluded, by suggesting that "the quick answer and easy generalization have been over-used in discussions about UFOs." Since the study was published in the 1970s, things have changed very little. During a wave of UFO sightings in and around Stephenville, Texas, in early 2008, national media fell back on the usual tired clichés. A Texas network TV station ran a feature on the sightings with the headline: "Grab Your Tin Foil Hat: UFO Fever Hits North Texas."

OBJECTIVITY

No one is without bias. We all have belief systems, or reasons for acting and behaving the way we do. Philosophers such as Jacques Derrida and Michel Foucault described ways of understanding our interpersonal communications in terms of post-structuralism and deconstruction. They suggested that in order to really understand what someone is saying, it is important to find out his or her motivation, ambition, intent, and bias. In other words, what does he or she really mean?

This is important in all aspects of life, and it is important in ufology. When someone makes a statement like, "UFOs do not exist," it is wise to use critical thinking to analyze what is being said, rather than taking the statement at face value. Obviously, an astronaut would have a different perspective on the issue than, say, a bank manager. Is one in a better position to make such a statement than the other? Is one more objective than the other?

Being objective is not taking a stand one way or another, but judging an issue strictly on the facts. It is very difficult to be objective, especially on issues of major importance. Should American military forces remain in the Middle East? Should the legal drinking age be lowered to eighteen everywhere? Should marijuana be legalized?

Your personal answers to these questions will vary depending on your own experiences, background, upbringing, peers, job, and many other factors.

It is no wonder, then, that the question, "Do UFOs exist?" will be answered differently by different people. Those who believe that aliens are visiting Earth or have a predisposition to do so, will tend to answer "yes," while those whose belief systems are such that the idea of alien beings is strictly science fiction will tend to answer "no."

This is particularly evident when UFO sightings are made public. Almost immediately, the general public takes sides, divided approximately into equal halves. Some will consider the UFO sighting to be a possible indication of alien visitation, while others will laugh off the sighting completely. Few will actually take the time to consider the report on its merits.

In late 2007, the video of a curious smoke trail was made public. The images were taken by a couple who watched a spiralling object falling obliquely through the sky, creating a black streak as it fell over Prince Edward Island, Canada. The couple sanely inquired with aviation authorities and the local weather office about it, showing them the video, but neither official institution could explain the object. They then sent it to Ufology Research, for which I am research co-ordinator, and I examined it at length.

When interviewed by a newspaper reporter about it, I suggested it could have one of several terrestrial explanations, including "a balloon experiment, satellite re-entry, or something atmospheric, perhaps. Not a celestial object or astronomical phenomenon, or a rocket or satellite fuel dump." I was quoted as saying that we were "definitely not sure what this object was," and that it was "very puzzling." An astronomer whom the reporter also asked for an opinion pointed out that a "definite scientific opinion is hard without firm data." In that sense, he agreed with my objective view that there was no definitive explanation at the time.

Although many scientists find it difficult to actually admit it, the answer "I don't know" is a perfectly valid, scientific statement. In fact, how many people are put off by a know-it-all? When someone seems to have an answer for everything, his or her audience tends to be suspicious.

The scientific community might be regarded less as denizens of ivory towers if they appeared to be more human by admitting their lack of complete knowledge, even in their specialized fields of study.

When I'm asked if I personally believe that aliens are visiting Earth, I state that I have not seen any incontrovertible evidence that they are, or that they are not. When prodded, I explain that my personal opinion is that sentient extraterrestrial civilizations probably do exist, but that as an astronomy educator, I know the limitations of distance and the difficulties with interstellar travel. It's not impossible to travel between the stars, just not easy.

I admit that I'm sitting on the fence on the issue. But this is a consequence of truly being objective. I simply don't *know* with certainty.

Fence posts are very uncomfortable, especially the ones with pointy ends.

PILOT CASES

One of the questions most often asked by skeptics as a challenge to ufologists is: "How come pilots don't report seeing UFOs?" After all, each day pilots and other air crew spend thousands of flight hours looking out cockpit windows, watching the skies. If UFOs were real, surely they would see them. Since pilots aren't reporting UFOs on a regular basis, UFOs must not exist.

This might be a reasonable assumption if pilots had no reservations about coming forward with information about seeing unidentified objects while flying, or if they had been asked if they had ever seen such objects and answered to the negative. The truth is that pilots do see UFOs and sometimes report them, often at the risk of their reputations.

In 2001, all pilots employed by one commercial American airline were surveyed about whether or not they had ever seen anything they could not identify while in flight. A remarkable 23.5 percent responded to the survey (a very good rate for surveys in general), and of those, 23 percent said they had seen an unidentified object. However, of those who indicated they had seen an unidentified object, only one in four had actually reported it to authorities.

While this may be interpreted as showing that about a quarter of all airline pilots have seen UFOs, the significant point is that some have seen them at all. Perhaps more significant is that most did not report their sighting of an unusual object to authorities. There seems to be reluctance on the part of pilots to report UFOs.

Dr. Richard Haines is a psychologist who has worked as a consultant to NASA on a number of programs related to simulating space environments, designing spacecraft, and other projects. When he left his full-time position at NASA in 1988 he began teaching psychology at San Jose State University, but still acted as a consultant on some NASA projects including the International Space Station.

Haines's passion since the 1980s has been instrumented UFO sightings and sightings by pilots. Haines wrote *Observing UFOs*, a textbook on the optics and psychological aspects of UFO reports, and he has published numerous articles and reports on UFO cases. He assisted colleague Ted Roe in creating the National Aviation Reporting Center on Anomalous Phenomena (NARCAP) as a way in which pilots could confidently and confidentially report their observations of UFOs, and also to allow the study of such reports.

The number of UFO reports by military, airline, and private pilots catalogued by NARCAP is currently around 1,500, spanning the years 1916 to the present. They come from all corners of the world, reporting objects seen over all continents. Yet, pilots face a great deal of peer pressure not to report their UFO sightings. Haines notes:

> Fear of ridicule, fear of having one's competence questioned, fear of losing one's career, fear of government reprisal, even fear of the phenomena itself are all cited as reasons why pilots are not officially reporting many observations, close pacing and near mid-air collisions, and even alleged collisions with unidentified aerial phenomena.

This atmosphere of reluctance for pilots to report UFOs is completely opposite to what military officials desire in terms of vigilance and security. During the Cold War when Soviet attack was a major concern, having all civilian and military pilots report sightings of possible enemy aircraft was most desirable. In 1954, military and commercial aviation officials produced the Joint Army, Navy, Air Force Publication 146 (known as JANAP 146), and a companion set of directives giving Communication Instructions for Reporting Vital Intelligence Sightings (CIRVIS), described earlier. Under the directive, all pilots were encouraged to report unusual activity, including UFOs, since they could be a matter of national security. Despite this, many pilots are unaware that their colleagues are making UFO sightings because it seems to have evolved into a taboo subject.

Part of the reason for this is that JANAP 146 evolved with time, and other official bodies such as the National Transportation Safety Board (NTSB), FAA, and NASA became the centres for collecting information on mid-air events such as near misses and accidents. The term "unidentified flying object" became unworthy of inclusion in the databases and so there was no official place to report such observations.

However, because pilots still make UFO sightings, the atmosphere of reluctance has been slowly dissipating. A courageous few come forward with their reports now and then and are highlighted in the media. Some pilots have come to realize that they can make official reports without reprisal. Indeed, pilots' UFO reports routinely make up part of the yearly accumulation of UFO cases recorded in international UFO databases every year, such as those of Ufology Research of Manitoba (UFOROM) and the National UFO Reporting Center (NUFORC) in Washington.

One remarkable official UFO report was made by a pilot on March 21, 2004. A brilliant fireball was seen by witnesses on the ground and in the air, including observers on the private jet carrying the Right Honourable Paul Martin, then the prime minister of Canada. An unidentified bright object was reported to air traffic controllers in Edmonton flying near Canadian Forces Base Suffield at 7:56 p.m. local time. The report, made available to UFOROM through Transport Canada, noted that pilots of three aircraft, including two commercial airliners and the government jet, all reported seeing "a very bright light falling from the sky, with smoke trailing."

In addition, pilots of several other aircraft flying near Westaskiwin, Alberta, also reported seeing the object. One of these pilots was said to have described it as "the brightest fireball he'd ever seen." It is not known if the Prime Minister was advised of the incident, or was also a witness to the event, but it is at least significant that his personal pilot saw and officially reported the object, which was likely a piece of cometary debris impacting the Earth's atmosphere.

Skeptics are quick to point out that pilots, even though they are considered excellent observers, are not infallible. Even though thousands of people place their faith in the observational capabilities of pilots every day, they do make visual mistakes, sometimes with tragic consequences. It is possible that pilots who report seeing UFOs are misidentifying other aircraft or atmospheric phenomena. But if so, then UFO observations by pilots must be considered of crucial importance to the Federal Aviation Administration (FAA) and other official bodies, because such observations might be indicative of serious safety problems within the airline industry. One would think that pilots' reporting of UFOs should be encouraged within the military and commercial aviation companies so that these errors of observation can be studied in greater depth. Instead of facing ridicule, pilots should be thanked for bringing visual interpretation problems to official attention.

But this scenario is not in evidence. What is more likely is that seeing UFOs is a natural and expected consequence of spending a great deal of time looking into the sky. In other words, it's normal for pilots to see UFOs.

QUESTIONS

"If they are here, then where are they?"
— Enrico Fermi

Ufologist Stanton Friedman recalls famous physicist Enrico Fermi's lectures at the University of Chicago in the 1950s. He remembers that Fermi would often pose questions as thought exercises, without expecting or requiring any answers. The famous quote that seems to sarcastically raise doubt that aliens exist at all is interpreted by Friedman as a serious question by Fermi, simply asking students to ponder the possibility of seeking and finding extraterrestrial life in the universe. His question, which has become known as the Fermi Paradox, was created in 1950 and has become one of the great questions asked about UFOs and aliens.

It's good to ask questions. It's how we learn about our world and our environment. Throughout the history of UFOs, many questions have been asked, often to poke fun at the subject or point out its flaws. Here are some of them:

Q. "Why don't pilots see UFOs, since they're the ones looking into the sky all the time?"
A. They do. See the previous section.

Q. "Why don't astronomers see UFOs? They're always looking into the night sky!"
A. Again, they do. Two major studies have been conducted to survey both amateur and professional astronomers about their views on UFOs. In 1977, Peter Sturrock published the results of his survey of 2,611 members of the American Astronomical Society, composed mostly of educators and researchers. Among other things, he found that more than 4 percent of those surveyed had seen UFOs. It is a fact that most professional astronomers spend very little time actually observing the sky above, instead using computers or devices such as spectrophotometers to examine very small areas of the sky, often in radio or other invisible wavelengths. Most ardent comet watchers

and asteroid trackers, who watch the sky frequently, are amateur astronomers (a misnomer, because many are highly specialized and experienced in observational astronomy). Many amateurs begin to make their observations at twilight and continue through the night, observing and photographing interesting objects.

In 1980, a study of the results of a survey of 8,526 amateur astronomers who were members of the Astronomical League, the Association of Lunar and Planetary Observers (ALPO), and the International Occultation Timing Association (IOTA) was published. (Another large group of amateurs, the American Association of Variable Star Observers, refused to participate in the survey at all, believing UFOs not to be worthy of study.) The study's author, Gert Herb, realized that these true skywatchers would have the best chance of seeing a UFO. The result was significant: out of the 1,805 amateur astronomers who responded to the survey, almost 24 percent answered "yes" to the question, "Have you ever observed an object which you could not identify, despite your best efforts to do so?" Even taking the entire sample, including those who did not respond to the questionnaire, this is still more than 5 percent of the total.

Herb went even further; he had asked respondents about their observing experience, qualifications, and background, and identified 261 senior observers who possessed higher-than-average abilities and knowledge, and who were most familiar with the night sky. Of these, 74 individuals had seen objects "which resisted most exhaustive efforts of identification." Of these objects, most were point or slightly extended sources, although 24 were observed "at short enough distance as to leave no doubt in the observer's mind that something strange was reported." Sixty-six were observed through a telescope, and 40 were seen with binoculars. There is no question, then, that astronomers do see UFOs, although, as with pilots, there is a reluctance to report sightings.

Q. "Why don't they just land on the White House lawn?"
A. This question implies that if aliens really existed and were visiting Earth, they would choose to make themselves known by initiating a formal diplomatic exchange with the primary head of the terrestrial

government. First of all, if a spacecraft were to try to get near the White House unannounced, it would certainly be the target of missiles and other weaponry. Second, there is no reason to assume that aliens would recognize the president of the United States as the leader of Earth. Perhaps they would instead choose a religious leader, such as the Pope or the Dalai Lama. Perhaps they would choose the leader of the most populous nation. Perhaps there are other criteria about which we cannot even begin to guess.

The question also suggests that aliens would want to deal directly with world governments and political parties, although there is no good reason that they should choose to do so. It could be that they are observing us as an anthropological study, noting our behaviour and development with time, perhaps selecting and tagging specimen occasionally. In that case, openly announcing their presence would not be in their plans. There are many possible reasons why aliens might not want to display themselves so openly. Of course, this question also assumes that UFOs are alien spacecraft, something that is still not resolved. If UFOs are a natural phenomenon, then this question is completely irrelevant.

Q. "Why are flying saucers shaped like saucers?"

A. They're not always shaped like that. As noted in the discussion of Kenneth Arnold's sighting in 1947, even the objects he saw weren't exactly saucers. One interesting point of note is that in August 1979, physicist Alan Holt published a little-seen research paper in which he proposes a method of interstellar travel based on a "field resonance" that involves a kind of "surfing" on magnetic fields. The proposed shape of the craft that would be able to travel in this way: a disc.

Q. "Where can I go to see a UFO?"

A. If I knew the answer to that, I would be a millionaire. However, I can predict with great confidence that if you go outside at about midnight, in a place away from city lights, and watch the sky overhead, you will soon see a small, star-like object that is moving slowly across the bowl of night. You'll probably have no idea what it is, so it is an unidentified flying object. Perhaps later we could work together to discover which satellite it was, but it was for a short while at least, a UFO.

From time to time, it would appear that certain places are UFO hot spots, where there seem to be an inordinate number of sightings. In January 2008, this was Stephenville, Texas. In 1954, it was France. In 1990, it was Belgium. In 1975, it was Manitoba. It is very difficult to predict where UFOs will appear, although there are some places that boast recurring lights or "spook lights" that may or may not have much to do with the UFO phenomenon in general. One of these is Hessdalen, Norway; others are Brown Mountain in Texas, and the Surrey Corridor in British Columbia.

RELIGION

For some people belief in UFOs has been called *religious* in the sense that it is a pervasive system of viewing the world. This is apart from several religious movements that are based on the idea that omnipotent extraterrestrials are guiding our lives and destinies.

In a technical sense, God is not an extraterrestrial because he is not apart from the Earth, but is part of everything we see. A term that has been used instead is "ultraterrestrial," but that too seems inappropriate. Some recognized religions accept at least some aspects of intervention of aliens from other planets, explicitly or otherwise.

Although some guides to alternative religions list ufology as a religion, this is as absurd as including birdwatching, vegetarianism, organic farming, or marathon-running in that category. People who are deeply involved may participate in any of these activities *religiously*, but not through devout worship as such. Certainly some fanatics involved in these areas might become immersed in their interests to the exclusion of all else, but this would not be true of most fans or adherents.

It would be fair, however, to include so-called New Age movements as religions, as many of them are exactly that. Some, like channelling, divining, astrology, tarot card reading, and Eastern mysticism have all been collected under the New Age label even though most have been around since biblical times.

Having said all that, some UFO believers inject significant religious fervour into their actions to the point that religiosity is the result. Fanatical UFO belief is essentially an anti-science movement that rejects the scientific evaluation and rational explanation for UFOs in favour of a more mystical and religious view. Spiritual UFO cults embrace omnipotent beings known often as the "Space Brothers," deities who are much more advanced than humans. Their levels of advancement are such that they almost always have apparently magical or mystical powers, often including ESP and other psychic abilities. In some cases, they appear to be more spiritually aware than humans, and they often impart mystical knowledge to contactees about how they must advance to a higher level of consciousness in order to reach their spiritual potential.

An early spiritual UFO cult was the Aetherius Society of Britain, founded by George King in 1954 after he heard a voice from heaven, telling him that he was to become the terrestrial appointee to an "interplanetary Parliament." King prepared himself for this role by adopting a healthier lifestyle, practising yoga, and meditating. Soon he began channelling an alien named Aetherius from Venus, who wanted to alert Earth to its demise should its denizens not straighten out immediately. He warned the growing number of King's followers of natural catastrophes and taught them about "cosmic energies" and the need for more "positive ions" in the world. Sometimes, King channelled Jesus, who had apparently been born on Venus and came to Earth in a flying saucer disguised as the Star of Bethlehem. According to King, Jesus is now on Mars, where he continues his teachings.

On November 20, 1952, at twelve-thirty, in the California desert, George Adamski and some friends saw a UFO land. Adamski went on ahead to investigate. He said he met a human-like alien with shoulder-length blond hair. This alien, too, was from Venus, and he also brought the message that the Space Brothers were concerned about the behaviour of humans. He said that they had chosen Adamski to help humans become more peaceful and civilized. Adamski travelled widely and attracted a huge following with groups around the world. He met with politicians and dignitaries, and travelled to Rome to meet the Pope. He called himself Professor George Adamski, claiming he lived and worked at Mount Palomar Observatory. In reality, he ran a small cafeteria halfway up the mountain road leading to the astronomical institution. He had a small portable telescope through which he took several photographs of aliens and their spaceships hovering nearby. Adamski died in 1965, but his groups continued meeting into the 1970s.

The Mark-Age movement still exists today in small groups who follow the teachings of aliens channelled by its leader, Mark. They believe that humankind was once part of an interplanetary spiritual communications system, but has turned away from spiritual matters, much to the detriment of everyone. Because of our fall from grace, the Hierarchical Board of the Solar System has clouded our ability to perceive spiritual reality, but some benevolent aliens are helping to increase our spiritual awareness through mental communications with Mark-Age members. Sometimes, they make themselves seen to us as flying saucers.

On December 13, 1973, French journalist Claude Vorhilon had an encounter with an alien that was similar to George Adamski's. The small olive-skinned humanoid with long, dark hair and almond-shaped eyes told Vorhilon that spacemen like himself created life on Earth through a series of genetic experiments. He said that the aliens were mistaken for gods, and that our Bible is a record of their activities. Vorhilon was told to take the name Rael, and the alien directed him to spread the word of the true origins of humankind and to establish an interplanetary embassy in Jerusalem in preparation for the aliens' second coming.

Rael has claimed that a UFO took him to their planet, where he met advanced beings such as Jesus and John F. Kennedy. While there, Rael was given explicit instruction in sexuality, which is an integral part of the aliens' master plan. He was also taught the secrets of cloning, which is one of the advanced scientific methods the aliens used in their development of our race.

The Raelian movement has attracted a significant following around the world, including many scientists and learned individuals. Rael announced that a team of scientists working at a Quebec laboratory had successfully cloned a human, and that the first baby created in this manner was born on December 26, 2002. Despite repeated requests, proof of the cloning was never provided, and the baby, Eve, has never been publicly introduced. Rael has stated that his Clonaid program is a way in which humans can become more like their alien ancestors.

According to revelations made to psychiatrist William Sadler in 1932, Urantia is the name of Earth. One of his patients, allegedly Wilfred Kellogg, a relative of the founders of the famous Battle Creek Sanatorium, claimed to have received divine revelations from space beings. *The Urantia Book*, a huge volume of more than two thousand pages, describes in great detail the hundreds of planets in the universe, and how we were created by an omnipotent alien being named Michael, who is better known as Jesus. *The Urantia Book* contains information on Havona, a planet that we call heaven, and various other worlds populated by spiritual beings in "superuniverses" beyond time and space. Urantia is apparently world number 606 of a planetary system called Satania, within which there are many more planets harbouring developing civilizations under the watchful eyes of alien Seraphim and their lesser ministers. *The Urantia Book* is densely packed with channelled information about minutiae regarding the unseen reality of alien administration. For example, Gabriel is the name of "the chief officer of execution for superuniverse mandates relating to non-personal affairs in the local universe."

Several recurring themes are present in the beliefs of most of these groups:

1. Mankind's spiritual awareness is missing or weak;
2. Space Brothers are trying to coax us back onto the path of spiritual understanding; and
3. Salvation is possible through adherence to the teachings of the terrestrial leader or appointee.

For the most part, UFO religious cults and groups are concerned with the welfare of the human race, and are spreading the teachings of their masters in the hope that humankind will be saved from itself. From a religious standpoint, they simply replace God with a physical being or beings from another planet. As a side effect, UFO cults reject science's dismissal of UFO reports, and therefore adopt an anti-science and sometimes anti-establishment or anti-government attitude that can make their followers outspoken against normal society.

On March 26, 1997, thirty-nine bodies were discovered in a house in California, dead as the result of a religious suicide pact among members of the Heaven's Gate UFO cult. Their leader, Marshall Applewhite, had taught his followers that suicide would allow their souls would be "grafted" into a "container" (or body) that is further advanced than humans, on board a spacecraft that was visible in the sky near Comet Hale-Bopp.

Like many contactee cult leaders before him, Applewhite received channelled communications from aliens who imparted spiritual teachings to him. Heaven's Gate followers believed that Jesus was an alien representative who was inviting humans to join his spiritual extraterrestrial kingdom.

Another example of cultish behaviour is the contactee named V, described earlier. She held actual church-like ceremonies and had a modest following that praised and offered prayers to benevolent Space Brothers. Her revelations from the omnipotent beings gave her the power to heal the sick and make proclamations on their behalf.

Other UFO religions arose from UFO sightings and experiences that made impressions on witnesses who later founded sects. Todd Jumper, who was raised as a Mormon, had many UFO-related experiences that he firmly believed were the result of satanic aliens invading our planet and negatively affecting our spiritual well-being. He created his own branch of the Church of Latter-Day Saints, grafting his own views onto the church to form an interesting mixture of Christianity and modern UFO beliefs. He recalls several abduction-style events that occurred in his youth, as well as many UFO sightings, including a large black triangle hovering over his house, and feelings of being watched. Jumper claimed many bedroom visitations of monsters and aliens, and remembered balls of light floating about his bedroom. In response, he prayed to God and found that Jesus would come and drive away the alien demons in both a spiritual and physical sense.

His theology expanded to include his interpretations of other insights obtained through prayer, including visions of the end of the world, cities on fire, wars, and "darkness upon the lands." Jesus visited Jumper and directed him to become a prophet and share his revelations with the world. He believes his mission is to help rid the world of satanic, grey-skinned aliens.

Jumper's theology borrows heavily from popular ufology and what is known as "ancient astronaut" theory, in which ancient writings, myths, and ruins are interpreted as our ancestors' records of meetings with aliens. To those fascinated with the concept of ancient astronauts, extraterrestrials visited Earth many eons ago, giving rise to myths about "strangers from the sky" and gods with powers beyond primitive understanding. Some were viewed as "angels" (which appropriately means "messengers") when they came to Earth, although some became wicked, having sex with women and creating hybrid aliens.

Many books have been written about the concept of alien intervention in early human history. Barry Downing, whose book *The Bible and Flying Saucers* set the tone for many later authors, may have borrowed ideas from previous authors such as Robert Charroux, who wrote extensively about ancient artifacts that may have alien origins. Downing's thesis is summarized in the following passage:

> If beings from another world came to Earth with the intention of molding a specific religious perspective on a group of people — chosen people, the Jews — and if these beings in their UFO caused the parting of the Red Sea, provided manna in the wilderness, put on a display of power at Mount Sinai while giving Moses various instructions, and finally led Israel through the wilderness to the Promised Land, hovering night and day over the Tent of Meeting, then I dare say that the people involved in this sequence, the people who were under the influence of the beings in the UFO, might very well record the events in which they were involved.

Downing's interpretation of biblical events as being caused or designed by extraterrestrial aliens is not unique; numerous others have explored the idea in depth, including Josef Blumrich, whose detailed analysis of the wheels seen by Ezekiel in a vision suggested that they were actually part of a landing module similar to the one that NASA sent to the moon. This wasn't surprising, since Blumrich was the chief of a NASA department at the time.

The most popular writer on the theme of ancient astronauts was Erich Von Daniken, whose wildly popular book *Chariots of the Gods?* took the world by storm when it was translated into English. It led to several sequels, a storm of controversy, skeptical analysis, and the creation of a tourist theme park in Europe, which is now closed. Von Daniken himself was preceded by several authors, including Morris K. Jessup, whose much earlier work suggested that the Bible "is a treasure house of UFO data." Modern UFO-related books continue the theme of aliens as our ancestors and the reason for our development of civilization. Many authors believe that the pyramids and other ancient monuments were either built by aliens or with their assistance.

Finally, mention should be made of another viewpoint regarding UFOs in religion, and that is the belief that UFOs are messengers of Satan. In principle, this is identical to those who believe UFOs and aliens are angels and that we are visited by them on a frequent basis for purposes completely out of our control.

UFO-based religious groups reflect anxieties about our present society, specifically the possibility of nuclear war or other catastrophe. They attract those who feel oppressed or left out, who are longing for acceptance and looking for someone to give them direction towards fulfillment. Since the Space Brothers come from planets free from war, poverty, and need, they appeal to individuals dissatisfied with the current world problems of pollution, violence, and injustice. These planets are desirable idyllic paradises far removed from earthly problems. By replacing a spiritual God with a more technological entity, UFO cults place humans on par with their saviours. If only we knew enough science, we too could be like the aliens.

Science Fiction and UFOs

When I began collecting UFO-related books and magazines in earnest in the 1970s, one of the items I found in a used bookstore was a copy of *Flying Saucers From Other Worlds*, a pulp magazine that had been published in the 1950s. I wanted to find more issues of the magazine and scoured other bookstores, but I was unable to locate any more copies.

As I began reading the yellowed and faded copy, I noticed an ad in the classified section at the back. It was about a regular weekly meeting of the Winnipeg Science Fiction Society in the home of its librarian, Chester Cuthbert. A science fiction society in my own city? Why, that could be a place to find more copies of the magazine! But would it still be in existence twenty-five years later?

Amazingly, I found a listing for Cuthbert in the phone book and called him up. I explained that I was a ufologist and described what I was looking for. He told me that he might have additional issues in his collection and invited me to come to the next meeting of the society at his home.

When I arrived at his house on the day of the meeting, I found a motley crew of individuals who turned out to be science fiction fans. I was surprised to find that in addition to several writers and people who worked at book publishing companies, there was also a nuclear physicist and a computer scientist. When Cuthbert introduced me to the group, I was initially rebuffed. "You don't really fit in with this group," one member said. "We're interested in science fiction, and you're only interested in — " he paused when he realized what he was saying. "Oh, okay, you can join the group."

The connection between UFOs and science fiction is obvious to some people, especially skeptics. Others who take the subject very seriously find little of merit in discussions about *Star Trek* and science fiction fandom. Speculative fiction (as opposed to fantasy) has dealt with the idea of encounters between aliens and humans for many decades, if not centuries. A classic work by Voltaire, *Micromegas* (1752), finds an alien being from Saturn and one from Sirius visiting Earth and marvelling at our primitive and illogical society. H.G. Wells' *War of the Worlds* (1898) may be the best-known alien invasion story, depicting profoundly alien aliens bent on conquering Earth. Orson Welles's radio broadcast of the story in 1938 sent people running panicked into the streets. Several movie versions of it have done reasonably well in the cinema.

Early in the development of science fiction literature, aliens were generally bug-eyed monsters, usually with a predisposition to destroy or enslave us. They were grotesque for the most part, wreaking havoc, and often threatening a damsel in distress who had to be rescued by a hero. As science fiction progressed however, writers allowed readers inside aliens' minds and the monsters became more humanized, with emotions and feelings. It seemed that writers were not content to look at space as a battleground or a place of confrontation, but more as a location for humanity's own destiny.

At one point, aliens became "nice." This is perhaps best exemplified by Ray Bradbury's *The Martian Chronicles* (1950), in which we learn about the demise of the aliens as humans settle their planet. Much later, we would read about highly evolved and sympathetic aliens in science fiction literature, although on television and in the movies, aliens were still portrayed as malevolent. It took until the 1970s and 1980s for nicer aliens, like E.T. and the spindly ones from *Close Encounters of the Third Kind*, to make it to the large screen. The pendulum has swung the other way again, and the "bad" aliens of *Alien, Independence Day, Invasion,* and *Mars Attacks!* dominate film.

Within science fiction literature and films, UFOs have formed a particular category. Science fiction films in general are recognized as being rooted in fantasy and pure speculation, whereas UFOs have been depicted in movies and literature as "real" or "possible." Audiences know that the events and action seen in *Star Wars* movies or the *Alien* franchise are fictional, but they also know that since UFO reports are in the news and in magazines, portrayals of saucer-shaped spaceships are "based on true stories."

A good example of the collision between science fiction and ufology is the latest entry in the Indiana Jones saga. In *Indiana Jones and the Crystal Skull*, our hero finds himself facing off against government agents who are covering up activities at Roswell. It is not only the swashbuckling character of Jones that makes the movie work, but the fact that the movie audience believes Roswell is a secret government base where aliens and UFOs are supposedly stashed (whether true or not).

With that in mind, let's look at my picks for the top ten UFO movies of all time:

1. *Close Encounters of the Third Kind* (1977)
    This was a grand tour of ufology, with pre-*X-Files* government conspirators, UFO fanatics, and early abduction themes. Richard Dreyfuss is outstanding as an average guy whose UFO experience turns his life upside down. The railway-crossing scene, where he is burned during a close brush with a UFO, is memorable and taken from narratives of actual close encounter reports.

    The movie is also noted for its attention to detail by people who study UFOs. The French scientist working with the American government is patterned after Jacques Vallee, while noted ufologist Dr. J. Allen Hynek actually makes a cameo appearance during the climactic scene towards the end when the "mother ship" finally lands. The movie's title refers to the most extreme of the UFO encounter categories defined by Hynek in his research: the first kind is a sighting within five hundred feet; the second is a case in which physical traces are noted; the third kind is an encounter that involves contact with aliens.

2. *The Abyss* (1989)
    Unidentified underwater objects (UUOs) turn out to be curious aliens in this movie. Given that much of the Earth is covered by water and much of the oceans' depths are still unexplored in detail, it makes perfect sense that aliens might choose to establish a base on the ocean floor, undisturbed by humans. Again, this is partly based on claims that there are underwater UFO bases off the eastern seaboard, at the bottom of

Lake Ontario, and within the Bermuda Triangle. The stunning effects and cinematography make this film an outstanding first-contact story.

3. *Uforia* (1980)

This is a sadly underrated story of a checkout clerk, played by Cindy Williams, who thinks she's been chosen by aliens to carry their message of peace to the masses. She attracts quite a following, and there is a resemblance to *Elmer Gantry* when her boyfriend begins exploiting her as a contactee who is acting as the aliens' ambassador. But the government seems to be taking her seriously for some reason ...

4. *The UFO Incident* (TV) (1975)

This television version of Fuller's *The Interrupted Journey* has wonderful, low-key, believable performances by Estelle Parsons and James Earl Jones as Betty and Barney Hill. A thoughtful portrayal of the granddaddy of all UFO abductions, this movie accurately portrayed the confusion and angst felt by the Hills as they tried to come to terms with memories of their experience.

5. *Earth Versus the Flying Saucers* (1956)

This was one of the best saucer movies of the 1950s, with excellent special effects for its time, including the frequently seen stock footage of plastic model saucers flying over Washington, D.C. The film portrayed malevolent aliens who were clearly here to take over the planet, using displays of force such as blowing up buildings. The film conveyed the fear and panic that many people expressed regarding the invasion of saucers over the United States in the 1950s, and the military response to the alien menace.

6. *The Day the Earth Stood Still* (1951)

A classic even beyond ufology, this film turns the alien invasion theme on its head. When Klaatu's saucer hovers over Washington, it creates absolute chaos, despite his good intentions. This is a story of hope and peace dashed by our inherent xenophobia, and the inappropriate and unwise use of military force when faced with what we might perceive as a threat to ourselves and our society.

7. *Hangar 18* (1980)

Probably the true forerunner of *The X-Files*, this movie out-Roswelled Roswell, revealing a military base where a crashed saucer is under study. Another example of fiction meeting fact, Hangar 18 was a real location at Wright-Patterson Air Force Base where the debris from a crashed flying saucer from Roswell was allegedly housed. In the movie, when a saucer collides with a NASA vehicle, it's all quickly hushed up because it's election time. Can the heroic astronauts find the saucer in time? Aliens = good. Government = bad. Thrash rock group Megadeth recorded two songs about aliens at Hangar 18, and neither story ended well for the humans.

8. *Communion* (1989)

This very strange film is less a UFO movie than it is a character study of abduction researcher Whitley Strieber. Christopher Walken goes over the top to portray Strieber's dissociation and paranoia when aliens seem to be haunting his life. The ultimate message seems to be that aliens are in complete control and that they will show us only what they want. The movie does convey many elements of abductees' experiences well, especially the multi-layered memories and confusion that are part of some stories.

9. *Fire in the Sky* (1993)

I panned this movie when it first came out, largely because of the end sequences in which Travis Walton is encased in goo, in a scene similar to one from *The Matrix* or *Invasion of the Body Snatchers*. Those scenes were not part of Walton's story, which to me was fantastic enough without Hollywood embellishment. My review led to many conversations with the film's screenwriter, Tracy Tormé, which provided me with insight into how "true" stories get fictionalized. Leading up to the final scenes, the film accurately portrays how UFO case investigations are conducted, and the difficulty in unravelling witnesses' testimony in complicated cases.

10. *The Brother From Another Planet* (1984)

In this low-key but sympathetic movie, the UFO is seen only at the beginning, but the story of an alien dealing with the reality of being stranded on Earth like a fish out of water again underlines our xenophobia. Yes, I liked *E.T.*, which had a similar theme, but this low-budget film gets my vote as a touching, yet powerful statement about our society.

Many other films could have made the list, including (in alphabetical order):

batteries not included (1987)
Cocoon (1985) and *Cocoon: The Return* (1988)
Dreamcatcher (2003)
E.T. (1981)
Escape to Witch Mountain (1975), *Return from Witch Mountain* (1978), and *Beyond Witch Mountain* (TV)(1982)
Flight of the Navigator (1986)
Flying Saucer Daffy (1958)

Foes (1977)
Glitterball (1977)
Independence Day (1996)
Invasion: UFO (1972)
Liquid Sky (1982)
Mars Attacks! (1996)
Men in Black (1997) and *Men in Black II* (2002)
Scary Movie 3 (2003)
Signs (2002)
Space Jam (1996)
Space is the Place (1974)
Spaced Invaders (1990)
Sphere (1998)
Stardust Memories (1980)
Starship Invasions (1977)
Taken (TV) (2003)
The Ambushers (1967)
The Cat From Outer Space (1978)
The Flying Saucer (1950)
The Man Who Fell to Earth (1976)
The Mothman Prophecies (2002)
The Thing From Another World (1951)
The X-Files (1998)
UFO Fever (2002)
War of the Worlds (1953)

A handful of documentaries on UFOs make my must-see list as well. These include:

In Advance of the Landing (1993)
Brilliant movie based on the book by Doug Curran. Basically, the cameras travel the continent filming people obsessed with aliens and UFOs, from Ruth Norman to the members of The Aetherius Society.

Flying Saucers are Real (1979)

Stanton Friedman's documentary ferrets out the facts on UFOs and the Roswell crash, with interviews with the original witnesses. There's also a little-seen biography of Stan titled *Stanton Friedman is Real!* (2002).

Six Days in Roswell (1998)

A film crew visits Roswell for its UFO Days celebrations. This movie does for ufology what the documentary *Trekkies* did for *Star Trek*.

UFOs: Past, Present and Future (1974)

Bob Emenegger's classic documentary that started when he was at Holloman Air Force Base and was shown a film of military UFO encounters. Did this actually happen, or did the United States government set it all up to cover up their ignorance of the subject?

Shag Harbour UFO Incident (TV) (2000)

Mike MacDonald's case study of the crash of something off the coast of Nova Scotia in 1967.

Best Evidence: Top Ten UFO Sightings (2007)

Paul Kimball's interesting examination of the top ten UFO sightings ever reported and investigated, as judged by a panel of ufologists from around the world.

Finally, I must recommend one delightful tongue-in-cheek short film:

Non-Abductees Anonymous (2002)

This is superbly brilliant satire, focusing on a support group for people who want to be abducted by aliens, but haven't. The best line of the movie is spoken as a group member role-playing as an alien tries to explain why he didn't abduct another group member: "I was busy."

TIME, MISSING

One of the first books on alien abductions was *Missing Time* by Budd Hopkins. In the book, Hopkins related the story of a woman who had UFO experiences while in an area he described as Manitoba and northwestern Ontario. Curious, and wanting to help with a case in my own backyard, I contacted Hopkins to see if he needed any assistance. He explained that he had changed the location of the events in order to protect the witness's anonymity and that the encounters did not take place in Manitoba at all. Nevertheless, it was a good chance to speak with a leading researcher on the subject and I was glad I had the opportunity to do so.

My own investigations into UFO abductions have led me to frequently consider the problem of missing time in these cases. Basically, the situation is that aliens somehow take humans out of their environment, spend time examining or talking with them, then take them back home some time later. The abductees, whose memories are tampered with by the aliens, do not recall being away for an extended period of time. In some cases they are told they will not remember their experiences.

The problem I have with this scenario is that abductees *do* remember their experiences — either on their own or with the assistance of hypnosis. If the aliens did not want their human subjects to recall what had transpired, they have failed miserably.

(This notion led me to write a satirical article in 1996 about the apparent incompetence of aliens. I was surprised by the responses I received. Most people enjoyed the humour, but several people berated me for daring to suggest that the Space Brothers were less than omnipotent. The entire work can be found at various sites on the Internet, and was reprinted in my earlier book, *Abductions and Aliens*.)

As noted in the review of the case of Barney and Betty Hill, it was only after some investigation that they realized a period of time was missing from their conscious memories. Since then, it has become almost a given that missing time will be an element in an abduction experience, although there are some exceptions. According to one abduction researcher, one indication that you have had an abduction experience is that you have periods of missing time in your life.

Missing time and memory loss are elements in many abductees' stories. In 1993, Kelly Cahill and her husband were driving home late one night from her girlfriend's home near Melbourne, Australia, when they saw a bright ring of light above a field beside the road. They both initially had conscious recall of seeing the object, but soon after, Kelly's memory faded and she had no recall of events that night. It was only after her memories spontaneously started to re-emerge some time later that the story of their abduction by aliens came back. Kelly went to her girlfriend's home on another occasion and as she drove past a certain spot, she was overcome by a feeling of terror and the memory of much of the experience surfaced. Kelly could still not account for a period of time, and she had to piece together her experience from a series of dreams and later flashes of imagery.

Another example is the case of Alan Godfrey, a police officer who had a strange experience while on patrol in Todmorden, West Yorkshire, in November 1980. Curiously, he had been investigating reports of cattle that had gone missing from their pastures. As he was driving at about five o'clock in the morning, he was surprised to see a large, spinning, car-sized grey object hovering over the roadway ahead of him. He stopped his vehicle to take a look at the object, but just as he began to do so, there was a flash of light and he found himself again driving down the road some distance further. Returning to the spot where he believed he had seen the object, he found a patch that was dry despite the heavy rain that had fallen the night before. When he went back to the police station to make a report, he discovered that about fifteen minutes of his time were missing. Later, through hypnosis, he recalled odd images of a tall, bearded man who spoke about religion, and a group of small robot-like creatures who confronted him while he was in a small room somewhere. Sadly, Godfrey suffered ridicule when his story was made public, and he eventually resigned from the police force.

Psychologists point out that a feeling of missing time can occur with dissociation, a common illusion that occurs as our brains try to multi-task in a repetitive situation. We have all experienced this while driving cross-country, when we realize that we somehow missed a turnoff or do not recall passing through a small town on the interstate. Other examples are getting "lost" while listening to music or reading a book, and being oblivious to your surroundings. Even daydreaming is an example of dissociation. More serious than dissociation are dissociative disorder and dissociative amnesia. A person experiencing dissociative amnesia is unable to remember important personal information, usually associated with a traumatic event, creating gaps in his or her personal history.

Dissociative disorders are usually caused by a major stress in one's life, such as a traumatic event like abuse or an accident. The brain copes with the stress by dissociating or separating the traumatic memories from our consciousness, protecting us from the emotional and physical pain caused by the trauma. These memories are buried within the brain but still exist, and can surface on their own or can be triggered by something.

Although most skeptics argue that alien abductions can be explained as the result of a dissociative disorder, it should be noted that such a disorder could be caused by an actual alien abduction. (In fact, given the shock that something like that had actually occurred, it might even be expected!) The result would be a missing time episode.

While most abduction researchers assume that aliens somehow implant or create the missing time by manipulating abductees' minds, or even by telling abductees that they will not recall the experience, one could speculate that the aliens might be aware that the experience will be traumatic and expect that dissociation will occur as a natural consequence of the event. When aliens tell abductees that they won't remember anything, they may simply be cautioning them that this loss of memory might occur because of the trauma of abduction, and not because they are going to do something to the abductees' brains.

This helps to explain the fact that abductees often spontaneously remember their experiences after undergoing clinical hypnosis and counselling. While memory erasure is something that human researchers are working on, a complete eradication of a specific memory seems difficult unless the brain is damaged, or a section of it is removed.

Missing time would seem to occur to UFO abductees (if they have indeed really been abducted), because it would naturally take a discrete amount of time for an abduction to take place. Physical examinations, talking with the aliens, and other processes would occur at a normal pace and could last several hours.

How aliens might actually abduct people from cars, apartments, or campsites is another issue entirely.

Ufology

In 1959, the term "ufology" was accepted into popular usage and recognized as a word in most dictionaries. *The American Heritage Dictionary* defines ufology in the following way:

ufology
> SYLLABICATION: u · fol · o · gy
> NOUN: The study of unidentified flying objects.
> ETYMOLOGY: UFO + -logy
> OTHER FORMS: ufo · logi · cal (yf-lj-kl) — ADJECTIVE
> u · folo · gist — NOUN

But what is a "study of unidentified flying objects," anyway? Are the objects still there for anyone to study after the fact? The Encarta entry makes this definition a bit clearer:

u · fol · o · gy [yoo fóllcjee] noun
> Definition: study of UFOs: the study of UFOs, especially the investigation of recorded sightings of them.

Ufologists study reports of UFOs, conducting analyses, reviewing literature, examining cases, and speculating on their nature. Ufology encompasses everything associated with the phenomenon, including books, magazines, fans, skywatchers, abductees, government documents, conferences, and on-line discussion groups.

What ufology is not is a separate science unto itself. Although it deals with a specific subject, I would argue that ufology is not a distinct discipline within the broader context of scientific knowledge. However, one can use scientific methodology within ufology to understand and categorize the phenomenon.

I have often said that if UFOs are not a real physical phenomenon, they are at the very least a psychological or sociological phenomenon. UFOs are therefore worthy of scientific study. I believe that a study of UFO reports can provide further insight and understanding about our world and the human condition. In fact, I would charge that it is unconscionable that science has failed to study the phenomenon adequately.

This is not to say that there have not been attempts to do so. The most widely known official American government investigation into UFOs is actually titled "Scientific Study of Unidentified Flying Objects." Although scientists from a variety of disciplines were consulted for their opinions on various aspects of the UFO phenomenon for the study, it concluded that there was no need to further study the issue because there was nothing of scientific interest to be gained by doing so. This would be analogous to suggesting there is no need to further study Shakespeare because, after all, he's dead, or that birdwatchers should hang up their binoculars because we already know that swallows prefer nesting in barns. An analysis of the UFO study found that:

> Most case studies were conducted by junior staff; the senior staff took little part, and the director took no part, in these investigations. The analysis of evidence by categories shows that there are substantial and significant differences between the findings of the project staff and those that the director attributes to the project. Although both the director and the staff are cautious in stating questions, the staff tend to emphasize challenging cases and unanswered questions, whereas the director emphasizes the difficulty of further study and the probability that there is no scientific knowledge to be gained.

The point that the study of UFOs is difficult cannot be overemphasized. In general, ufologists have no funding for their investigations or research.

There is no accrediting body from which a ufologist can obtain credentials or a post-secondary degree in UFO studies. Ufologists tend to be independent and have unique investigative approaches and views on the phenomenon; there is no consensus among ufologists as to what the phenomenon represents. Speculation and theories abound, ranging from ideas that UFOs are alien spacecraft (with some ufologists claiming knowledge of which specific planets they are from), to ideas about UFOs being vehicles piloted by time travellers, ethereal beings from higher dimensions, or spiritual demons. With such diverse beliefs among ufologists, it is no wonder that a "science of ufology" has not been developed.

Within ufology, though, advances are being made and theories tested. Recurring mystery lights near Hessdalen, Norway, are being studied with devices that produce spectrograms that allow interpretation of chemical constituents. Demographics and characteristics of UFO reports are annually catalogued and statistically analyzed by Ufology Research in Canada. Studies on earthquake lights are demonstrating that the energy released by seismic events is not completely understood and may generate moving patches of light in the atmosphere.

I would suggest that other established fields of science, and the topics that are studied within these fields can be examined for questions that might lead to a more rigorous understanding of UFO reports:

Earthquake Lights:
> Geophysicists have been examining reports of luminous phenomena associated with major seismic events. The mechanism for these odd lights is not fully understood, and there are many questions about their propagation, energy source, and movement. Many UFOs are seen near seismically active areas, including those classified as nocturnal lights. Are these actually earthquake lights in disguise?

Earthquake Prediction:
> This follows from the previous paragraph, but is quite a separate issue. Researchers of earthquake precursors

have noted that disparate phenomena may possibly indicate impending seismic events. These include sudden increases in the number of lost pets, electrical interference, and unusual lights in the sky. If these lights are reported as UFOs, then studies of UFOs may have value in helping to formulate and design methods of earthquake prediction. One cannot underestimate the importance of studying possible earthquake precursors.

Tectonic Strain Theory:

Much has been made of a theory proposed by physiological psychologist Michael Persinger that underground crustal strain deep within the Earth causes electromagnetic fields which either: a) affect the brain directly and cause people to think they have been abducted by aliens, or b) create luminous phenomena that are perceived as UFOs by unsuspecting witnesses. Curiously, the theory seems to have few supporters outside of Persinger's Laurentian University laboratory. Other scientists should independently test the theory for its viability; after all, if Persinger is right, his idea has implications well beyond UFOs.

Ball Lightning:

This is another poorly understood and rarely observed natural phenomenon. Some UFO cases may be due to ball lightning discharges. It is only through a detailed examination of UFO data that possible candidates for ball lightning can be located. Geophysicists should be gathering UFO data as a matter of course, trying to learn if plasma discharges can be found often in nature.

Dissociative Disorders:

Dissociative Identity Disorder (DID) has been described in psychological literature as a tendency to have periods of time missing from one's life. This has been used to explain UFO abductions. But what really occurs in DID? How widespread is tuning out in our society? Surely this has implications in many professions, especially if it can account for UFO abductees' experiences.

Fantasy-Prone Personality:

This psychological condition is also sometimes cited as an explanation for abduction experiences. People with such personalities have a tendency to imagine elaborate life scenarios and have, literally, flights of fancy during their waking hours. How prevalent is this trait, and what are the implications in our culture?

False Memory Syndrome (FMS):

This condition is the subject of intense debate. Victims of the FMS defence in a court of law vigorously oppose its use on the grounds that there is no incontrovertible evidence that it exists at all. However, FMS proponents argue that it is a profoundly important phenomenon that may bring criminals to justice, since some people might deliberately implant or manipulate memories in victims for their own reasons. Also, could it be possible that an interrogator might convince witnesses of certain events that they never happened, or that completely different events did?

Perceptual Ability:

Why do people report that stationary nighttime lights such as stars and planets are actually dancing and jumping around? While autokinesis and autostasis are well known to perceptual psychologists, much more study on people's abilities to judge distance, altitude, and movement would be useful for a variety of investigations.

Media Influence:

> The media has always been suspect in its coverage of UFOs. We can still wonder, however, how the advent of tabloid TV and UFO-themed programs like *The X-Files* affect public opinion. And if newspapers are now reporting fewer UFO sightings as news, why are there more UFO reports? (Or are there?)

Group Behaviour:

> What, exactly, are the dynamics of UFO reporting? Can one person's sighting and subsequent report really become contagious and influence others to report banal phenomena as something more mysterious?

Aerospace Development:

> If, as many believe, UFOs represent observations of secret tests of highly advanced technology, then records of such observations can provide avionics experts with information about what and where such technology is under development. Aviation insiders have long been using data from professional aircraft spotters to determine the characteristics of aircraft under development.

Meteoritics

> The search for meteorites is very important to geologists and xenobiologists. Astronomers and meteoriticists await reports of brilliant fireballs in the hope that a recovery may lead to an important find. Some countries have used all-sky cameras to monitor bolides and meteors in order to assist meteorite hunters in their quest for cosmic debris.

Epilepsy Research:

> It has been suggested that some abductees have actually experienced petit mal or even grand mal events and

interpreted them as something more exotic. Are there any indicators that would unequivocally prove that some abduction experiences are caused by epilepsy or temporal lobe epilepsy?

Psychopathology:

John Mack and others insist that abductees are normal with respect to the rest of the population. That is, their MMPI (Minnesota Multiphasic Personality Inventory) and other psychological tests show that they are no different from those who have not claimed abduction experiences. Is this assertion true? Can independent tests on larger samples of the population support this contention?

Belief Systems:

Why is it that UFOs elicit such impassioned debate? Public opinion is highly polarized, and yet people's belief in the reality or non-reality of UFOs seems to be largely unchangeable. Why do skeptics and believers attack one another with such vigour when arguing this subject? Why is a belief or disbelief in UFOs so similar to religious fundamentalism, unlike other subjects that may seem less provocative?

Venusians, V, and Lizard People

There are many similarities between individual UFO reports, and attempts have been made to statistically study UFO report characteristics to get a handle on what a typical UFO case looks like. Yet cases contain enough differences that it is proving difficult to gain a complete understanding of the UFO phenomenon. Some seem to be explainable as misidentifications of ordinary objects. Some seem to have psychological explanations. Others do not seem to have simple explanations at all.

The same can be said about abduction cases. If each abductee reported seeing essentially the same kind of aliens, described the same kind of spaceship, and said that they had received the same imparted message, then the UFO abduction phenomenon would be much easier to accept and understand. Alas, this is not so. Although there are general similarities in abductees' beliefs they were being watched or that they had an experience aboard a spaceship, the details of their accounts vary substantially. Some report aliens with round eyes, some with almond-shaped eyes, and some that are human in appearance. Some aliens are grey-skinned and small in stature, while others are tall, blond-haired, and lanky. Some aliens give abductees unpleasant medical examinations while others take them on tours of heaven. Some pilot flying saucers while others are spiritual travellers on the astral plane and appear not to need any physical transportation. There's even the problem of the mixed-up wisdom imparted to abductees and contactees by supposedly omnipotent extraterrestrials.

As noted earlier, UFO witnesses have rarely reported green-skinned aliens. The grey-skinned variety is most common, although the blonds (or Nordics) are quite popular as well. In the 1950s, contactees almost exclusively described contact with human-like aliens, most often with blond hair. These aliens were usually benevolent, taking people on trips to Mars and Venus, but also commissioning contactees as their intergalactic ambassadors. Their messages for humankind were often admonishments about our pollution of the environment or our inhumane treatment of one another. Chastising us for our nuclear tests was also high on their agenda.

Among the few reports of green-skinned aliens, the most remarkable claims are those made by conspiracy theorist David Icke. In a collection of books, audio tapes, and videos, he has laid out his thesis that lizard-like aliens have infiltrated the population of Earth. He believes that alien reptiles from Draco live inside the Earth and "manipulate humanity from another dimension by 'possessing' human bodies." His oddest claim is that the members of the British royal family belong to the "reptilian Brotherhood," and control much of the free world through corruption and manipulation of governments.

This last idea may have originated with a science fiction television miniseries that later spawned a large following. In *V* (1983), enormous alien flying saucers appear over most major cities on Earth. They are controlled by a race of aliens that look identical to humans and claim that they come in peace, seeking only friendly co-operation and the exchange of ideas. As these apparently benevolent visitors possess superior technology and weaponry, terrestrial governments and military powers quickly agree to co-operate with them. However, journalist Mike Donovan and medical student Julie Parrish discover their real intentions and the disguised reptile appearance of the aliens, and organize a resistance movement against these hostile invaders.

Icke believes he is on a mission to warn everyone on Earth about the global conspiracy between reptilian aliens and terrestrial governments. His claims skirt paranoia, and his anti-government stance has made him a very controversial figure indeed. He goes far beyond where early contactees of the 1950s ventured, stringing together ancient astronauts, UFOs, conspiracies, aliens, and radical fundamentalism.

Despite their superiority, aliens who have accosted contactees have been unable to give them a single clear photograph of their spaceships or to impart some useful knowledge, such as a cure for any specific disease or a new kind of rocket fuel. Contactees, then and now, are resigned to spreading the word through appearances at conventions and on lecture circuits throughout North America. Some early contactees became so popular that they went on speaking tours around the world.

Other contactees claimed that they were aliens incarnated in human form so that they could live and work among us. Contactee Howard Menger not only received communication from aliens, but he even married a Venusian female who took on the appearance of a beautiful woman. Menger revealed that he himself was actually from Saturn and that he had entered his human body when it was only one year old.

Venus appears to be a very popular alien destination and origin. T. Lobsang Rampa, the British mystic who was born Cyril Henry Hoskin, wrote extensively about Tibetan culture and ancient knowledge until it was revealed he did not speak Tibetan or Chinese and had never visited Asia. He wrote a book titled *My Visit to Venus* in which he described how he and other monks were taken up in a flying saucer by two wise aliens and given a tour of Venus's "fairy cities' and a "beautiful sparkling sea." George King thought that Aetherius, the alien he channeled, lived on Venus, and believed that Jesus did as well. Even L. Ron Hubbard, founder of Scientology, described visiting a thetan "implant station" on Venus in one of his religious documents.

Venus has been known as Earth's twin, even though it is much hotter and closer to the sun. Astronomers now know that Venus is completely inhospitable to terrestrial life, with a toxic atmosphere and a boiling surface that makes our own global warming look like an ice age. Because Venus is shrouded in thick cloud, it reflects the sun's light very efficiently and shines brilliantly in the night sky. It was certainly observed by prehistoric humans, and mythologies were developed to explain its appearance. Early astrologers undoubtedly used Venus as a guide, and as a sign of important events. In the Bible, Jesus describes Himself as "the bright and morning star" (Revelation 22:16), an allusion to Venus, which is predominant in the morning (and sometimes evening) sky.

It's no wonder then, that Venus has been the focus of so many UFO-related stories and cases. In fact, Venus is perhaps misidentified as a UFO more often than any other celestial body. Even the military isn't immune from making such a mistaken identity. On December 5, 1963, a rocket was launched from Vandenberg Air Force Base in California at 1:54 p.m. into a clear blue sky. Tracking cameras showed a bright, star-like object "apparently passing the missile," and the UFO seemed to be moving upwards as the rocket headed towards the horizon. Analysis of the film showed that Venus was in the exact location in the sky at that moment, and the Condon Committee explained the UFO conclusively.

In the 1970s, a report was made to Canadian ufologists that police had chased a bright, star-like UFO for dozens of miles along a highway, but the object kept receding and could not be caught by its pursuers, despite speeds of up to 190 kilometres (120 miles) per hour. It was eventually found that the object they pursued was Venus, setting low on the horizon.

Ufologist Allan Hendry related two classic anecdotes about Venus in his major work on ufological investigation: During the Second World War, the USS *Houston* once tried to "shoot down" Venus. According to Hendry, "as the crew fired 250 rounds at the planet, the gunnery officer kept shouting. 'Lengthen your range! Lengthen your range!'" And when asked about odd objects seen by air traffic control officials at Detroit Metropolitan Airport, one FAA officer offered, "Do you know how many times we've cleared Venus to land?"

WATER

Water is a separate listing in "Ufology from A to Z" because many researchers have placed special emphasis on sightings of UFOs on, over, or in the water. Since the Earth is mostly covered by water, it is logical that if UFOs are a truly global phenomenon, a huge number of potential sightings are made over the oceans.

Some UFO buffs have even speculated that aliens might be visiting Earth for its water, since water is a very scarce commodity in the universe. Conditions have to be just right for a planet to retain its hydrogen and oxygen in the amounts necessary for water to form, and even then, it might disappear through climatic evolution as it may have done on Mars. A water-rich planet may indeed be hard to find in the galaxy.

Most evolutionary biologists believe that water was a requirement for life to form on Earth. They believe life evolved through many stages over millions of years, much of it in the oceans, until land-living creatures eventually bred and survived. It took many more millions of years before intelligent life formed relatively recently on the geologic time scale (although I would not be the first to suggest we are still awaiting this development).

If liquid water is necessary for a civilization to develop on a planet, then Earth fits the bill. Furthermore, since astronomers think it's likely that a watery planet like ours is rare, it's all the more reason for aliens to seek us out. In fact, one thing that a moon colony would likely engineer once established to help it become self-sustainable is a way to extract water from moon rocks.

There are, as a matter of fact, UFO cases in which aliens seemed to be taking an extraordinary interest in the Earth's water. One supposedly occurred on July 2, 1950, in Sawmill Bay on Steep Rock Lake in northwestern Ontario, Canada, according to an anonymous writer who sent a letter to a small local newspaper. The story said that an amorous couple was having a picnic when "the air seemed to vibrate as if from shock waves." They looked down at the lake and saw a large object that looked like "two saucers, one upside down on top of the other," floating on the water. On its upper deck was an open hatch, and walking around on top were several small creatures wearing some kind of metallic uniform.

While the creatures went about their business (whatever that was), the witnesses crouched behind a large rock and watched. They noticed a large hoop-shaped antenna rotating slowly on top of the craft, making sure that the coast was clear. At one point a deer walked by the shore near the couple, and the antenna stopped rotating, focusing on the animal. The creatures froze in their tracks but as soon as the all-clear was somehow given, they once again began their work. As the couple watched in amazement, they saw that one of the creatures was holding a green hose that hung down into the lake. A loud humming noise could be heard, and they assumed it meant that the craft was taking on a supply of water. After a while, the couple watched the saucer take off with a blast of air and disappear. Unfortunately, the story was later found to be a hoax.

Nevertheless, stories about UFOs and aliens' interest in water are reported in great numbers. Carl Feindt, a Delaware ufologist, has devoted much of his time to cataloguing and studying reports of water-related UFO cases. His main web page (waterufo.net) is a veritable treasure trove of UFO sightings that occurred in, over, or on the water. He notes:

"Intrigued by the fact that aircraft cannot emerge or submerge into water, I started assembling water-related UFO cases, which has grown into a data base of this aspect of the mystery." Convinced that UFOs are physical alien craft, he notes: "Just as ground traces such as broken tree limbs, swirled grasses, ground imprints and burned plant roots can give us some fleeting clues to the 'operation/field' of these craft, I feel that the observed reaction between the envelope surrounding this craft, and the water, might further our understanding of the principles behind it."

As of October 2, 2007, Feindt had managed to create a huge database of 1,112 water-related UFO cases. These include some very odd reports, many of which are much more substantiated than the Steep Rock non-incident. Canada's version of Roswell, for example, is the Shag Harbour crash of 1967, in which many good witnesses watched an object fall into the Atlantic Ocean off the coast of Nova Scotia.

Many other examples of water-based cases exist on record. On July 15, 1993, the USS *Eisenhower*, an aircraft carrier, was north of Puerto Rico on a routine mission. Two seamen on watch at about three in the morning saw a bright ball of orange light, as "big as the Moon," approach the ship from behind, bathing the flight deck and parked aircraft in an eerie glow. It was completely silent, and was only about seventy-five feet above the water as it flew past the ship. Once it passed the bow, it sped up and shot up into the sky until it was lost to sight.

Late one night in January 1980, ten people watched a disc-shaped object shine a beam of light down onto the Tapajos River in the Brazilian Amazon. They were camping at a beach thirty miles south of Santarem and many were still awake at eleven o'clock when the saucer came towards their campsite, flying about seventy-five feet above the river. It stopped about one hundred feet away from them and shone a beam of light on the surface of the water. It hovered in place briefly, then moved slowly over the river, heading north, parallel to the shore. As it moved, the beam seemed to leave a luminescent trail on the water, which faded after a short time. The object was lost to sight after it had travelled about half a mile.

A curious story about another aircraft carrier was reported in the *Chicago Tribune* in the 1990s. The USS *Midway* was in the Indian Ocean heading for the Gulf of Oman to protect oil tankers that had been under fire in the summer of 1989. One day, an officer in the radar room of the ship saw three strong blips on the screen that moved very far between sweeps and yet maintained a perfect triangular formation. Ruling out high wave crests and low aircraft because of the high speed with which they were travelling, he considered that they were missiles. He contacted another radar operator and learned that no missiles had been launched and no aircraft were in flight at the time.

During the next minute, the blips continued to approach until two of them turned away from the ship, while the third headed directly towards it. The radar officer contacted lookouts on the upper deck of the ship and asked them if they could see the "bogie." But when the blip had come within a mile of the ship, it suddenly vanished from the screen, and the lookouts never saw any object at all. After a few minutes, the blips reappeared at their original starting point, and the entire scenario was repeated. There was no explanation for the incident.

Many other cases of water UFOs could also be listed. While in the middle of the Atlantic Ocean, the famed seagoing explorer Thor Heyerdahl reported seeing a UFO fly along the horizon for several minutes very early one morning in 1970, before it disappeared in a "bright orange flash." Investigators believe the sighting may have been a U.S. Navy missile launch.

In January 2008, it was reported that Lake Erie was a UFO hotspot, and that some people believe that there is an underwater UFO base somewhere offshore. Similarly, people living on the north shore of Lake Ontario have been seeing orbs of light hovering over the water and dropping into the waves near the Toronto Island Airport. This has led some UFO buffs to suggest that there is an underwater alien base near there, too, although it's much more likely that they're seeing the lights of terrestrial craft refracted and reflected off the turbulent water and smog. A typical report can be found at orbwatch.com: "Sunday, January 15, 2006. We saw a lot of 'orbs' in the sky. They appeared to be over or in front of the CN tower and the Toronto skyline as seen from Wilson, NY. We have never seen this before as we are only in that area from time to time. They are not aircraft because we saw airplanes also."

One of the first researchers to specifically name the Great Lakes as "hotbeds of UFO activity" was Ivan T. Sanderson. In *Invisible Residents*, his classic work on water-related UFOs and oddities, he noted that Lake Erie is the best example. He added: "One wonders what goes on in all the millions of lakes around which no people live and which, in the majority of cases, they never visit. Just look at the map of Canada!" The subtitle of his book, a heavily annotated, greatly detailed overview of water-related anomalies, is *A Disquisition Upon Certain Matters Maritime, and the Possibility of Intelligent Life Under the Waters of This Earth*.

Finally, it should be noted that some people have speculated that UFOs are aliens returning to Earth after their continent of Atlantis sunk beneath the waves eons ago. As one writer suggests:

> One popular theory has it that Atlantis was a super-civilization in Earth in some dim epoch of history that was endangered by an impending catastrophe — the advent of an ice age, earthquakes, the gradual shifting of the polar regions, or nuclear war. Whatever the danger, the technologically advanced country attempted to send colonists to another planet, and a few thousand survivors found an Earth-like planet in outer space … If the Atlanteans did escape to another star, they would return periodically to Earth to check up on our progress.

I hope they were not disappointed.

THE X-FILES

One of the most frequent questions I am asked as a ufologist is: "Are you an *X-Files* fan?" I always have to answer, "No."

I watched very little of the popular TV series, mostly because during the nine years it was on the air, I was somewhat busy raising a family, and for much of it I was a single parent. I saw the occasional episode, more during the early seasons when it was a fresh and new concept.

The main premise of the entire series was that the government (or the Syndicate) had formed an allegiance between humans and aliens who wanted to return to Earth as a completion of a colonization program. Fox Mulder was the FBI agent assigned the thankless task of tracking down bizarre incidents that fell outside of ordinary police jurisdiction, such as monsters, mutants, and psychopathic aliens who wanted to play by their own rules. Dana Scully was originally the voice of reason in the investigations, coming up with plausible but incorrect explanations for the cases. She later became a believer and helped Mulder uncover a multi-layered conspiracy at the highest military and official levels that was trying to both stop and aid the invasion.

"I want to believe," the most popular tag line from the series, was featured on posters and other paraphernalia. *The X-Files* was a sweeping homage to conspiracy theories, touching on many paranormal concepts, such as telepathy, mind control, spirit possession, and voodooism. The secret to its success was including parallel story ideas about scientific concepts that were under discussion by media and taken directly from the news and pop culture, such as genetic mutations, Big Brother, implanted tracking devices, advanced weaponry, and of course, UFOs from outer space.

At the root of *The X-Files* is the belief that somewhere there is an office within a classified or secret organization that monitors or investigates reports of UFOs and other strange phenomena. A version of this existed as part of the now infamous Project Blue Book, the U.S. Air Force program that collected and investigated UFO reports. However, Blue Book was nowhere near as well-funded and co-ordinated as the X-files seemed to be. At one point Project Blue Book consisted of a single officer and a secretary at one base; they were barely able to file the cases on hand, let alone carry out extensive investigations. For this reason and others, Blue Book has been considered by some ufologists as only a public relations exercise.

Curiously, Blue Book itself was the topic of a major network television series, *Project UFO*, which ran in 1978 and 1979. The series played up the ability of the air force to solve all the UFO cases it was given in spectacular and sensational fashion; this was done using a *Dragnet*-style approach, underlining that hard facts and cool heads can solve a seeming mystery.

Another precursor to *The X-Files* was the Gerry Anderson British TV series simply called *UFO*. In this show, a super-secret organization is in charge of protecting Earth from invasion by aliens who want to use our bodies for replacement parts. The series ran from 1970 to 1971, and supposedly took place in the future — the 1980s. The mod sets and outlandish costumes made it look very silly, but the actors played it straight and the show featured generally good writing and dramatic effects.

Finally, we must also recall the wildly popular, albeit short-lived TV series, *Invaders*, which ran in 1967 and 1968. On the show, a witness to a UFO landing discovers that "they" really are among us, and he's the only one that knows. The paranoia displayed in this show certainly influenced the writers of *The X-Files*, which carried it to the extreme. For that matter, so did the unsuccessful humorous science fiction series *The Chronicle*, which ran from 2001 to 2002, just as *The X-Files* was winding down. Its premise was that a tabloid newspaper really did publish the truth: aliens, monsters, and Elvis all walk the Earth. It was a version of the well-conceived *Night Stalker* starring Darren McGavin; his character worked at a newspaper, and his employer frowned on his consistently finding ghosts, monsters, demons, and aliens when out on routine news assignments. He usually managed to save the world in the process.

The X-Files built on these and many other TV series. Its producer, Chris Carter, created an intelligent and sophisticated show about paranoia and government conspiracy that was both entertaining and thoughtful. And usually, fun.

Young Children

In parapsychology young children are traditionally more sensitive to phenomena such as ghosts and poltergeists. In fact, poltergeist activity is said to be precipitated or enhanced by children. Whether or not this has any basis in fact, the same has been said about children and UFOs — that they are more apt to see them than adults. One study has suggested that children may see UFOs more often than adults because their attention is drawn to a UFO's high-pitched whining noise which adults have trouble detecting.

It's possible that the reason is more prosaic; because children have less experience observing the sky than adults, more things they see will be mysterious. Of course, children also possess wonder and innocence that gets lost along the way to becoming grown-ups, so perhaps their ability to gaze at a scene and see something delightful is a positive attribute that adults sadly lack.

One collection of stories about children's encounters with UFOs notes that: "Kids have reported incredible incidents in which aliens terrorized them or even kidnapped them for a few horrifying hours. Other kids say they have made contact with friendly aliens who claim they want to help save our planet."

Because children have been the focus of many UFO cases, I have rewritten accounts of some incidents from their standpoint to give a better understanding of the bewilderment they must have experienced. The following cases were taken from the files of UFO investigators:

Almost Kidnapped by a UFO

"You can't catch me!" shouted Diana as she ran between the houses.

"Yes I can!" laughed Peter as he gave chase.

"Me, too!" yelled Brad.

Her skirt flapping in the breeze, Diana disappeared behind a hedge, giggling, with Peter and Brad in hot pursuit.

It was 1967 and the afternoon was hot for Manitoba in June. Everyone in the neighbourhood was taking advantage of the good weather by barbecuing for supper.

Eight-year-old Diana Lipton and her thirteen-year-old brother Brad were playing out in their yard with Peter Valentine and his twin sister Cassie from across the street. Diana and Brad's little sister Becky was playing in a sandbox by herself, sitting in the middle of a mound that used to be a carefully made castle.

"No, Becky," sighed Cassie. "Now look what you've done! It took me a whole hour to build that for you and you sat right on top of it!"

Cassie grabbed a shovel out of Becky's hand and began filling a pail again.

"Now watch how I do this!" she said.

But Becky was offended. She had decided she didn't want any more help, and she shrieked loudly, demanding her shovel back.

"Is everything all right out there?" her mother called, stepping out the back door of their house.

"Yes, Mrs. Lipton," Cassie replied. "We're okay."

"Now, don't get me into any more trouble, like last time," she whispered curtly to Becky

Becky stuck her tongue out and made a triumphant face. "My shovel!" she said, reaching for it as an angry Cassie looked on.

"I hope none of you kids are fighting or anything," said Bonnie Lipton, with her hands planted firmly on her hips. "It's only a half hour or so before our supper and your mother just called, Cassie. Yours is almost ready."

"Yes, Mrs. Lipton," Cassie said, looking at her feet.

"My shovel!" Becky said, nodding.

Bonnie Lipton looked around the yard, squinting in the bright sun. "Where are Diana and the boys?" she asked.

Cassie shrugged. "I dunno. They ran off that way," she replied, pointing.

"Well, you tell them that supper's ready when they come back in the yard," the woman ordered.

Bonnie Lipton went back into the house and started getting plates out of the cupboard. Her husband, Gord, should have been home by now, since he insisted on lighting the barbecue. He claimed he had a special technique for getting the coals to just the right temperature, and that his burgers tasted so good because of his expertise.

She smiled thinking of the last time he barbecued, when the expert accidentally singed his favourite fishing hat.

Suddenly, an odd sound filled the room. It seemed to be a slow, beeping noise, starting quietly but gradually getting louder.

Bonnie went over to the radio, but it was off. She checked in the living room and walked up to the television set, but it was off too. The sound was still there. She twisted the TV dial and heard the familiar click as it came on. No, that wasn't it.

She looked around, but couldn't figure out where the unusual sound was coming from. Then she looked out the kitchen window.

She let out a small gasp, raising a hand to her mouth.

Dirt, leaves, and other debris were flying by the window, as if there was a hurricane outside. She turned and looked out a window in a different part of the house and saw that the wind was there too. It was whipping around the house in a counter-clockwise direction.

It's like there's a tornado over our house, she thought to herself.

Running outside, she found herself inside a whirlwind centred on the house. Her hair was blown into her face and dirt stung her eyes. "Becky!" she yelled above the sound of the rushing wind.

*　　*　　*

When they had turned the corner of the house, Peter and Brad had nearly caught Diana in the front yard. She veered suddenly, taking them by surprise and forcing Brad to stop and turn. Peter ran headlong into him, and the two of them fell unceremoniously into a hedge.

"Owww!" Peter cried in pain, a bloody scrape starting to appear on his knee.

"Ha!" Diana gloated as she stopped on the driveway watching them. "You missed!"

"Why you little … " Brad began, ready to give chase again. But he stopped and looked up into the sky. "Diana, what's that above you?" he said, perplexed.

But she wasn't going to fall for that old trick. "Oh, no you don't, Brad Lipton," she said defiantly. "You're not going to get me that way!"

A strong wind had suddenly started blowing. Her hair and clothes were flapping in the draft. Dirt blew into her face and she began coughing. She started to turn and run, but found that her legs didn't want to work.

"Wha … what's happening?" she stammered.

Peter forgot about his injury and stood up, pointing. "What is that thing?" he asked.

Diana was starting to get frightened. Try as she might, she couldn't seem to run away. Panicking, she looked up.

There, not more than twenty feet above her head, was a huge cube-shaped object, with alternating silver and black sides. Its bottom surface was very black, as if she was looking inside a box, and the entire thing was slowly rotating counter-clockwise. It seemed as if the strange object was somehow causing the wind to blow. Dust and old newspapers were being tossed in the air, swirling in a giant circle around them.

Without warning, Diana felt herself getting lighter and she was shocked to find that her feet were no longer touching the driveway.

"Help!" she screamed as she rose towards the cube.

That was enough to spur the boys into action.

"Hey! Let go of her!" Brad shouted. He glanced down and found a large rock near the driveway and carefully took aim. He threw it as hard as he could towards the cube, but it had already started to rise and he fell short of his target. In fact, Diana was already three feet in the air and her clothes were being pulled up on her body as if she was being sucked up by a vacuum cleaner.

"I'll get her!" Peter said and ran towards her. In his best imitation of a defensive football player, he launched himself in the air and tackled Diana around her knees. He held on tight, and felt a strong tug that suddenly released them both. They both fell, sprawling onto the grass.

* * *

Gord Lipton was nearly home, driving along his street when he noticed that the wind had picked up considerably. "That's funny," he said aloud.

"The weather forecast said it was going to be calm and clear today."

When he pulled into his driveway, he saw Peter, a boy who lived across the street, laying on top of Diana in the yard. Then he saw Brad pile on top, too.

He stopped the car and rolled down the window. Dirt and leaves blew in. "What's going on?" he demanded.

In answer, Brad pointed into the sky. "Look at that thing," he said, trembling.

As he opened the car door, a shout made him turn away.

"What's happening?" said Cassie, with Becky in tow. "We heard Diana screaming."

"That thing was sucking her up into the air," Peter offered, shaking and still in shock.

Gord Lipton noted the two boys were ghostly white, trembling, and very scared. Obviously something very odd had occurred.

He turned his gaze upward and saw a peculiar box-like object hanging in the air, and moving slowly away from them. It looked hollow on the bottom. It didn't look like any aircraft or helicopter he had ever seen. As it flew further away, the wind died down.

"What the heck is that?" he wondered aloud.

He ran over to Diana as the boys stood up. "Diana," her father pleaded. "Say something. Are you alright?"

Dazed, Diana blinked her eyes and moaned softly. "What's going on?" she asked after a while, looking at the small crowd that had gathered around her. "Why am I on the ground? Did Peter catch me?"

* * *

Bonnie Lipton ran out from around the house. "Becky! Diana! I was calling for you! Are you all right?" she exclaimed, nearly out of breath. She looked down at Diana. "I was worried you were all outside in that wind," she said, with worry in her voice.

"What wind?" asked little Becky.

Sure enough, the wind had died down as the object ascended, and the air was once again still and silent. The strange craft was now tilted at a forty-five-degree angle and was flying away over the trees and neighbouring houses. As they all watched, it moved soundlessly away and eventually disappeared in the distance.

"Diana, what was it like being in the air like that?" asked her brother.

Still a bit dazed, Diana frowned and looked at him, glassy-eyed. "What do you mean?" she replied. "You were chasing me and I fell."

Brad's eyes widened. "Don't you remember being sucked up?" he asked, incredulous. "Peter had to grab you and pull you back down!"

Horrified, she shook her head. "No, all I know is that it suddenly got very windy," she said. "But … how did everyone get here? I don't remember Dad getting home."

Her father called to them all. "Look at this," he said, pointing to the ground near the house when they walked over to him. "There's a big circular area of dirt and leaves around our house, but nothing on anyone else's yard. And I just raked yesterday."

"It's like a big dome of some sort was over top of us," said his wife, puzzled.

*　　*　　*

Later, they checked with other neighbours and found no one else had seen or heard the whirlwind. No one had seen the cube. And no one else had seen Diana's levitation.

The airport had no record of any aircraft being in the vicinity that afternoon and no other unusual objects had been reported. Investigators could not find any explanation for the case.

Only Brad and Peter had seen Diana almost kidnapped by a UFO.

ATTACKED BY ALIENS

It was almost dark, but Lorenzo Flores and Jesus Gomez were determined to shoot a rabbit that night. They had been out hunting all afternoon and were hot and tired from climbing across the rocky outcrops of the paramos, the swampy highlands along the Andes Mountains in southern Venezuela.

The sun had set a short time ago, but they still thought they could catch something before it got too late, even if was only a small ground squirrel.

That afternoon, December 10, 1954, they had walked out of their village near Chico and followed the Transandean Highway for a few miles until they decided they were in a good hunting spot. Then they marked their entry point carefully before heading into the bush.

Now, they were nearing the highway again as they retraced their trail. Both were good trackers and knew they value of safety in the wilderness. Only once had they become lost and that was a long time ago, before they had learned to take more care and blaze their trail carefully.

Jesus, with his rifle slung on his back, was in the lead now as he usually was, always wanting to be the first in everything. He was also the older of the two, having just turned sixteen. His tall frame allowed him to take bigger strides and maybe that's why his companion seemed to fall behind so much.

But Lorenzo, although a year younger, was easily a match for Jesus's speed. He was nearly a foot shorter, but was extremely agile and nimble and able to dart among the rocks and spiny cacti with ease.

Jesus stopped when he reached the highway and sat down on a flat rock beside the road. "Come on," he shouted to Lorenzo, "I think there's a truck coming. Maybe we can get a ride back home."

Lorenzo walked into sight and looked down the road. "Oh, are you too weak to walk?" he jibed. "You should have eaten more lunch today!"

Jesus grinned and said, "No, I'm fine. I was worrying more about you having to carry your rifle much longer!"

He ducked when Lorenzo kicked some dirt at him. Jesus knew Lorenzo was very proud of his new rifle. He had just bought it with money he had earned by selling birds and monkeys to pet store buyers from America. It had taken him a year to get the amount the cantina store manager wanted for the gun. He did not have a sling for it, but carried it carefully, only occasionally letting it out of his grasp when resting it gently against a tree.

"So where is this truck?" Lorenzo asked, impatiently. He was unhappy about not catching a rabbit that day and wanted nothing more than to go home to bed.

Jesus looked down the road to where he thought he had seen a set of headlights. "That's funny," he said. "I was sure there was something on the road there." He squinted, but could not see any light on the roadway. There was another light, just off to the side, not far off the highway. "There. What's that?"

Lorenzo looked to where Jesus was pointing at a light that seemed to be in some low trees not far away. The yellow glow seemed to be getting brighter and was shimmering, as if it were underwater. "Come on!" he shouted excitedly. "Maybe a truck ran off the road and the people need help!" He grabbed his rifle and started running down the road, this time in the lead.

Jesus ran after him, finding some new energy through his excitement. He remembered that two years ago a bus had turned over near there and many people were hurt in the accident.

The boys almost flew down the dirt road, following its snaking path over gently rolling hills until they reached a point that was nearest to the light.

"Look here," Lorenzo said. "There's no tire tracks or any sign that something drove off the road into the trees."

Jesus agreed. "But what else could the light be? No one lives near here."

"Perhaps a night spirit," Lorenzo replied with a big grin. "Your mother is always talking about such things!"

Jesus laughed, but then became serious. "Maybe an airplane crashed! Let's find it, then we can go for help."

"Good idea."

The two walked into the brush and started weaving their way towards the source of the light. After only a few minutes, they came upon a clearing. They froze in total shock at what they saw.

There before them was a shiny, metallic object that looked like two soup bowls joined rim to rim. It was as large as a car and seemed to be hovering about three feet above the ground. The strange thing was glowing and there was an orange flame coming from somewhere underneath it.

"What is this thing?" whispered Lorenzo, very scared.

Jesus could barely answer. "I don't know! I've never seen any pictures of airplanes that look like this!"

They both stood watching the object, unable to move because of their fear. Suddenly, things got much worse!

Four small creatures came out from behind the craft and started coming towards them. The beings looked like small men, were only about three feet tall, and were covered with long dark hair. Their eyes were huge, round discs the size of saucers, and they stared at the boys with an unnerving quality. The creatures had long, thin arms. Their hands had four fingers with long, sharp claws, like a hawk. As they came towards the boys, the monsters reached out to them with their talons.

Although frightened, Jesus and Lorenzo snapped out of their frozen panic and realized they were in danger.

"Run!" screamed Lorenzo.

They both turned and started scrambling back the way they had come. Lorenzo strode quickly between some shrubs and rocks and was making some headway when he heard a cry behind him. He looked back just in time to see Jesus stumble and fall. "Jesus!" he shouted! "Get up! They're right behind you!"

He watched helplessly as Jesus tried to regain his footing, but it was too late. The creatures reached Jesus and bent over him.

"Aiieeee!" Jesus cried when the beings stretched their arms towards him.

Lorenzo sprang into action to save his friend. He ran back to where the creatures had Jesus pinned on the ground. Even though they were small, they appeared to have great strength. The five of them were too much for Jesus to handle. One of the beings had Jesus in a headlock while the other four were trying to hold on to his legs and arms. Jesus was putting up a good fight, flailing his limbs and managing to get them with some kicks.

The creature that had its arms around Jesus's head was making some low, snarling sounds. His mouth was open slightly and Lorenzo could see some sharp teeth inside.

"Get away from him!" Lorenzo shouted angrily. "Let him go!"

He grabbed the arm of the one closest to him. Its hairy body was well muscled, despite its size, and it fought Lorenzo off easily. It pushed him away with a strength Lorenzo had never seen before.

The other beings did not take any notice of him, but continued attacking his friend. One had a firm grip on Jesus's leg now, and they all started dragging the struggling boy towards the strange craft.

Looking around on the ground for something to hit them with, Lorenzo realized his rifle was not far away, where he had dropped it among some small shrubs. He ran to where it lay and picked it up quickly.

Lorenzo held up the rifle. He realized it was not loaded and that by the time he was able to get ammunition into the chambers, it might be too late. But — he could still use it as a weapon!

He moved behind the creature who had Jesus's head and raised his gun in the air, holding it by the shaft. The hairy dwarf took no notice of him. He brought the rifle down hard on the monster's head.

The rifle broke in two, as though it had struck a rock or something very solid. The creature let out a loud yelp and let go of Jesus, who slumped to the ground. The others stopped trying to pull Jesus with them and also let him go. They all turned to look at Lorenzo, who had a desperate expression on his face and was brandishing what was left of his gun.

"Get away, I said!" ordered Lorenzo. "I'll take you all on!"

The creatures seemed to confer with each other soundlessly, and then started running back through the bush to the craft.

Lorenzo, not bothering to wonder why they did that, bent over Jesus, who was now unconscious. He slapped his face gently, saying, "Jesus! Jesus!"

Jesus started moaning and moving his head from side to side. He was scratched on his face and arms and his shirt was ripped and torn in several places. Lorenzo looked down at his own clothes and saw that his shirt had also been torn by the creatures' claws.

He heard a loud roar and looked up to see the strange craft rise into the air. It paused for a moment, glowed a brilliant white, then zipped away across the hills, almost too fast to follow. In a few seconds, it was gone, leaving the boys alone in the bush, with only the sounds of the night to keep them company.

* * *

"I'd say you had a run-in with a wild boar," said Dr. Mendez after dressing Lorenzo's wounds.

After Jesus had recovered, he and Lorenzo had slowly trekked back to their village, where their worried parents were waiting for them. Upon seeing their condition and hearing their bizarre tale, the local doctor was called.

"But Papa," Lorenzo insisted, "it did happen! Those creatures attacked us and were going to take Jesus with them!"

His father frowned and turned to Jesus, whose own family was in the same room. Since the boys returned, they had been hysterical and told their families their wild story about flying ships and little monsters. It was all he and Lorenzo's mother could do to calm them down, and Jesus's parents were just as puzzled by their son's behaviour. Neither boy had ever acted this way before, or made up tall tales.

"Is this true?" he asked the boy. "Were there really any small little men?"

Jesus had many bruises, and blood was oozing from several deep gouges on his arms and legs. He was no longer dazed, but was very adamant that his experience had been real. "Yes!" he said firmly. "I was fighting with them, but then I must have blacked out. I don't remember how they left. I was sure I was going to be taken by them!"

"Ridiculous!" the doctor snorted. "You two are lying! There are no such things as hairy dwarves or flying craft like you described!"

"We'll prove it!" Jesus shouted. "We'll take you there and show you!"

"Yes, right now!" Lorenzo chimed in.

Lorenzo's father thought for a minute, then turned to the other boy's father. "What do you say, Hector?" he asked. "Shall we go now?"

Hector Gomez nodded immediately. "Yes, but only if the doctor goes with us too!"

Mendez stood up. "All right!" he exclaimed. "If only to prove there is nothing to this foolishness!" He added, "But let's get the police sergeant to come with us, too."

"Yes, good idea!" said Lorenzo. "He can protect us if they come back!"

Dr. Mendez was startled by the boy's remark. He was sure threatening to bring the police along would make the boys change their story and own up to the truth.

A small army of people from the village went out to the spot that night. All were able to see crushed grass and disturbed dirt where there had obviously been a struggle of some sort. There were even long gouges in the earth that might have been made by the heels of a young boy's shoes as he was dragged along the ground.

What's more, they found pieces of Lorenzo's gun. The wood had shattered from some impact and the metal was twisted.

But there was no sign of the creatures or the unusual flying craft.

*   *   *

"I don't know what to think of this," said Hector Gomez to Lorenzo's father when the group had returned to the village. The men were sitting in the kitchen, talking about the incident. "Why would they make up such a story?"

"I don't know," was the reply. "Lorenzo has never been this upset before. And how do you explain their injuries?"

Dr. Mendez coughed. "I still say they made it all up. There is one thing that bothers me."

"What is that?" Hector asked.

The doctor thought for a minute before answering. "Did you not say Lorenzo had saved all his money to buy that rifle?" he asked aloud. "Was it not his most valued possession?"

"Yes it was."

"Then why would he deliberately break it just to support a tall tale?" Mendez wondered.

Zoo

"I think we're property."

So goes a famous quote from Charles Fort, an eccentric recluse who spent much of his life collecting news clippings about strange and wondrous events happening around the world. He gathered documented cases of frogs falling from a clear sky, out-of-place artifacts, strange objects seen by astronomers and meteorologists, squid swimming in upstream rivers, and stories about people's bizarre talents. An entire subculture of Forteans sprung following his death in 1932. There are newsletters, conventions, and a major magazine, *Fortean Times*, which carries on his chronicling of weird phenomena.

During his lifetime, Fort accumulated a huge amount of information, classified and categorized in myriad ways. The strangeness spurred him to write several books that speculated on what it all means in the grand scheme of things. His first book, *The Book of the Damned*, made a huge impression when it was published in 1919, shocking some people with its frank and tangential style of freely bouncing from one thought to another without apparent logic. "By the damned, I mean the excluded," Fort wrote in the way of explanation. "A procession of data that science has ignored."

He was of the opinion that the universe held many wonders, at least one of which was extraterrestrial life. And he, too, pondered the reason why "they" didn't just come out and make themselves known:

> The greatest of mysteries: Why don't they ever come here, or send here, openly?
>
> Why not missionaries sent here openly to convert us from our barbarous prohibitions and other taboos, and to prepare the way for a good trade in ultra-bibles and super-whiskeys…
>
> The answer that occurs to me is so simple that it seems immediately acceptable…
>
> Would we, if we could, educate and sophisticate pigs, geese, cattle? Would it be wise to establish diplomatic

relations with the hen that now functions, satisfied with mere sense of achievement by way of compensation?

I think we're property. I should say we belong to something. That once upon a time, this earth was No-man's Land, that other worlds explored and colonized here, and fought among themselves for possession, but that now it's owned by something:

That something owns this earth — all others warned off.

Fort's exposition was considered "way out" in 1919, as it still is today. What's interesting is that even in scientific examinations of the Fermi Paradox, the possibility that the Earth is a galactic zoo is actually given some consideration. In a remarkable recent meta-analysis of the possibility of contact with extraterrestrial life, futurist and diplomat Michael Michaud listed more than a dozen reasonable explanations why we don't see any incontrovertible and obvious evidence of aliens. Michaud explained: "If an alien presence is in our Solar System, it may be deliberately hidden. Extraterrestrials could be monitoring or studying us without revealing themselves. We may be in an anthropological research area, a preserve, a wilderness, or a zoo; we may be under quarantine; we may be in a sphere of influence that excludes others." He further notes: "Some extraterrestrial civilizations may observe a principle of noninterference toward less powerful intelligences because contact might wreck their usefulness as suppliers of unique information, or for ethical reasons."

This last point is, of course, the *Star Trek* scenario. Although a science fiction concept, the prime directive as formulated in the *Star Trek* universe is in fact based on standard anthropological rules and guidelines about being careful not to interfere with your subjects' natural development and culture. Now, one could easily argue that if there was a Martian or Reticulian version of these terrestrial principles governing the limits of contact with humans, then the aliens appear to have violated their own ethical standards. We are definitely conscious of some kind of alien contact, whether it is real or speculative. They haven't done a good job of hiding themselves from us, if that was their intent.

IF YOU SEE A
UFO

POLLS HAVE INDICATED ABOUT 10 PERCENT OF ALL NORTH Americans have seen UFOs, and there is reason to think that the same percentage would be true for the rest of the world. If so, you're not alone if you believe you have seen a UFO. Chances are that if the topic of UFOs was raised in a group of people at a dinner party, in a pub, a church meeting, or a family gathering, at least a few individuals would admit to having seen an unidentified flying object at one time in their lives. Several more would say they had friends or acquaintances who had seen UFOs, and nearly everyone in the room would have an opinion on the subject one way or another.

Suppose you were on a long driving trip or were camped out in a field late at night, and were looking up at the heavens. Suddenly, you see a bright light moving across your view, looking different from other objects with which you are familiar. What would you do?

If you are like most people, you would do nothing. You would likely say, "It's just one of those things," and leave it at that. Others would point the object out to a companion or someone nearby, and they would watch together, perhaps commenting on it. Some would be completely fascinated by the sighting and make mental note of the time and exact location, and perhaps details of the object's physical appearance, its shape, colour, and direction of movement.

Maybe you would be one of the 10 percent of all UFO witnesses who would actually go to the trouble of reporting your sighting, either by phone to a local authority or through an e-mail to a UFO organization.

Without records of people's observations of UFOs, proper investigation cannot be done. Your sighting may be explainable as an interesting astronomical event, or a secret military aircraft test, or a natural, rare geophysical phenomenon. Without reporting it, without investigation and without research, we would never know. Your UFO would always remain a mystery. Even with investigation, a definitive answer may not be possible, but at least your report would allow researchers to compare it with other cases from around the world, helping to piece together the puzzle that is the UFO phenomenon.

Please consider reporting your UFO sighting to: myuforeport@gmail.com.

Provide some details of what you have seen, including:

1. Date of sighting.
2. Time you first saw the object(s).
3. Time you last saw the object(s).
4. How long the object(s) was/were in sight.
5. What direction you were looking when you first saw it/them.
6. What direction were you looking when you lost sight of it/them.
7. Where were you? (i.e. what town or where in a city?)
8. How did the object(s) move, if at all?
9. Describe what the object(s) looked like.
10. What was the weather like at the time?
11. Did anyone else see this with you? (Have him or her or them provide details too.)
12. In your own words, describe your UFO sighting, including any information that you think would be relevant or important. Draw the object(s), if possible, even if just a rough sketch.

That's it. That's all that is needed for a preliminary UFO sighting report. You may have additional details, such as sounds you may have heard, whether or not animals noticed the UFO, or if you felt anything else out of the ordinary. But the information given in response to the questions above would be enough for an investigator to go on, at least initially.

This kind of information is considered private. We understand that some people are hesitant to come forward with information on their UFO sightings, fearing ridicule or awkward questions from friends or family. Normally, your name and contact information are required so that a follow-up can be done if it seems like the case warrants further investigation. Also, if you live near a good investigator, your contact information should be passed on to him or her so that you can be reached for possible follow-up. Unless you specifically give permission for an investigator to do so, your name will not be released to news media by an investigator. Details of what was seen, but not who saw it, will often be given to other UFO researchers or investigators so that comparisons can be made with other cases and studies can be conducted.

Ufology Research is a non-profit, volunteer association of ufologists and other interested researchers who co-operate in research and discussion to better understand the UFO phenomenon. Ufology Research can be contacted at: myuforeport@gmail.com.

Other places where you can report a UFO sighting:

1. Your local police
2. The FBI
3. The Center for UFO Studies: www.cufos.org
4. The Mutual UFO Network: www.mufon.com
5. The National UFO Reporting Center: www.ufocenter.com
6. UFOINFO: www.ufoinfo.com
7. The Houston, British Columbia, Centre for UFO Research: www.hbccufo.org

Where to Look
For More Information

IF YOU WANT MORE INFORMATION ABOUT UFOs, THERE IS
no dearth of sources or resources. Libraries have shelves full of books on
the subject, and there are literally millions of web pages on the Internet
that can be found using the search term "UFO." Because web pages
appear and disappear so quickly, it would be inappropriate to provide a
list of them for you to check out. Similarly, it may be frustrating to search
for books from a list because many excellent volumes are either out of
print or difficult to find.

Having said that, the bibliography at the end of this book lists many
books and links to web pages that were used in the preparation of these
chapters. I would urge you to seek them out if you have additional
questions or are perplexed by what you have read.

I would also recommend an excellent on-line resource that is
accessible to anyone who is interested in the subject of UFOs. Ufologist
Isaac Koi has compiled a large collection of on-line resources and web
pages, as well as downloadable books and articles that will help casual
readers appreciate and understand the complex UFO phenomenon. His
site is called "Free UFO Researcher Starter Pack," and can be found at
abovetopsecret.com.

LAST WORDS

NONE OF THE UFO CASES DESCRIBED IN THIS BOOK HAVE been made up; they come from an assimilation of information from other sources or from actual cases from investigators' files. Some information has come directly from the files of Ufology Research of Manitoba (UFOROM), now usually just called Ufology Research.

I would like you to consider reading materials that represent both sides of the UFO phenomenon. Although most thorough UFO researchers consider all possible explanations before making claims about UFO cases, it is best to get other opinions. Seek out critical comments about the claims and the cases, but do not be quick to explain away evidence simply because the alternate explanations *sound* scientific and rational. That would be like a Republican politico hearing a Democrat's party platform and then quickly jumping on the Democratic bandwagon. An appropriate position or response might be one or the other, a mixture of the two, or neither.

It's one thing for someone to pronounce that UFOs are alien spaceships, or that they are all misidentifications. It is another thing for that person to prove his point, and simply citing opinion or presenting arm-waving arguments isn't enough. Don't always believe the believers, but also be skeptical of skeptics.

I would encourage you to do some research of your own — gather information, explore ideas, debate issues, and talk with others about aspects of the UFO phenomenon that you find interesting. Ultimately, some of the questions that will arise will be about our own world, our place in the universe, and understanding our place within a world of UFOs.

CONFIDENTIAL

SUMMARY OF INFORMATION	DATE 17 Nov 49

PREPARING OFFICE

Field Area Office #5, W. Jackson, Miss. , 111th CIC Detachment

SUBJECT

"FLYING SAUCER" - Seen Near University of Miss. Campus, Oxford, Miss.

CODE FOR USE IN INDIVIDUAL PARAGRAPH EVALUATION

OF SOURCE:		OF INFORMATION:	
COMPLETELY RELIABLE	A	CONFIRMED BY OTHER SOURCES	1
USUALLY RELIABLE	B	PROBABLY TRUE	2
FAIRLY RELIABLE	C	POSSIBLY TRUE	3
NOT USUALLY RELIABLE	D	DOUBTFULLY TRUE	4
UNRELIABLE	E	IMPROBABLE	5
RELIABILITY UNKNOWN	F	TRUTH CANNOT BE JUDGED	6

SUMMARY OF INFORMATION

On 16 Nov 1949, at about 0915 hours, a cylindrical object, judged to be between 30 and 50 feet long, was sighted by three farmers, J. J. Brite, James A. Brite, and Carl Flanagin, a general store manager, Mr. Alex Coffey, and a housewife, Mrs. Ruth Gilmer. This object was sighted between Oxford, Miss. and Batesville, Miss. on the route of Miss. Highway #6, and was reported to be flying at an altitude of about 200 feet, traveling at a speed of approximately 30 miles per hour. All five of the above named individuals agreed on the approximate size and the shape of said object, and reported that it looked like a "beam of light that stayed level all the time". Informants also stated that this object gave off an exhaust that had the appearance of phosphorus. The weather was a clear, bright day. (c-3)

A check with authorities of the Civil Aeronautics Administration, Jackson, Miss. failed to reveal any further information re the above sighted object. According to Mr. George Fish, Official in Charge, U. S. Weather Station, Jackson, Miss., it is very improbable that object sighted was any of the various instruments sent up by the weather bureau to test weather conditions, etc., provided that object was anywhere near the size it was described to be by those who saw same. (B-2)

1. A USAF file on a cylindrical "flying saucer" seen near Oxford, Mississippi, on November 16, 1949.

UNCLASSIFIED

DETAILS:

1. This investigation was initiated by the District Commander, 9th OSI District (IG), Barksdale AFB, La., upon receipt of clipping from the Times-Picayune newspaper, New Orleans, La., indicating that Mr E.N. FOLSE had sighted an unconventional aircraft in the vicinity of Raceland, La., on 18 November 1949.

AT RACELAND, LOUISIANA:

2. Mr E.N. FOLSE, a retired insurance agent of Raceland, La., advised during an interview that at approximately 0930 hours, 18 November 1949, he had observed an object in the skies from a point approximately one mile south of Raceland, La. The "Essential Elements of Information" obtained from Mr. FOLSE are included in Paragraph #3.

3. ESSENTIAL ELEMENTS OF INFORMATION:

    a. Date of sighting: Friday, 18 November 1949
    b. Time of sighting: 0930 hours
    c. Where sighted: The object was sighted in the air from a point on the ground approximately one (1) mile south of Raceland, Louisiana.
    d. Number of objects: One (1)
    e. Distance of object from observer: Observer was unable to determine or estimate, due to lack of experience in such matters
      (1) Angle of elevation from horizon: Observer unable to determine or estimate due to lack of experience in such matters
    f. Time in sight: Approximately thirty (30) minutes
    g. Appearance of object:
      (1) Color: Shiny, aluminum type appearance
      (2) Shape: Similar to fuselage of aircraft, without protruding appendages of any type. (See attached sketch, labeled Exhibit "A".) Observer insisted object was not a blimp or dirigible.
      (3) Apparent construction: Unable to establish though appeared to be similar to aircraft.
      (4) Size: Estimated larger than large cargo type aircraft.
    h. Direction of flight: Southwest when first observed, executed 90 degree turn to Northwest, then another 90 degree turn to Northeast and proceeded in that direction until disappearance.
    i. Tactics or maneuvers: Object proceeded on level plane except when executing turning maneuver. Tail section seemed to be split when object entered turning maneuver. (See attached sketch.)
    j. Evidence of exhaust: No exhaust was observed.
    k. Effect on clouds: No clouds were in the area at the time of sighting.
    l. Lights: No lights were visible. Object was observed in daylight hours.
    m. Support: No wings or any other type of support were discernible.

UNCLASSIFIED

2. USAF file on a tadpole-shaped object seen on November 18, 1949, near Raceland, Louisiana.

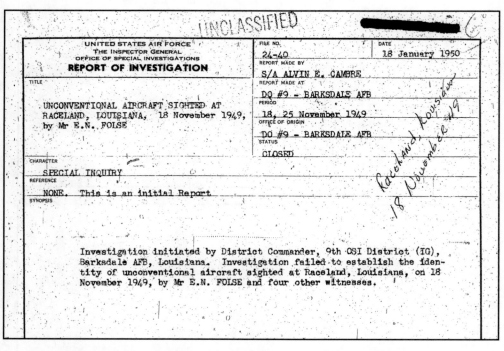

UNCLASSIFIED

UNITED STATES AIR FORCE	FILE NO.	DATE
THE INSPECTOR GENERAL OFFICE OF SPECIAL INVESTIGATIONS	24-40	18 January 1950
REPORT OF INVESTIGATION	REPORT MADE BY	
	S/A ALVIN E. CAMBRE	
TITLE	REPORT MADE AT	
	DQ #9 - BARKSDALE AFB	
UNCONVENTIONAL AIRCRAFT SIGHTED AT RACELAND, LOUISIANA, 18 November 1949, by Mr E.N. FOLSE	PERIOD	
	18, 25 November 1949	
	OFFICE OF ORIGIN	
	DQ #9 - BARKSDALE AFB	
	STATUS	
	CLOSED	
CHARACTER		
SPECIAL INQUIRY		
REFERENCE		
NONE. This is an initial Report		
SYNOPSIS		

Raceland, Louisiana
18 November '49

Investigation initiated by District Commander, 9th OSI District (IG), Barksdale AFB, Louisiana. Investigation failed to establish the identity of unconventional aircraft sighted at Raceland, Louisiana, on 18 November 1949, by Mr E.N. FOLSE and four other witnesses.

3. USAF report noting investigators could not "establish the identity" of the "unconventional aircraft" seen near Raceland.

4. Witness's sketch of metallic object seen over Raceland, Louisiana, in 1949.

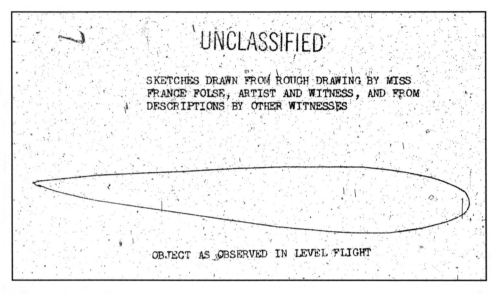

UNCLASSIFIED

SKETCHES DRAWN FROM ROUGH DRAWING BY MISS
FRANCE FOLSE, ARTIST AND WITNESS, AND FROM
DESCRIPTIONS BY OTHER WITNESSES

OBJECT AS OBSERVED IN LEVEL FLIGHT

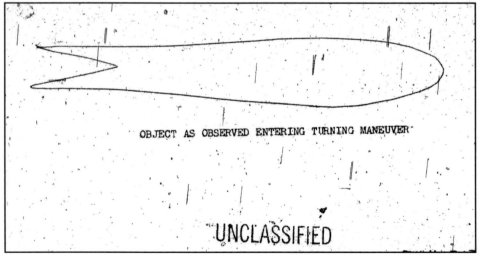

OBJECT AS OBSERVED ENTERING TURNING MANEUVER

UNCLASSIFIED

5. Side view of object seen near Raceland, Louisiana, in 1949.

SOURCES

THE ROSWELL CRASH

Author unknown. "The Walter G. Haut Affidavit." *UFO Updates*, 2007. http://www.virtuallystrange.net/ufo/updates/2007/jul/m01-007.shtml (accessed January 17, 2008).

Author unknown. "1947 Roswell UFO Incident." Undated. http://www.ufoevidence.org/documents/doc384.htm (accessed May 1, 2007).

Air Force Web Information Service. "Air Force News Special Report. Roswell Report: Case Closed." June 24, 1997. http://www.af.mil/library/roswell/ (accessed May 1, 2007).

Berlitz, Charles, and William Moore. *The Roswell Incident*. London: Granada, 1981.

Carey, Thomas, and Donald Schmitt. *Witness to Roswell: Unmasking the 60-year Cover-Up*. Franklin Lakes, NJ: Career Press: 2007.

Friedman, Stanton, and Don Berliner. *Crash at Corona: The U.S. Military Retrieval and Cover-Up of a UFO*. New York: Paragon, 1992.

Hardy, Rufus. "Famous Cases Revisited: Roswell." *Beyond Magazine*, No.4 (2007): 74–82.

Jeffrey, Kent. "Roswell: The Whole Story." 2004. Centre for UFO Studies (CUFOS). http://www.cufos.org/ros2.html (accessed May 1, 2007).

Korff, Kal K. *The Roswell UFO Crash: What They Don't Want You to Know*. New York: Dell, 2000.

Randle, Kevin and Don Schmitt. *UFO Crash at Roswell*. New York: Avon Books, 1991.

Redfern, Nick. *Body Snatchers in the Desert*. Toronto: Paraview, 2005.

Stringfield, Leonard. *UFO Crash/Retrievals: The Inner Sanctum. Status Report VI*. Cincinatti: privately published, 1991.

Yenne, Bill. *UFO: Evaluating the Evidence*. Rowayton, CT: Saraband, 1997.

BARNEY AND BETTY HILL

Friedman, Stanton, and Kathleen Marden. *Captured! The Betty and Barney Hill UFO Experience*. Franklin Lakes, NJ: New Page Books, 2007.

Fuller, John. *The Interrupted Journey*. New York: Dial Press, 1966.

Klass, Philip. *UFOs Explained*. New York: Vintage Books, 1976, 297–301.

Randles, Jenny. *Aliens: The Real Story*. London: Robert Hale, 1993, 28–33.

Schwarz, Berthold. *UFO Dynamics*. Moore Haven, FL: Rainbow Books, 1983, 273–300.

Story, Ronald. *UFOs and the Limits of Science*. New York: William Morrow, 1981, 194–205.

Webb, Walter. *A Dramatic UFO Encounter in the White Mountains, New Hampshire. The Hill Case: September 19–20, 1961*. Privately published, 1965.

THE RENDLESHAM FOREST INCIDENT

Butler, Brenda, et al. *Sky Crash*. London: Grafton Books, 1986.

Randles, Jenny, et al. *The UFOs That Never Were*. London: London House, 2000, 164–222.

Randles, Jenny, and Peter Hough. *The Complete Book of UFOs*. New York:

Sterling Publishing Co., 1996, 212–218.

Randles, Jenny. *From Out of the Blue*. New York: Berkley, 1993.

Warren, Larry, and Peter Robbins. *Left at East Gate*. New York: Marlowe & Co., 1997.

THE TEHRAN INCIDENT

Fawcett, Lawrence, and Barry Greenwood. *Clear Intent: The Government Cover-Up of the UFO Experience*. Englewood Cliffs, NJ: Prentice Hall, 1984, 81–86.

Good, Timothy. *Above Top Secret*. Toronto: Macmillan, 1988, 318–321.

Klass, Philip. *UFOs: The Public Deceived*. Buffalo: Prometheus Books, 1983, 111–124.

Shough, Martin *Radar Catalogue: A Review of Twenty-One Ground and Airborne Radar UAP Contact Reports Generally Related to Aviation Safety for the Period October 15, 1948 to September 19, 1976*. National Aviation Reporting Center on Anomalous Phenomena (NARCAP), Technical Report 6. http://www.narcap.org/reports/TR6pt1.htm (accessed June 18, 2007).

THE PHOENIX LIGHTS

Davenport, Peter. "UFO Events Over Arizona, March 13, 1997." 1997. http://www.ufocenter.com (accessed January 18, 2008).

Greenewald, John Jr. "FOIA Request on Phoenix Lights." May 1, 1997. http://www.blackvault.com (accessed January 14, 2008).

Kean, Leslie. "Symington Confirms He Saw UFO 10 Years Ago." *Arizona Daily Courier*, 18 March 1997.

Kitei, Lynne. *The Phoenix Lights*. Charlottesville, VA: Hampton Roads Publishing, 2004. 58, 66–67.

Ortega, Tony. "The Great UFO Cover-Up." *Phoenix New Times*, 26 June

1997. http://phoenixnewtimes.com/1997-06-26/news/the-great-ufo-cover-up/ (accessed January 18, 2008).

Printy, Tim. "The V-Formation of Lights and My Analysis." 1998. http://members.aol.com/tprinty/azconc.html (accessed January 18, 2008).

The Kelly-Hopkinsville Close Encounter

Clark, Jerome, ed. *The UFO Encyclopedia, The Emergence of a Phenomenon: UFOs from the Beginning Through 1959*. Detroit: Omnigraphics, 1992, 214–216.

Hynek, J. Allen. *The UFO Experience: A Scientific Inquiry*. Chicago: Henry Regnery, 1972, 150–155.

Spencer, John. *UFOs: The Definitive Casebook*. London: Hamlyn, 1992, 38–39.

Joe Simonton's Pancakes

Keel, John. *Why UFOs: Operation Trojan Horse*. New York: Manor Books, 1976, 164–165.

Randles, Jenny. *Alien Contact: The First Fifty Years*. New York: Sterling Publishing, 1997, 42.

Riccardi, Frank. "Alien Flapjacks." http://www.eyepod.org/AlienFlapjacks.html (accessed January 18, 2008).

Vallee, Jacques. *Passport to Magonia*. Chicago: Henry Regnery, 1969, 23–25.

The Tully Saucer Nests

Chalker, Bill. "Tully and other UFO nests." In *The UFO Encyclopedia*, 2nd ed. Vol. 2, L–Z, edited by Jerome Clark, 903–906. Detroit: Omnigraphics, 1998, 903–906.

Story, Ronald. *UFOs and the Limits of Science*. New York: William Morrow, 1981. 93–94.

ANTONIO VILLAS-BOAS

Evans, Hilary, and Dennis Stacy, eds. *UFOs 1947–1997*. London: John Brown, 1997. 9–10.

Fontes, Olavo and Martins, Joao. "Report on the Villas-Boas Incident," in *Flying Saucer Occupants*. Edited by Coral Lorenzen and Jim Lorenzen. Toronto: Signet, 1967, 42–72.

Granchi, Irene. *UFOs and Abductions in Brazil*. Madison, WI: Horus House Press 1995, 32.

Randles, Jenny. *Alien Contact: The First Fifty Years*. New York: Sterling Publishing, 1997, 34–35.

Randles, Jenny, and Peter Hough. *The Complete Book of UFOs*. New York: Sterling Publishing Co., 1996, 141–146.

THE MANHATTAN ABDUCTIONS

Hopkins, Budd. *Witnessed*. Toronto: Pocket Books, 1997.

Randles, Jenny, and Peter Hough. *The Complete Book of UFOs*. New York: Sterling Publishing Co., 1996, 261–266.

Reeves-Stevens, Garfield. *Nighteyes*. New York: Doubleday, 1989.

FATHER GILL

Clark, Jerome, ed. *The UFO Encyclopedia. The Emergence of a Phenomenon: UFOs From the Beginning Through 1959*. Detroit: Omnigraphics, 1992, 177–180.

Hynek, J. Allen. *The UFO Experience: A Scientific Inquiry*. Chicago: Henry Regnery, 1972, 146–150.

Menzel, Donald. "UFOs — the Modern Myth," in *UFOs: A Scientific Debate*. Edited by Carl Sagan and Thornton Page. New York: Norton, 1972, 146–153.

Story, Ronald. *UFOs and the Limits of Science*. New York: William Morrow, 1981. 185–193.

THE BELGIAN TRIANGLES

Printy, Tim. "Belgium 1990: A Case for Radar-Visual UFOs?" 2002. http://members.aol.com/TPrinty/Belg.html (accessed January 18, 2008).

Randle, Kevin. *Project Moon Dust*. New York: Avon Books, 1998, 215–230.

Van Utrecht, Wim. "The Belgian 1989–1990 UFO Wave," in *UFOs: 1947–1997*. Edited by Hilary Evans and Dennis Stacy. London: John Brown: 1997, 165–174.

von Ludwiger, Illobrand. *Best UFO Cases — Europe*. Las Vegas: National Institute for Discovery Science, 1998, 31–33.

TRINDADE ISLAND

Clark, Jerome, ed. *The UFO Encyclopedia. The Emergence of a Phenomenon: UFOs From the Beginning Through 1959*. Detroit: Omnigraphics, 1992, 326–330.

Gevaerd, A.J. "Interview With Witness to Trindade Island UFO." *UFO Updates*, February 13, 2008. http://www.virtuallystrange.net/ufo/updates/subscribers/2008/feb/m13-003.shtml (accessed January 18, 2008).

Gevaerd, A. J. "Almiro Barauna." *UFO Updates*, January 28, 2008. http://virtuallystrange.net/ufo/updates/subscribers/2008/jan/m29-005.shtml (accessed January 18, 2008).

Menzel, Donald, and Ernest Taves. *The UFO Engma: The Definitive Explanation of the UFO Phenomenon*. New York: Doubleday, 1977, 193–194.

Story, Ronald. *UFOs and the Limits of Science*. New York: William Morrow, 1981, 121–128.

TRAVIS WALTON

Berry, Bill. *Ultimate Encounter.* New York: Pocket Books, 1978.

Clark, Jerome, ed. *The UFO Encyclopedia*, 2nd ed., Vol. 2, *The Phenomenon From the Beginning: L–Z.* Detroit: Omnigraphics, 1998, 981–998.

Klass, Philip. *UFOs: The Public Deceived.* Buffalo: Prometheus Books, 1983, 161–222.

Walton, Travis. *The Walton Experience.* New York: Berkley, 1978.

THE GIANT YUKON SAUCER

BBC. "Mexico Pilots Release 'UFO Film.'" BBC News, May 12, 2004. http:// news.bbc.co.uk/go/pr/fr/2/hi/americas/3707057.stm (accessed January 18, 2008).

Jasek, M. *Giant UFO in the Yukon Territory. UFO*BC Special Report*, No. 1. Vancouver: privately published, 2000.

ASIA

Author unknown. "India Victims Blame UFO Aliens — 'Experts' Blame Weird Bugs." 2002. http://www.unsolvedmysteries.com/usm288272.html (accessed January 17, 2007).

Corrales, Scott. "UFOs in the Land of the Rising Sun." 2003. http://www. rense.com/general34/UFOsintheland.htm (accessed January 18, 2008).

Dong, Paul. *The Four Major Mysteries of Mainland China.* Englewood Cliffs, NJ: Prentice Hall, 1984.

Fowler, Ray. *UFOs: Interplanetary Visitors.* Englewood Cliffs, NJ: Prentice Hall, 1979, 101–103.

Gindilis, L., et al. *Observations of Anomalous Atmospheric Phenomena in the USSR: Statistical Analysis.* [Translation]. NASA Technical memorandum No. 75665. February 1980.

Good, Timothy. *Above Top Secret*. Toronto: Macmillan, 1988, 206–249.

Gross, Patrick. "UFOs at Close Sight: Quotes From Known Personalities." 2003. http://ufologie.net/htm/quotes.htm (accessed July 18, 2003).

Huneeus, Antonio. "UFOs Behind the Great Wall." *Fate Magazine* 50, No. 9 (September 1997).

Mookerji, Madhumita. "Did a UFO come over Kolkata?" DNA India, October 31, 2007. http://www.dnaindia.com/report.asp?newsid=1130823 (accessed February 23, 2008).

Ostrander, Sheila, and Lynn Schroeder. *Psychic Discoveries Behind the Iron Curtain*. New York: Bantam, 1971. 95–96.

Paljor, Karma. "Were there UFOs of PM's house?" CNN-IBN, March 14, 2007. http://www.ibnlive.com/news/were-there-ufos-over-pms-house/36030-3.html (accessed February 23, 2008).

Randles, Jenny. *Aliens: The Real Story*. London: Robert Hale, 1993. 85–88.

Spencer, John. *UFOs: The Definitive Casebook*. London: Hamlyn, 1992. 126–140.

Stonehill, Paul. *The Soviet UFO Files*. London: CLB International, 1998.

Wilce, Matt. "Close encounters of the Japanese kind." *Japan Today*, November 8, 2003. http://www.japantoday.com/news/jp/e/tools/print.asp?content=feature&id=544 (accessed January 14, 2008).

Yanyan, Zheng. "UFO Enthusiasts in Dalian for Conference." *China Daily*, 9 September 2005.

Ziegel, Felix. "Nuclear Explosion Over Siberia." In *On the Track of Discovery*, edited by D. Skvirsky and V. Talmi. 26–37. Moscow: Progress Publishers, 1965.

AUSTRALIA AND OCEANIA

Booth, Billy. "1993: Kelly Cahill Alien Abduction." about.com, 1993. http://

ufos.about.com/od/aliensalienabduction/p/cahill1993.htm (accessed January 18, 2008).

Brookesmith, Peter. *UFOs: The Complete Sightings*. London: Brown Books, 1995, 116–117.

Cahill, Kelly. *Encounter*. Sydney: HarperCollins, 1996.

Chalker, Bill. *Hair of the Alien*. New York: Paraview Pocket Books, 2005, 49–67.

Good, Timothy. *Above Top Secret*. Toronto: Macmillan, 1988, 160, 175–181.

Richardson, G. "The Controversial New Zealand Film." The Why Files, 2004. http://www.thewhyfiles.net/newzealand.htm (accessed January 18, 2008).

Spencer, John. *UFOs: The Definitive Casebook*. London: Hamlyn, 1992, 169–173.

Europe

Clark, Jerome, ed. *The UFO Encyclopedia*, Vol. 3, *High Strangeness: UFOs from 1960 through 1979*. Detroit: Omnigraphics, 1996, 161–165.

Devereux, Paul (1982). *Earthlights: Towards an Understanding of the UFO Enigma*. Wellingborough: Turnstone Press, 1982.

Good, Timothy. *Above Top Secret*. Toronto: Macmillan, 1988, 60–64.

Gross, Loren. *The Mystery of the Ghost Rockets*, 2nd ed. Fremont: privately published, 1982.

Hauge, Bjørn. "10 Years of Scientific Research of the Hessdalen Phenomena." Comitato Italiano per il Progetto Hessdalen, 2005. http://www.loscrittoio. it (accessed January 18, 2008).

Leone, Matteo. "On a Triangulation of an Alleged 'Hessdalen Light.'" Comitato Italiano per il Progetto Hessdalen, 2007. http://www.loscrittoio.it (accessed January 18, 2008).

Maillot, Eric, and Jacques Scornaux. "Trans-en-Provence: When Science and

Belief Go Hand in Hand." In *UFOs 1947–1997*, edited by Hilary Evans and Dennis Stacy. London: John Brown, 1997, 151–159.

Michel, Aimé. *Flying Saucers and the Straight-Line Mystery*. New York: Criterion Books, 1958.

Randles, Jenny, et al. *The UFOs That Never Were*. London: London House, 2000, 163.

Randles, Jenny. *Alien Contact: The First Fifty Years*. New York: Sterling Publishing, 1997, 30–31.

Randles, Jenny, and Peter Warrington. *UFOs: A British Viewpoint*. London: Robert Hale, 1979, 108–110.

Spencer, John. *UFOs: The Definitive Casebook*. London: Hamlyn, 1992. 86, 94, 99, 110.

von Ludwiger, Illobrand. *Best UFO Cases — Europe*. Las Vegas: National Institute for Discovery Science, 1998.

Wade, Mark. "Peenemunde." 1997. www.astronautix.com/sites/peeuende.htm (accessed February 23, 2008).

North and South America

Author unknown. "Stephenville UFO Report." Mutual UFO Network (MUFON), 2008. http://www.mufon.com/mufonreports.htm (accessed February 21, 2008).

BBC. "Mexico Pilots Release 'UFO Film.'" BBC News, May 12, 2004. http://news.bbc.co.uk/go/pr/fr/2/hi/americas/3707057.stm (accessed January 18, 2008).

Gallart, Henry. "Flying Saucers Over Cuba," in *UFOs Around the World*. Edited by Edward Babcock and Timothy Beckley. New York: Global Communications, 1978, 60.

Gillmor, Daniel, ed. *Scientific Study of Unidentified Flying Objects*. New York; Dutton, 1968, 316–324.

Good, Timothy. *Above Top Secret*. Toronto: Macmillan, 1988, 315–316, 324.

Granchi, Irene. *UFOs and Abductions in Brazil*. Madison: Horus House Press, 1995, 11–14, 39–41.

Hall, Richard. "The UFO Evidence." National Investigations Committee on Aerial Phenomena (NICAP), 1964. http://www.nicap.org/580505dir.htm (accessed January 18, 2008).

Joiner, Angela. "Stephenville Lights." 2008. http://www.stephenvillelights.com (accessed February 18, 2008).

Pratt, Bob. "Dog Dies." Mutual UFO Network (MUFON), 1995. http://www.mufon.com/bob_pratt/dogdies.html (accessed February 21, 2008).

Sheaffer, Robert. "The Campeche, Mexico, 'Infrared UFO' Video." *Skeptical Inquirer*, September 2004.

Spencer, John. *UFOs: The Definitive Casebook*. London: Hamlyn, 1992, 184.

Strieber, Whitley. *Confirmation: The Hard Evidence of Aliens Among Us*. New York: St. Martin's Press, 1998.

AFRICA

Fawcett, Lawrence and Barry Greenwood. *Clear Intent: The Government Cover-Up of the UFO Experience*. Englewood Cliffs: Prentice Hall, 1984, 119–121.

Hind, Cynthia. "UFOs in Africa: Changing Ways in Changing Days," in *UFOs 1947–1997*. Edited by Hilary Evans and Dennis Stacy. London: John Brown, 1997, 194–199.

Hind, Cynthia. *UFOs: African Encounters*. Zimbabwe: Gemini Publishers, 1982.

The Arctic and Antarctic

Dittman, Geoff, and Chris Rutkowski. "The 2007 Canadian UFO Survey."
Ufology Research of Manitoba, 2008. http://survey.canadianuforeport.
com (accessed September 1, 2008).

Good, Timothy. *Above Top Secret.* Toronto: Macmillan, 1988, 309–310.

The Unexplained

Gillmor, Daniel, ed. *Scientific Study of Unidentified Flying Objects.* New York: Dutton,
1968, 260–266.

Kimball, Paul. "The Other Side of Truth." 2008. http://redstarfilms.blogspot.
com/ (accessed January 18, 2008).

Klotz, Jim, and Robert Salas. "The Malmstrom AFB UFO/Missile Incident."
CUFON, 1996. http://www.cufon.org/cufon/malmstrom/malm1.htm
(accessed January 18, 2008).

Ledger, Don, and Chris Styles. *Dark Object: The World's Only Government-Documented
UFO Crash.* New York: Dell, 2001.

Abductions

Author unknown. "Alien Abduction Test. What's Your Score?" 2006. http://www.
abovetopsecret.com/forum/thread222759/pg1 (accessed February 9, 2008).

Bryan, C.D.B. *Close Encounters of the Fourth Kind: Alien Abduction, UFOs, and the
Conference at M.I.T.* New York: Alfred A. Knopf, 1995.

Fowler, Raymond. *The Watchers.* New York: Bantam Books, 1990.

Hopkins, Budd. *Intruders.* New York: Random House, 1987.

Hopkins, Budd. *Missing Time: A Documented Study of UFO Abductions.* New York:
Richard Marek, 1981.

Klass, Philip. *UFO Abductions: A Dangerous Game*. Amherst: Prometheus Books, 1989.

Mack, John. *Abduction: Human Encounters With Aliens*. New York: Charles Scribner, 1994.

Randles, Jenny, and Peter Warrington. *Science and the UFOs*. Oxford: Basil Blackwell, 1985.

Rutkowski, Chris. *Abductions and Aliens: What's Really Going On?* Toronto: Dundurn, 1999.

Strieber, Whitley. *Communion: A True Story*. New York: Beech Tree Books, 1987.

Strieber, Whitley. *Transformation: The Breakthrough*. New York: Beech Tree Books, 1988.

CONTACT

Friedman, Stanton. "The UFO 'Why' Questions." 2006. http://www. vjenterprises.com/sfufowhy1.html (accessed January 18, 2008).

Sagan, Carl. *The Demon-Haunted World: Science as a Candle in the Dark*. New York: Ballantine Books, 1996.

DEBUNKING

Kurtz, Paul. "Debunking, Neutrality, and Skepticism in Science," in *Science Confronts the Paranormal*. Edited by Kendrick Fraser. Buffalo: Prometheus Books, 1986, 5–12.

EVIDENCE

Canada. DND Flight Information Publication — GPH 204. *Flight Planning and Procedures, Canada and North Atlantic*, No. 57, May 20, 1999.

Flying Saucers

Arnold, Kenneth. "What Happened on June 24, 1947," in *UFOs: 1947–1997*. Edited by Hilary Evans and Dennis Stacy. London: John Brown, 1997, 29–34.

Arnold, Kenneth, and Ray Palmer. *The Coming of the Saucers*. Amherst: privately published, 1952.

Clark, Jerome, ed. *The UFO Encyclopedia*, 2nd ed., Vol. 1, *The Phenomenon From the Beginning: A–K*. Detroit: Omnigraphics, 1998, 139–143.

Dittman, Geoff, and Chris Rutkowski. "The 2007 Canadian UFO Survey." Ufology Research of Manitoba, 2008. http://survey.canadianuforeport. com (accessed September 1, 2008).

Government

CNN. "Poll: U.S. Hiding Knowledge of Aliens." CNN, June 15, 1997. http:// www.cnn.com/US/9706/15/ufo.poll/ (accessed January 18, 2008).

COMETA. "UFOs and Defense: What Should We Prepare For?" Undated. http:// www.ufoevidence.org/topics/Cometa.htm (accessed January 18, 2008).

Cameron, Grant and T. Scott Crain, Jr. "UFOs, MJ-12 and the Government," in *Tales of Charlie Red Star*. Edited by Grant Cameron. Winnipeg: privately published (CD), 2004.

Craig, Roy. *UFOs: An Insider's View of the Official Quest for Evidence*. Denton, TX: University of North Texas Press, 1995, 177.

Gillmor, Daniel, ed. *Scientific Study of Unidentified Flying Objects*. New York; Dutton, 1968.

Good, Timothy. *Above Top Secret*. Toronto: Macmillan, 1988, 34, 280.

Greenwood, Barry. "UFOs: Government Involvement, Secrecy, and Documents." 1997. http://www.project1947.com/bg/ufogov.htm (accessed January 18, 2008).

Pope, Nick. *Open Skies, Closed Minds*. New York: Dell, 1998.

Swords, Michael. "Project Sign and the Estimate of the Situation." *Journal of UFO Studies*, No. 7. http://www.ufoscience.org/history/swords.pdf (accessed January 18, 2008), 27–64.

United Kingdom. *Unidentified Aerial Phenomena in the UK Air Defence Region: Executive Summary*. Scientific & Technical Memorandum, No. 55. Defence Air Intelligence Staff. December 2000.

HOAXES

Author unknown. "The Great Internet UFO Hoax." 2005. http://www.museumofhoaxes.com/hoax.weblog/permalink/the_great_internet_ufo_hoax (accessed September 18, 2007).

Davidson, Leon. *Flying Saucers: An Analysis of the Air Force Project Blue Book Special Report No. 14*. Ramsey: Ramsey-Wallace Corporation, 1967.

Hynek, J. Allen and Jacques Vallee. *The Edge of Reality: A Progress Report on UFOs*. Chicago: Henry Regnery, 1975, 167–171.

INVESTIGATION

BUFORA. *UFO Investigation: A Field Investigator's Handbook*. London: British UFO Research Association, London, 1976.

Fowler, Raymond. *MUFON Field Investigator's Manual*. Seguin: Mutual UFO Network, 1983.

Hendry, Allan. *The UFO Handbook*. Garden City: Doubleday, 1979.

J. ALLEN HYNEK

Hynek, J. Allen. *The UFO Experience: A Scientific Inquiry*. Chicago: Henry Regnery, 1972.

Hynek, J. Allen. *The Hynek UFO Report*. New York: Dell Publishing, 1977.

Hynek, J. Allen and Jacques Vallee. *The Edge of Reality: A Progress Report on UFOs*. Chicago: Henry Regnery, 1975.

KLASS, PHILIP J.

Clark, Jerome. *The UFO Book*. New York: Visible Ink, 1998, 368–370.

Klass, Philip. "The Last Will and Testament of Philip Klass." *Saucer Smear*, 10 October 1983.

Klass, Philip. *UFOs: The Public Deceived*. Buffalo: Prometheus Books, 1983.

Klass, Philip. *UFOs Explained*. New York: Vintage Books, 1976.

Rutkowski, Chris and John Timmerman. "Langenburg 1974: A Classic Historical CE2 and a Crop Circle Progenitor?" *International UFO Reporter* 17, No. 2 (1992): 4–11.

LITTLE GREEN MEN

Aubeck, Chris. "Little Green Men." 2007. http://caubeck.tripod.com/littlegreenmen/index.html (accessed December 2, 2007).

Clark, Jerome. Private communication, November 28, 2007.

Rojcewicz, Peter. *The Boundaries of Orthodoxy: A Folkloric Look at the "UFO Phenomenon."* PhD diss., University of Pennsylvania, 1984.

Sherman, Harold. *The Green Man and His Return*. Amherst, TX: Amherst Press, 1979.

MUTILATIONS OF CATTLE

Blann, Tommy Roy. *Special Criminal Investigation Report on Livestock Mutilations prepared for Royal Canadian Mounted Police*. Privately published, 1979.

Clark, Jerome. *Unexplained!* Detroit: Visible Ink, 1993, 56–60.

Duplantier, Gene. *The Night Mutilators*. Willowdale, ON: SS & S Publications, 1979.

Kagan, Daniel and Ian Summers. *Mute Evidence*. New York: Bantam Books, 1984.

Nation, Nick, and Elizabeth Williams. "Maggots, Mutilations and Myth: Patterns of Postmortem Scavenging of the Bovine Carcass." *Canadian Veterinary Journal*, Vol. 30 (September 1989): 742–747.

NEWS MEDIA

Strentz, Herbert. *A Survey of Press Coverage of Unidentified Flying Objects, 1947–1966.* PhD diss., Northwestern University, 1970.

Thomas, Joel. "Grab Your Tin Foil Hat: UFO Fever Hits North Texas." CBS TV 11, January 18, 2008. http://cbs11tv.com/local/UFO.Fever. Stephenville.2.633468.html (accessed January 19, 2008).

Winnipeg Free Press, "Mystery of the Flying Discs Deepens," 7 July 1947.

Winnipeg Tribune, "Dr. Murray Scientific Expedition Probes 'Flying Saucers,'" 8 July 1947.

OBJECTIVITY

Thomson, Andrew. "Experts 'Very Puzzled' by Sighting in PEI." *Ottawa Citizen*, 5 January 2008.

PILOT CASES

Haines, Richard. *Observing UFOs: An Investigative Handbook*. Chicago: Nelson-Hall, 1980.

Haines, Richard, and Ted Roe. "Pilot Survey Results." National Aviation Reporting Center on Anomalous Phenomena (NARCAP), Boulder Creek, California. www.narcap.org (accessed January 18, 2008).

Weinstein, Dominique. *Unidentified Aerial Phenomena: Eighty Years of Pilot Sightings. Catalog of Military, Airliner, Private Pilots sightings from 1916 to 2000.* February 2001 edition. National Aviation Reporting Center on Anomalous Phenomena (NARCAP). www.narcap.org (accessed January 18, 2008).

Questions

Herb, Gert. "Survey of Amateur Astronomers." *Center for UFO Studies Bulletin,* Fall 1980, 1–5.

Holt, Alan. *Field Resonance Propulsion Concept.* NASA Technical Memorandum TM-80961. Houston: NASA, 1979.

Rutkowski, Chris. "The Gert Herb Report." *Royal Astronomical Society of Canada, National Newsletter,* Vol. 75, No.1. February 1981, L12–L13.

Religion

Bergier, Jacques. *Extraterrestrial Visitations From Prehistoric Times to the Present.* New York: Signet Books, 1974.

Beverley, James. *Religions: A to Z.* Nashville: Thomas Nelson, 2005.

Blumrich, Josef. *The Spaceships of Ezekiel.* New York: Bantam Books, 1974.

Brasington, Virginia. *Flying Saucers in the Bible.* Clarksburg, WV: Saucerian Books, Clarksburg, 1963.

Charroux, Robert. *One Hundred Thousand Years of Man's Unknown History.* New York: Berkley Publishing, 1971.

Dibitonto, Giorgio. *UFO Contact From Angels in Starships.* Tucson: UFO Photo Archives, 1990.

Dione, R. L. *God Drives a Flying Saucer.* New York: Bantam Books, 1973.

Downing, Barry. *The Bible and Flying Saucers.* New York, Lippincott, 1968, 114–115.

Drake, W. Raymond. *Gods and Spacemen of the Ancient Past*. New York: Signet Books, 1974.

Gardner, Martin. *Urantia: the Great Cult Mystery*. Amherst: Prometheus Books, 1995.

Jessup, Morris. *UFOs and the Bible*. Clarksburg, WV: Saucerian Books, 1970.

Leon, Dorothy. *Is Jehovah an E.T.?* Huntsville, AR: Ozark Mountain Publishers, 2003.

Rutkowski, Chris. *Abductions and Aliens: What's Really Going On?* Toronto: Dundurn Press, 1999.

Tyson, Basil. *UFOs: Satanic Terror*. Beaverlodge: Horizon House Publishers, 1977.

Uversa Press. *The Urantia Book: A Revelation*. Indexed Version. New York: Urantia Book Fellowship, 2003.

Von Daniken, Erich. *Chariots of the Gods?* New York: Bantam Books, 1971.

TIME, MISSING

Hopkins, Budd. *Missing Time: A Documented Study of UFO Abductions*. New York: Richard Marek, 1981.

Leslie, Melinda. "52 Indicators Of Encounters Or Abductions By Aliens." 1999. http://www.geocities.com/Area51/Sadowlands/6583/abduct011.html (accessed January 18, 2008).

Miller, John. "Dissociative Disorders." 2000. http://www.athealth.com/Consumer/disorders/Dissociative.html (accessed January 18, 2008).

UFOLOGY

Gillmor, Daniel, ed. *Scientific Study of Unidentified Flying Objects*. New York: Dutton, 1968.

Persinger, Michael, and Gyslaine Lafrenière. *Space-Time Transients and Unusual Events*. Chicago: Nelson-Hall: 1977.

Rutkowski, Chris. *Abductions and Aliens: What's Really Going On?* Toronto: Dundurn, 1999.

Sturrock, P. "An Analysis of the Condon Report on the Colorado UFO Project." *Journal of Scientific Exploration*, Vol. 1, No. 1 (1987).

Tributsch, Helmut. *When the Snakes Awake*. New York: MIT Press, 1982.

VENUSIANS, V, AND LIZARD PEOPLE

Gillmor, Daniel, ed. *Scientific Study of Unidentified Flying Objects*. New York; Dutton, 1968, 434–436.

Hendry, Allan. *The UFO Handbook*. Garden City: Doubleday, 1979, 27.

Icke, David. *The Biggest Secret*. Scottsdale: Bridge of Love Publications, 1999.

Malko, George. *Scientology: The Now Religion*. New York: Delacorte Press, 1970, 106.

Moore, Patrick. *Can You Speak Venusian?* London: Wyndham Publications, 1976, 102–103.

Rampa, T. Lobsang. *My Visit to Venus*. Kitchener, ON: Galaxy Press, n.d.

WATER

Clark, Jerome, ed. *The UFO Encyclopedia*, 2nd ed., Vol. 2, *The Phenomenon From the Beginning: L–Z*. Detroit: Omnigraphics, 1998, 506.

Feindt, Carl. "Why is this Web Page Necessary?" 2008. http://www.waterufo. net (accessed January 11, 2008).

Lakser, John. "Lake Erie UFOs are Stars on YouTube." Wired News, 2008. http://www.wired.com/entertainment/theweb/news/2008/01/erie_ufos (accessed January 18, 2008).

Ledger, Don, and Chris Styles. *Dark Object: The World's Only Government-Documented UFO Crash*. New York: Dell, 2001.

Ledger, Don. *Maritime UFO Files*. Halifax: Nimbus Publishing, 1998.

Sanderson, Ivan. *Invisible Residents*. New York: World Publishing Co., 1970. 53.

Steiger, Brad. *Atlantis Rising*. New York: Dell Books, 1973, 173–174.

YOUNG CHILDREN

Randles, Jenny, and Peter Warrington. *UFOs: A British Viewpoint*. London: Robert Hale, 1979, 82–83.

Zullo, Allan. *UFO Kids*. Mahwah, NJ: Troll Associates, 1995.

ZOO

Fort, Charles. *The Book of the Damned*. New York: Holt, Rinehart & Winston, 1941, 155–156.

Michaud, Michael. *Contact with Alien Civilizations*. New York: Copernicus Books, 2007.

INDEX

Other Books by Chris A. Rutkowski

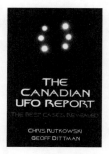

The Canadian UFO Report
The Best Cases Revealed
978-1-55002-621-4

$24.99

This popular history of the UFO phenomenon in Canada is something that has captured the imaginations of young and old alike. The book is drawn from government documents and civilian cases and includes a chronological overview of the best Canadian UFO cases.

Of Related Interest

UFOs Over Canada
Personal Accounts of Sightings and Close Encounters
John Robert Colombo
978-0-88882-138-6

$15.99

Presents, in highly readable style, 60 eyewitness accounts of UFO activity over Canada. For the first time, in one book, contributors from across the country recount their personal experiences in their own words.

Abductions and Aliens
What's Really Going On?
978-1-55002-210-9

$22.99

We can't escape them; aliens are everywhere. Based on his own investigative files and almost twenty-five years of research, science writer Chris Rutkowski asks hard questions, looking critically, yet compassionately, at the stories of abductees. Rutowski presents case histories of many abductees, showing both their diversity and similarities, and examines how our understanding is shaped by media, by science, and by society itself.

Tell us your story! What did you think of this book? Join the conversation at www.definingcanada.ca/tell-your-story by telling us what you think.

Available at your favourite bookseller.

DUNDURN PRESS
www.dundurn.com